Praise for *Freeing Tibet: 50 Years of Struggle, Resilience, and Hope*
by John B. Roberts II and Elizabeth A. Roberts

"The more we learn about Tibet, the beauty of her people and their culture, and the agony of her brutal subjugation under Chinese occupation, the more we feel committed to 'Freeing Tibet'—and we learn a lot from John and Elizabeth Roberts in this compelling book. The Tibetan people are the still-not-yet fully appreciated heroes of one of the great struggles for freedom of our time—especially great because of their overriding commitment to maintain the exacting discipline of nonviolence. The Buddhist principle of nonviolence is not merely a blind rush to martyrdom; it is also pragmatic. Forceful self-defense is justified only if it prevents more violence than it employs. The Roberts' tale gives a detailed and moving account of the Tibetan warriors who tried to defend their homes and families and monasteries, saved the Dalai Lama from capture by the Chinese military, then ignored his teaching and took up arms in a tragically doomed guerrilla war, and ultimately sacrificed their lives for their country. And the authors further describe how the Dalai Lama since has won the hearts of the world's people for the cause of Tibet, even though governments still have not found the insight and resolve to get the leaders of China to change their genocidal policy into the more realistic live and let live appropriate for this global century. *Freeing Tibet* is an absorbing read, and I heartily recommend it to all those who will never give up on their determination to see peace and justice prevail in our world."

—Robert A. F. Thurman
Jey Tsong Khapa Professor of Buddhist Studies,
Columbia University
President, Tibet House US
Author of *Why the Dalai Lama Matters*

"Shortly after he won the Nobel Peace Prize, I interviewed the Dalai Lama. It was a hopeful moment for Tibet. The Soviet Union's collapse meant freedom for scores of millions and expectations were high that China might follow the path of democracy. Until this book, those hopes seemed a distant memory. But this remarkable panoptic history of the Tibetan struggle, from its Cold War origins to global cause célèbre, rekindles optimism. *Freeing Tibet* is a call to action for concerned people everywhere to use the leverage of global economic interdependence to achieve freedom and democracy for Tibet and China. This is the greatest civil rights cause of the 21st century."

—Dr. John McLaughlin,
Executive Producer and Host
The McLaughlin Group

"China's remorseless goal of conquering Tibet and replacing its gracefully spiritual culture with collectivist rule threatens all mankind. During the ten years between 1951 and 1961, the CIA, supported by three presidents, waged a major and thoughtful covert war against China's depredations in Tibet. Two obdurate intelligence professionals, Desmond FitzGerald and Howard Bane (to whose memory the book is dedicated) were real-life heroes in the drama. FitzGerald and Bane thwarted every bureaucratic obstacle to achieve their own ideal of an autonomous Tibet. Arguably, this largely unheralded endeavor to mold a part of our future with assistance from thousands of Tibetan freedom fighters and spiritual leaders will ultimately be remembered as the Agency's purest, and possibly as its most sequacious, exploit. These same warriors, with their Agency comrades and sponsors, swept the Dalai Lama from Lhasa to safety in India, enabling him to emerge as one of the world's great teachers of Knowledge, Compassion, and Nonviolence. *Freeing Tibet* tells the story of how CIA 'meddling' in China's 'internal affairs' not only kept His Holiness and His Message from disappearing without a trace in March 1959, but set in motion the chain of events which gave global prominence to the cause of a Free Tibet."

—Robert H. Campbell
27-year veteran of the CIA's Clandestine Service

Freeing Tibet

*50 Years of Struggle,
Resilience, and Hope*

John B. Roberts II

Elizabeth A. Roberts

ᴀMACOM

American Management Association
New York • Atlanta • Brussels • Chicago • Mexico City
San Francisco • Shanghai • Tokyo • Toronto • Washington, D. C.

This publication is designed to provide accurate and authoritative information in
regard to the subject matter covered. It is sold with the understanding that the publisher is not engaged in rendering legal, accounting, or other professional service. If
legal advice or other expert assistance is required, the services of a competent professional person should be sought.

Library of Congress Cataloging-in-Publication Data

Roberts, John B.
    Freeing Tibet : 50 years of struggle, resilience, and hope / by John B.
Roberts II, Elizabeth A. Roberts. — 1st ed.
        p.   cm.
    Includes bibliographical references and index.
    ISBN 978-0-8144-0983-1
    1. Tibet (China)—History—Autonomy and independence movements.
I. Roberts, Elizabeth A.   II. Title.
DS786.R568 2009
951'.505—dc22

                                                              2008042427

Printing number

10 9 8 7 6 5 4 3 2 1

This book is dedicated to Howard Thomas Bane
Friend, Mentor, Spy
August 5, 1927 – July 27, 2007

NEVER GIVE UP

No matter what is going on
Never give up

Develop the heart
Too much energy in your country
is spent developing the mind
instead of the heart
Develop the heart

Be compassionate
Not just to your friends but to everyone
Be compassionate

Work for peace
in your heart and in the world
Work for Peace

And I say it again
Never give up
No matter what is happening
No matter what is going on around you

Never give up

His Holiness the XIVth Dalai Lama

Contents

PART TWO: RESILIENCE

PART THREE: HOPE

Foreword

Not too many years ago I read an account of a conversation His Holiness the Dalai Lama had with some of the West's finest scientists. One of the scientists candidly asked the Dalai Lama, in a manner clearly reflecting the mutual respect and trust they had developed over time, something like the following question: "Why is it, Your Holiness, that you have the keenest of interest in the latest advances in modern science, can ask the most penetrating questions about esoteric aspects of scientific theory and practice, and yet you maintain at the same time beliefs in such things as reincarnation and the existence of oracles who are spirits to be consulted in certain situations?"

The questioner sought assistance in understanding, what to him, was a blatant contradiction among conflicting worldviews and a sort of cognitive dissonance within a man whose powers of rational thought were known to be remarkably astute. The Dalai Lama's response, however, was not likely to solve the issue for the perplexed questioner. He answered, in effect, that there is no contradiction whatsoever in coupling a profound knowledge of and interest in modern scientific methods with belief in the continuation of consciousness beyond death or the existence of conscious beings invisible to the eye. In fact, he continued, the problem lies within the limitations that dogmatic scientific materialism can impose on one's imagination and, hence, on one's capacity for broader awareness of our actual and vast world. In the Dalai Lama's thinking, the apparent contradiction could be resolved if the scientist would simply consider the possibility that there might be dimensions of reality that cannot be measured by existing scientific equipment.

The simplicity and directness of his response is very typical of His Holiness' style. And the giggle that very likely emanated from his smiling face as he gently prodded his fellow thinker to try to expand his relatively rigid paradigms would also have been characteristic. He is a man very comfortable with himself and with others. And he is at ease when he deals in remarkably facile ways with both the people and ideas of the modern West and those of his Tibetan Buddhist tradition, with its well-preserved worldview rooted in the ancient teachings of a sage who called himself a Buddha, an awakened one, from India millennia ago.

It is no simple coincidence that the Dalai Lama, who is one of the finest trained Buddhist philosophers on the planet, has been spearheading dialogs with scientists from the likes of Stanford, Princeton, Harvard, and M.I.T. for the past twenty years. His lifetime of monastic training—decades of rigorous study of Buddhist philosophical traditions that include logic, ethics, epistemology, psychology, and much more—makes him not only exceedingly capable of engaging in the most sophisticated of conversations, and even debates, with Western scientists. His lifelong interest in science is what draws so many Westerners to want to talk with him. It is as if they see in him someone with the potential to reflect back to them the best in their tradition and, beyond that, to help them find ways of sharpening and expanding their scientific tools to deal most effectively with the many pressing issues of technology, bioethics, ecology, and so on. An up-to-date resource on these dialogues can be found at www.mindandlife.org, which includes links to a dozen books detailing the more than twenty meetings that have taken place and to the ongoing research that has emerged from these conversations.

It is also no simple coincidence that this "bridge" between two worlds, the Dalai Lama, was raised in Tibet. Tibetan culture has preserved what is arguably the broadest range of Buddhist teachings and practices in Asia. As an exile from his native Tibet, from which he escaped to India in 1959 after living nearly ten years under Chinese occupation, he has shared the many riches of his remarkable civilization with millions of people across the world. And this he has done while simultaneously working tirelessly, and courageously, to seek a peaceful resolution to the profound difficulties facing the Tibetan people. For five decades, their very culture and religion has been systematically destroyed by an occupying government that seems incapable of listening to, or of itself expressing, good reasoning regarding the dire situation of millions of Tibetans whose human rights and freedom and livelihood have been horribly damaged. And while so many of the great powers in the world seem fundamentally indifferent (there is rhetoric but little action) to the plight of this incredibly rich culture, the Dalai Lama keeps steadily working for a solution, just as he keeps conversing with scientists and with leaders and practitioners from many of the world's religions. He multitasks on an enormous scale, working across the planet on various levels for the benefit of so many people.

It is also no simple coincidence that I was asked to write these words. The authors, John and Elizabeth Roberts, and I met just one year ago. We had lived on the same street for two years, but our paths did not cross until a neighbor suggested I attend a "block party" at the Roberts' house. I hesitated to arrive at the home of people I had yet to meet but went anyway, small gift in hand, with my trusted neighbor. Let's just say John, Elizabeth, and I hit it off in surprising ways. I naturally found their company a delight. But, what was most memorable was that when they heard I was a specialist in Buddhist studies, they told me about the book they were writing on Tibet. It turned out that John (as he indicates in his Introduction) had first come into contact with the Tibetan freedom movement nearly eighteen years ago when writing questions for an interview John McLaughlin would have with the Dalai Lama on his television show, *One-on-One*. Then, in 1991, a friend and confidant, Howard Bane, told John of his involvement in the CIA's covert war in Tibet. It was that story that spurred John to write an article about Tibet that appeared in *George* magazine in 1997.

Serendipity brought the three of us together. Elizabeth had only recently begun to explore her interest in Tibetan Buddhism when the suggestion to write this book about Tibet's 50-year history since the Dalai Lama's exile came to the forefront. Our first meeting occurred shortly after the Roberts agreed to write this book. And, as we talked, the three of us were flabbergasted by the "connections" that emerged, particularly as I reported my own long history with things Tibetan and my close affiliation with leading Tibet scholars in the United States. We soon became friends, and I was delighted to share with them, on various occasions, information and contacts that might help with their project. I am even more delighted now that their book is complete. I know intimately that *Freeing Tibet* has been a labor of love for these dedicated authors.

The special book you are now reading is both remarkable and timely. It is remarkable because of its vast compass, and it is timely because it seems that just now, when the 2008 Beijing Summer Olympic Games have recently ended, China is emerging as a great power once again. Highly organized protests in Tibet have occurred for the past several months unlike anything witnessed in the past twenty years, so the potential for focused global attention on the tragedy in Tibet is exceedingly ripe. The very impressive DVD documentary, entitled *The Unwinking Gaze: The Inside Story of the Dalai Lama's Struggle for Tibet*, has just been released, as has Robert Thurman's latest book, *Why the Dalai Lama Matters*. Although His Holiness will sometimes say in regard to resolving the tragic situation of the Tibetan people, "all we can do is wait," this is not a fatalistic statement. Rather, it is an expression of a profound realism, one that recognizes that we need to keep planting seeds, tilling the soil, and providing fertilizer until the rains finally come and new life flourishes. His Holiness remains indefatigable in his efforts to negotiate a diplomatic solution. For those of us with knowledge and concern for the Tibetan people, we fervently wish for their freedom—not necessarily full political independence, for which the Dalai Lama no longer calls—and we might pray that such life-giving rains will soon fall—rains of reason and of justice that will benefit not only Tibetans but the many Chinese people who share their land. Let us seize this time to make a difference.

The vast compass of this book surely provides further favorable conditions for such a "rain of peace" in Tibet. This book tells a remarkable story based on many remarkable stories. It weaves together narratives of the lives of people from ancient and modern Tibet; narratives of Tibetans in exile; narratives of Westerners who are deeply concerned about Tibet's situation; narratives of people in the U.S. government from the 1940s until the present, who have been involved in making important decisions about Tibet; narratives of CIA operatives and directors who helped the Dalai Lama escape from Tibet in 1959 and who for a short time supported and trained Tibetan resistance fighters; narratives of American poets and scholars, such as Allen Ginsberg, who helped promote great interest in Tibetan spiritual culture; narratives of important Tibetan teachers of Buddhism in the United States; and narratives of various Buddhist practitioners and teachers among those non-Tibetan Americans, who have taken refuge in the Buddhist tradition. While a few of these tales have been told in other publications, *Freeing Tibet* not only introduces fascinating new narratives but also connects all of these intriguing and inspiring narratives in a way that is entirely unprecedented.

However, this book is not merely unprecedented, it is important. Here we get the story of a myriad of different people across the planet and across the decades who have been unified, some invisibly so, by their engagement on one level or another with the tragedy of the Tibetan people and their culture. *Freeing Tibet* presents a major historical perspective that reveals the primacy of the plight of Tibetans in the minds of so many people across time and space. And the authors demonstrate fine judgment in their decision not to attempt to explicitly "connect all the dots" in their account. Some connections they make for us in most helpful and brilliant ways. But in other cases, they have chosen simply to lay before the reader multiple accounts of people and institutions, allowing the reader to draw his or her own conclusion. This impressionistic aspect of their approach is laudable and reflects, it seems to me, the manner in which we usually gather information and come to conclusions ourselves about most things in life. We witness the force of accumulated data and begin to "see" a pattern that then guides our own vision and action.

It is my hope, and the hope of the authors, that the reader will draw from these fascinating accounts a profound appreciation for the many great efforts that have been and continue to be made on behalf of the Tibetan people and their culture. And it is our hope that readers will become motivated to learn more and will find ways to educate others about the importance of securing the precious and inalienable right to self-determination for the people of Tibet. The way that people acquire enough knowledge to become actively engaged in working to solve a problem is rarely the result of simple coincidence. A variety of causes and conditions accumulate until the will to be involved emerges. *Freeing Tibet* is about the power of knowledge and the power of effort. But it is especially about the almost mysterious way in which "events unfold" within human minds and communities as a result of accumulated knowledge and the work of individual actors. It is also, I believe, about the power of compassion.

I think this is a deeply hopeful book. Chapter 13 contains a remarkable quotation from Hu Yaobang, the Secretary of the Communist Chinese Party in the early 1980s. After inspecting conditions inside occupied Tibet, he constructed a political vision called the Six-Point reform program. Hu wrote:

> . . . vigorous efforts must be made to revive and develop Tibetan culture, education and science. The Tibetan people have a long

history and a rich culture. . . . All ideas that ignore Tibetan and weaken Tibetan culture are wrong. . . . The Tibetan people's habits, customs, history and culture must be respected.

While it turned out that not all of China's Communist leaders shared Secretary Hu's vision, he appears to have been well respected in more progressive circles for his effort to redress some of the terrible excesses of Mao's Cultural Revolution. Although, to this day, his push to permit Tibetan self-determination within China has yet to bear significant fruit, we must still hope that this time will come soon. Some of China's new leaders might see the wisdom of releasing their paradoxical grip on things Tibetan. While China claims in a steady stream of propaganda that all Tibetans are happy with the changes brought about by the Communist takeover, the government nonetheless continues to relentlessly spy on multitudes of Tibetans, tightly suspicious of their every word and action. This contradiction—which is typical of the official Chinese posture on Tibet and reflects a profound cognitive dissonance—is not only perilous to the Tibetan people. It also represents a gigantic knot of confusion at the heart of an important policy of the Chinese government. A reform of China's Tibet policy would have an even greater benefit than serving to free Tibetans to practice their own religion and to elect their own local leaders. Providing the Tibetans with the right of self-determination would free up enormous energies within the halls and minds of the Chinese Communist bureaucracy, energies that for so many decades have been tangled up in sustaining an illusion of justice and of peace in Tibet. Once freed, these energies could be employed in so many useful ways to help China become once again one of our great world powers, as it clearly has the vast resources to do this. And once freed, the Tibetan people would continue to provide themselves and the world with the fruits of their own rich and beautiful culture. Let us all work toward freeing both these bountiful resources. Let us work for a rain of peace and freedom that will nurture more well-being in the lives of people in China, as well as in Tibet.

David L. Gardiner
Chair of the Religion Department, Colorado College
Colorado Springs, CO

Acknowledgments

So many people have helped us in so many ways that it is hard to know where to begin to give thanks. First and foremost, we are grateful to the millions of Tibetans who endure until their freedom is restored and to the millions in Tibet and around the world who have taken action toward that end. There are thousands of people who have worked very hard on many of the developments cited in this book, from defending Tibet's towns and borders to fighting for its freedom to preserving its culture and religion during this period of exile and hardship. It is impossible to know or name all of these individuals but without them there would be no book to write.

Robert Campbell was extraordinarily generous with his time and his intelligence in helping us frame the book and keeping us current on fresh developments. His knack for cultivating contacts and leads is uncanny. Without his assistance, all of which he did out of friendship, the book would have suffered badly. We hope he is proud of the result.

Philip Bane was extremely helpful in encouraging us to write the book and unfailingly responsive in checking facts and details. We are grateful to Philip and his entire family for their support and for their permission to use the photographs of Howard Bane that appear in the book. Thanks also go to Roger E. McCarthy, his son Kevin McCarthy, and Duane Clarridge for their assistance.

Peter Volz was immensely helpful, not only in enlightening us to the spread of Tibetan Buddhism in America, but in making arrangements and helping with logistics for travel to Dharamsala. The resulting interviews added significantly to our understanding of the Tibetans' reality. Professor David L. Gardiner and Lama Sarah Harding gave generously of their time and insight into Tibetan Buddhism, and we are extremely grateful to them for sharing their experiences and adventures with us. David Gardiner has been munificent in his willingness to share his knowledge and his wide range of friends and colleagues. Dr. Robbie Barnett, professor of Modern Tibetan Studies at Columbia University's Weatherhead East Asian Institute, was extremely kind and gave liberally of both his time and expertise.

We would like to express special gratitude to the Office of His Holiness the Dalai Lama. We would also like to thank John Ackerly and Bhuchung Tsering of the International Campaign for Tibet. Among those who generously gave their time in interviews, we would like to thank the Venerable Tsering Phuntsok, Minister of the Department of Religion and Culture; Sonam Dagpo, Secretary of the Department of Information and International Relations; Karma Yeshi, Editor-in-Chief of the *Voice of Tibet*; Dr. Tenzin Namdul of the Men-Tsee-Khang; Tsewang Rigzin, President of the Tibetan Youth Congress; Tenzin Norgay of the Tibetan Centre for Human Rights and Democracy; and Tenzin Tsundue, Friends of Tibet.

Thanks also to Bhuti Shungpa for her help in making arrangements in Dharamsala and to Dawa Gangpa Dhekyi for generously taking time away from his many endeavors to translate during interviews.

Special thanks go to Kelsang Tsering, for whom we have a particular fondness that Buddhists call a "heart connection." Kelsang gave freely of his time in arranging interviews and making our Dharamsala trip productive. Most importantly, he shared his life and experiences and welcomed us into his family. He and Pasang Norbu were steady companions whose sharp intellects, intelligent conversation, and good humor made the trip to Dharamsala a pleasure to be cherished. They deserve extra thanks for keeping us up to date during the fast-breaking developments of March, 2008, when fresh duties were pressing on them both in their work for the Tibetan Central Administration. Shiv Singh, who made the demanding drive between New Delhi and Dharamsala and stayed throughout the trip, had unfailing good humor and was excellent company for the journey even in trying circumstances.

Valoise Armstrong of the Dwight D. Eisenhower Library was instrumental in locating National Security Council Directive 5412/2 and making it available for the book. This document clears up longstanding confusion regarding the true purpose of American assistance to the Tibetans. Hers is an invaluable contribution to setting the record straight.

Lhasang Tsering was especially helpful in understanding the Tibetan perspective on independence and generously gave us permission to reprint his poetry. Carolyn Gimian of Shambhala was particularly helpful in identifying photographs for use in the book. She cheerfully fielded our vague requests and fulfilled them with wonderful images. Lama Sarah Harding graciously shared her personal photographs with us. Joshua and Diana Cutler of the Tibetan Buddhist Learning Center and Natalie Hauptman were helpful in tracking down the portrait photo of Geshe Wangyal. Thanks also to Eric Olason, who created, on short notice, a map of Tibet.

Special thanks go to Bob Shuman and Jennifer Holder, our editors, for their support. Without them, this book would never have happened. Bob Shuman's sharp recommendations on structure were invaluable. Every writer should be so lucky as to have an editor with Bob's insight and patience. We would also like to thank Barbara Chernow for her expertise and assistance with the final manuscript. To all the others who helped with the many tasks necessary to publish this book and should have been named but were not, please accept our gratitude.

Introduction

R arely has a cause like the movement to free Tibet had such unusual allies. It began during the Cold War as a Central Intelligence Agency (CIA) covert operation. In the 1960s and 1970s, just as the U.S. government interest in Tibet began to wane, the movement was adopted by the counterculture. The spread of Tibetan Buddhism in the West, coinciding with the Dalai Lama's emergence from his isolation in India to become an international spiritual leader, transformed the movement into a popular global cause. At each phase in the movement to free Tibet, individual lives of unlikely allies—spies and statesmen, Beatnik poets and writers, gurus and seekers, students and performers—intersected in ways that combined to keep the hope of Tibetan freedom alive.

This book is the story of how the free Tibet movement was born, nurtured, and continues to endure. It is not a foreign policy history or an encyclopedic account of the Dalai Lama's efforts to preserve Tibet's religion, culture, and civilization. It is about a movement sustained by millions of people across the world, on whose shoulders the fate of Tibet's ancient civilization depends.

My interest in Tibet's struggle for liberation goes back two decades. Shortly after the Dalai Lama won the 1989 Nobel Peace Prize, he visited Washington, D.C., and was interviewed by Dr. John McLaughlin for his television program *One on One*. Steve Tuemmler, who is now a producer at CNN, landed the interview using contacts he made in Dharamsala in 1988. At the time an intern for UPI, Tuemmler had taken the overnight train from New Dehli to Dharamsala. On the trip into the mountains, he was pickpocketed by passengers who pretended to fall asleep and slump into him. Fortunately, most of his cash was stowed in a moneybelt, and his visit to the seat of the Tibetan government-in-exile, now called the Tibetan Central Administration, was not ruined. He got three bylined articles after the Dalai Lama granted him an interview.

As a consulting producer, I helped Steve formulate questions for McLaughlin's broadcast. It was the year following China's crackdown on democracy activists in Tiananmen Square, and we focused on the Dalai Lama's views toward Beijing. The most intriguing aspect of the half-hour interview was his unwillingness to harshly criticize China, despite thirty years of repression inside Tibet.

A year or so later, I was in South Africa with Howard Bane, who had a long and distinguished career in the CIA, training party activists, who had never before been allowed to vote or participate in elections because of their race. One afternoon, we sat on a verandah at the Oyster Box Hotel in Umhlanga Rocks, South Africa, watching the waves on the Indian Ocean break on the shoreline a few yards away. Out of the blue, Howard told me about his involvement with a CIA operation to arm the Tibetan freedom fighters. Nodding in agreement to his hushed tones, rarely rising much above the noise of the nearby breakers, he said,

"You gotta keep this secret, John."

It was the first I had heard about his work with the Tibetans. Over the next week, before Howard and I parted—he to Botswana for a camping safari with his wife, Anita, and their son Chris, and I to return to Washington, D.C.—we continued to talk about the CIA's far-ranging covert program supporting the Tibetans.

Then, in the mid-1990s, the U.S. government began to declassify many details of Cold War history. Policymakers were talking about a "peace dividend" and cutting budgets for defense and intelligence agencies. The late Senator Daniel Patrick Moynihan went so far as to propose abolishing the CIA because it was no longer necessary after the fall of the Soviet Union. The CIA wanted credit for its Cold War successes, not so much to burnish its reputation as to maintain its funding, and began to declassify a surprising volume of information.

In 1996, an editor named Rich Blow at John F. Kennedy, Jr's magazine, *George*, asked if I would contribute an article to a special edition of the magazine called "The Spy Issue." Tony Blankley, who was then a columnist at *George*, had worked with me at the White House Office of Planning and Evaluation and told Blow about my intelligence connections. I called Howard and asked if I could write about the Tibetan operation. To my surprise, provided I shielded his name, he agreed to allow some details to be published. Helpful archivists at the State Department and CIA pointed me to newly declassified documents, chiefly diplomatic cables regarding contacts between Tibetan emissaries and U.S. officials, which shed further light on the operation, and I wrote the first feature article about the true extent of the CIA's covert aid to Tibet. Elizabeth Hurley appeared on the October 1997 magazine cover, posing like James Bond.

Despite my best intentions, the article created a nasty stir. Some saw it as embarrassing to His Holiness the Dalai Lama; others felt disclosing the CIA's abandonment of Tibetan guerrillas was a blemish for the Agency. John F. Kennedy Jr. was scheduled to see the Dalai Lama in Dharamsala shortly after the special edition of *George* hit the newsstand. His interview was almost canceled because of the article.

I came under pressure to disclose my sources from several quarters, but I refused to do so. Other writers went so far as to suggest I did not have any CIA sources at all. I wondered how badly I had blundered and if I misjudged political sensitivities. Howard reassured me. An intermediary who met with the Dalai Lama's brother, Gyalo Thondup, reported back to Howard that no serious damage was done. Moreover, Gyalo had been impressed that I had the inside story.

"You should write that in your journal," Howard said, and I did.

This book results not only from my twenty-year interest in the Tibetan freedom fight, but also from personal experience of political repression. As a kid, I lived in Spain during the dictatorship of Generalissimo Francisco Franco. Despite my youth, living in a country where freedom was restricted made an indelible impression. While a student at Oxford University, I returned to Spain after Franco's death to study the country's political transition to democracy.

Spain is an example of how Tibet and China can reconcile. Statutes of political autonomy for Spain's Basque and Catalan minorities, granted in 1979, mirror the Dalai Lama's demand for political autonomy for Tibet. Most visitors to Barcelona or Bilbao may not realize it, but in those cities they are experiencing the same kind of political arrangement the Dalai Lama proposes for Tibet. The Basques and Catalans have their own regional governments, parliaments, police forces, power to tax, and languages, yet they remain a part of the Spanish nation. This is precisely what the Tibetans now want from Beijing—autonomy, within the framework of the Chinese state.

When I studied the Spanish political transition in the mid-1970s, it was far from certain that the Basques and Catalans would receive autonomy. Spanish government-sponsored death squads eliminated political opponents, and groups like ETA—Euskadi ta Askatasuna, or Basque Homeland and Liberty—carried out terrorist attacks. Researching in the field was sometimes hazardous.

A key question was whether Basque and Catalan culture could flourish again after thirty years of Franco's regime, during which the use of the Basque and Catalan languages was outlawed in schools and the media. As it is in Tibet with its flag, displaying the Basque flag or even wearing a jacket with the national colors of green and red was a crime under Franco. But after the collapse of Franco's dictatorship, the cultural vibrancy of Spain's minority regions quickly returned. The Spanish example gives hope for Tibet.

Spain is not the only case of political transition from dictatorship to democracy that I have experienced. After working in the White House, I spent a decade as an international political consultant advising foreign governments and political leaders and working on election campaigns around the world. I was drawn primarily to societies in transition, those just emerging from military juntas, one-party Marxist rule, or civil unrest and guerrilla war. This exposed me to the turning points, the moments when old orders collapse and freedom arises, in many different countries. I experienced it firsthand in Argentina, Uruguay, Romania, Chile, Russia, Kazakhstan, Kyrgyszstan, Ukraine, and South Africa. Even countries which had been dominated for seventy years and experienced religious and cultural repression similar to Tibet sprang back like saplings just released from melting snowpacks in the high mountains.

Ever since Howard Bane told me about his Tibetan experiences, I have wondered why he chose the moment he did to reveal his story. In writing this book, an answer came to me. Freedom for South Africa's blacks inspired him, but the way in which that country's black majority achieved it is the underlying reason for his disclosure that day at Umhlanga Rocks.

Consumer boycotts, trade sanctions, and a divestment campaign targeting corporate interests finally forced South Africa's apartheid regime to concede to majority rule. Today, the economic linkages between China and the rest of the world make it possible to use the same tools to compel China to grant autonomy to Tibet. Just as Spain represents the solution, South Africa's example shows us the means toward the goal of liberating Tibet.

Elizabeth, my wife and coauthor, shares a passion for politics, freedom, and human rights. Her background as a campaign worker on a U.S. Senate race and a journalist covering candidates and elections for the highly respected *Cook Political Report* gave her insight into the inside maneuverings of the nation's capitol. Her perspective on the intertwining of policy and politics was instrumental in writing this book, as were her interviewing skills. Elizabeth's commitment to Tibet includes a personal boycott of products and apparel made in China, and she has a flourishing interest in Buddhism.

In the conclusion to the book, we urge a change in tactics to focus economic pressure on China. There is a growing sense of urgency among Tibetans and their supporters that time could be running out and that if freedom for Tibet does not become a reality within the next decade, it may be too late to save this ancient civilization from disappearing.

People make history. Tibetans have been struggling against China for fifty years. They have been aided by the United States and India, student movements, celebrities, individual politicians, human rights groups, Buddhists worldwide, and sympathetic individuals as different from one another as CIA officer Howard Bane and the Beatnik poet Allen Ginsberg. This account of Tibet's fifty-year struggle for freedom follows the threads of many individual lives that intersect in surprising ways. The final chapter in the story of Tibet's fight for liberation remains to be written by you, the readers, and the many others worldwide willing to take action to free Tibet.

—John B. Roberts II
www.FreeingTibet.com

Greater Tibet
Map By: Eric Olason.www.ericolason.com

Part One: Struggle

Chapter 1

Warriors of the Fortress of Faith

EASTERN TIBET, JANUARY, 1956, NYARONG DISTRICT, KHAM PROVINCE

orjee Yudon pulsed with rage when she heard about the slaughter of Gyurme's family. A squad of Chinese soldiers had gone to his house with orders to confiscate the weapons—rifles, usually antiquated flintlocks, and swords, traditionally carried by Khampas, as the people of the Kham province were called. Gyurme was away on a business trip in the town of Dartsedo, the local administrative center of the Nyarong district, when the People's Liberation Army (PLA) troops barged through the wooden gate and crossed the courtyard of his home.

His wife, their young son, and his mother were alone, except for a family domestic servant. The soldiers demanded to be shown where the guns were stashed. Gyurme's wife pleaded, telling them that there were no arms other than those her husband had taken along on his trip. No sensible person traveled in Nyarong without some means of self-defense against the banditry common in the region.

The Chinese commander became incensed. He screamed at her to turn over the weapons. She protested that she didn't have any to surrender. He replied by ordering his troops to shoot everyone in the house—the boy, the grandmother, the servant, and Gyurme's wife.

Dorjee knew that the soldiers would come to her house soon, if not next. Like Gyurme, her husband, Gyari Nima, was a local leader. He was a tribal head of the Gyaritsang, one of the clans of Nyarongwa people who had inhabited this land for centuries. Nyarong was one of the Tibetan districts closest to the border with China.

In the five-and-a-half years since the PLA invaded Tibet on October 7, 1950, the Chinese military had kept troops based in Eastern Tibet. The initial fighting lasted less than two weeks. Tibet's army, outnumbered ten to one, was decisively defeated at the battle of Chamdo on October 17, and a formal surrender was signed the next day. Until now, the PLA had generally behaved well, leaving the Khampas to handle their own affairs. Soldiers were even known to help peasants harvest barley and other crops.

Dorjee realized something had changed to put her family and neighbors in danger. Chairman Mao Zedong, founder of the People's Republic of China (PRC) and head of the all-powerful Chinese Communist Party, had ordered "democratic reforms" imposed in Eastern Tibet. Mao's objective was to radically transform Tibetan society, replacing it with socialist rule from Beijing. Party cadres were to strip power from local leaders like Gyurme and Gyari Nima. To minimize resistance, the PLA was seizing weapons.

Tibet's government, headed by the 20-year-old Dalai Lama, was powerless to stop the Chinese in Kham. Remnants of Tibet's army were far away to the west in the province of U-Tsang and clustered mainly near the capital city of Lhasa. There would be no help from it.

Dorjee was Gyari Nima's youngest wife, agile on horseback, strong spirited, and beautiful. She had no way of knowing when her husband would return from Dartsedo. There were no telephone or telegraph lines in Eastern Tibet. The only way to communicate was by courier, and there was little time to act.

Dartsedo was under Chinese control, and her husband might be detained indefinitely. She would have to be the one to take action. Writing notes telling of the massacre at Gyurme's house, she gave them to riders to carry by horseback to other clans and tribes across Eastern Tibet. Dorjee urged the men to join her in a coordinated revolt against the PLA.

Twenty-three leaders responded. Under the banner of the Warriors of the Fortress of Faith, Dorjee organized meetings throughout Kham to plan an uprising. When the Chinese authorities got word of her activities, they enlisted the aid of Tibetan collaborators. Two Nyarongwa men, accompanied by two soldiers, tried to kill her in her home but were thwarted by guards. The foiled attack increased her fame, and her determination.

Dorjee knew that the assassination attempt would be followed by another if she didn't act first. Her uprising began four days earlier than originally planned. Its scale took the Chinese by surprise. On horseback, with a pistol holstered by her side, and wearing a turquoise-studded charm box bearing protective amulets around her neck, Dorjee lead the assaults against Chinese convoys and outposts. In battle after battle the PLA was pushed back. The Chinese retreated into Drugmo Dzong, an ancient castle called the Fortress of the Female Dragon.

As a fighter, Dorjee was fearless and relentless. Over the course of a month-long siege of the stone fortress, she led several attempts to storm the walls. When the PLA sent some six hundred reinforcements, the Khampas attacked them at Upper Nyarong. Four hundred soldiers were killed. A few hundred managed to break away and reach the fortress, where they too were soon under siege.

China responded with maximum force. The next troops to march into Kham numbered between 18,000 and 20,000. Dorjee and her fighters were forced to withdraw. Some returned home, melding into the population. Others took refuge in the mountains and operated as guerrilla bands, harassing the PLA with hit-and-run tactics.

Dorjee's 1956 uprising had lasted months. More than 2000 Chinese troops were killed at the siege of the Fortress of the Female Dragon alone. The Warriors had shown that the people of Tibet were determined to resist the attempts by Chairman Mao to destroy their culture, their religion, and their society. They would not be alone in their struggle.

ROOTS OF THE TIBET—CHINA CONFLICT

Before Dorjee's revolt, the PLA and the Tibetans had gotten along fairly well. There had been no major conflicts since the 1950 invasion. The initial fighting had stopped short of the capital city of Lhasa, and the Tibetans had been largely left to govern themselves. Most Tibetans were mystified by Mao's decision to invade. His excuse was to rid the country of foreign imperialists, but there were no imperialists in Tibet. There were less than a dozen outsiders in the whole land, including Austrian

mountaineer Heinrich Harrer and two British citizens, Robert Ford and
Reginald Fox, employees of the Tibetan government who ran radio communications. To the Tibetans, the Chinese were the foreigners.

Tibet's government was unique. Tenzin Gyatso, the Fourteenth Dalai
Lama, was both the head of state and the highest religious authority. As
monarch and spiritual leader, he was guardian of an ancient civilization,
making him unique among world leaders. This system of government
was established in 1642 by Ngawang Lozang Gyatso, the Fifth Dalai
Lama. It had endured more than 300 years when China invaded in 1950.

From 1642 onward, Tibet governed herself. It had its own army, language, currency, and postage stamps. Tibet issued passports to its citizens,
although this was rare because few Tibetans traveled abroad. The country's history, ethnicity, culture, and political structure were distinct from
China's and the rest of its neighbors. In fact, there was no other civilization like it, with its thousands of Buddhist monasteries that functioned as
centers of finance, education, social welfare, and spiritual study, anywhere else in the world.

Other nations also saw Tibet as independent. In the late nineteenth
and early twentieth centuries, when the mandate of the British Empire
stretched across India to the borders of Afghanistan, British officials
sought to align Tibet with their imperial interests. In 1904, British and
Sepoy troops (Indians trained to serve in the colonial army) invaded Tibet
under the command of Colonel Francis Younghusband. After concluding a treaty establishing bilateral relations and commercial trade between
Tibet and the British Empire, Younghusband and his army withdrew.

The treaty Tibet signed with the British Empire had two important
implications. First, and foremost, it confirmed Tibet's independence from
any other nation. Had the British believed that Tibet was, in fact, governed by the Manchu sovereigns (the foreign conquerors who also ruled
China), it would have been a simple matter for British diplomats to negotiate directly with Beijing. The second consequence was that by signing a
treaty with the British, the Tibetan government had allied itself with foreign imperialists.

Tibet's territory extended over two-and-a-half-million square kilome-
ters and was divided into three provinces. Amdo was in the northeast and
closest to China. Kham province lay south of Amdo and was home to the
Khampas, nomadic herders renowned for their horsemanship and physical prowess. In the western province of U-Tsang, the capital city of Lhasa

was located. Ringed with mountain ranges like the Himalayas, Kara-korum, and Kunlun, its central feature is the Tibetan Plateau, situated at 14,000 feet.

Tibet and China coexisted in a fragile symbiosis. The main route into China ran through the province of Kham. And it was common for Tibetans and Chinese merchants to import and export their goods. Tibet's chief import from China was tea, but silk, horses, cotton, and goods like matches and buttons were imported as well. The Tibetans either paid in gold or bartered wool, deer horns, medicinal herbs, furs, and sheepskins.

At various times throughout history, both China and Tibet were under the dominion of foreign rulers. From 1644 until 1911, China was ruled by the Manchu Qing emperors. During the eighteenth century, when the Manchu Empire was still vibrant, its reign briefly extended to Tibet. By the middle of the nineteenth century, Manchu influence waned and, in 1911, there were coordinated uprisings in Hankow and Wuchang in China. When the Manchu sent General Yuan Shih-Kai to quash the Chinese revolt he, instead, switched sides and joined the rebels. A new provisional government was established in Nanking in December 1911 and, by February 1912, the Manchu renounced all right to govern China and recognized the Republic as the lawful successor regime.

It was Mao Zedong, a Marxist revolutionary, who would eventually claim Tibet as a part of China. The son of peasants from Hunan, Mao could recruit men to his revolutionary cause simply by the power of his oratory. In 1921, he had the brilliant insight that revolution in China would not be brought about by industrial workers, as classic Marxist-Leninist theory held, but by landless farmers and villagers. Embittered by generations of social injustice, the peasantry was an irresistible force for fundamental change.

From 1921 through 1948, Mao and his followers fought what he called the Long March. On October 1, 1949, standing on the main gate to Tiananmen Square, he announced the founding of the People's Republic of China (PRC). It had taken nearly 28 years and hundreds of thousands of lost lives, but Mao finally had what he sought: power over China. He now felt his Revolution could finally begin in earnest. Mao's indispensable deputy, Zhou En-lai, called the task before them the "next Long March."

Consolidating control over the territories on China's fringes was the first step in the next Long March. To build the modern revolutionary power Mao envisioned, China needed resources. The Tibetan Plateau, larger than a quarter of China's land mass and rich in minerals, was necessary to his success. Broadcasts on Radio Beijing announced that "the People's Liberation Army must liberate all Chinese territories, including Tibet, Xinjiang, Hainan, and Taiwan."

In Tibet, the broadcasts were heard with alarm. The Tibetan Foreign Office promptly sent a blunt response to Chairman Mao. The Foreign Office communiqué stated: "Tibet had from the earliest times up to now been an independent country whose political administration has never been taken over by any foreign country and Tibet also defended her own territories from foreign invasion."

The message, devoid of diplomatic finesse, was an act of bravado. Tibet's army numbered a mere 8,500 troops. It had outmoded artillery, lacked modern rifles and machine guns, and had no radio communications to link its soldiers. There were no mechanized infantry, no armored units, and no air force. Mobile units consisted of cavalry and swordsmen. The Tibetans were no match for the battle-hardened veterans of the PLA, and Mao knew it. The United States and other governments denounced Mao's invasion of Tibet, but no one took immediate action against the PLA.

PRESIDENT EISENHOWER
AND THE 5412 SPECIAL GROUP

Dorjee Yudon could not have known that the President of the United States had decided to support guerrilla movements, like hers, against the Chinese. It was a few days after Christmas in December 1955, when President Dwight D. Eisenhower signed a secret presidential directive ordering the Central Intelligence Agency (CIA) to step up covert activities against Communist regimes on a global basis. His directive became known as National Security Council (NSC) Directive 5412/2.

NSC 5412/2 was an extraordinarily broad and aggressive response to the Cold War challenge posed by the Soviet Union, the People's Republic of China, and their satellite states. In the top secret document, all were lumped together under the rubric "International Communism." Distributed to the Secretary of State, Secretary of Defense, Chairman of the

Joint Chiefs of Staff, Director of Central Intelligence, and the Executive Officer of the Operations Coordinating Board, access to the directive was ordered strictly controlled on an "absolute need to know basis." NSC 5412/2 said to:

> Create and exploit troublesome problems for International Communism . . . complicate control within the USSR, Communist China, and their satellites . . . discredit the prestige and ideology of International Communism . . . and to the extent practicable in areas dominated or threatened by International Communism, develop underground resistance and facilitate covert and guerilla operations and ensure availability of those forces in the event of war, including wherever practicable provision of a base upon which the military may expand those forces in time of war. . . .

To leave no doubt about what Eisenhower wanted the CIA to do, NSC 5412/2 was explicit about covert operations:

> Specifically, such operations shall include any covert activities related to: propaganda; political action; economic warfare; preventive direct action, including sabotage, anti-sabotage, demolition; escape and evasion and evacuation measures; subversion against hostile states or groups including assistance to underground resistance movements, guerrillas and refugee liberation groups; support of indigenous and anti-communist elements in threatened countries of the free world; deception plans and operations; and all activities compatible with this directive necessary to accomplish the foregoing. . . .

The responsibility for overseeing covert plans and approving their operational details fell to an ultra secret White House committee known as the 5412 Special Group. It was an unusually powerful White House committee. The job of the 5412 Special Group wasn't to make foreign policy; it was to take action. The group's authority derived directly from broad covert directives that had been drafted by the NSC and approved by the President. Gordon Gray, Eisenhower's Special Assistant for National Security Affairs, was given the power to approve the CIA's covert action plans and its interagency coordination with other departments of the U.S. government.

In addition to Gray, the 5412 Special Group's members included CIA Director Allen Dulles and the deputy secretaries of the State Department and Defense Department. Thomas Parrot, who served as special assistant to Dulles, was the 5412 Special Group's secretary and sole staff member.

TIBETAN RESISTANCE GROWS

Resistance to the Chinese spread throughout Eastern Tibet in 1956. In addition to Dorjee's uprising, there were rebellions among the Golok tribespeople and in Litang, where a charismatic 25-year old named Yunri Ponpo rallied a force of thousands to make a stand against the PLA. Using the Great Monastery as a base, Ponpo's fighters inflicted heavy damage on surrounding Chinese troops. The Chinese counterattacked with artillery and Soviet-made Ilyushin 28 bombers. Battering the walls of the monastery from land and by air, they finally forced the Khampas to surrender. Yunri was among the last defenders left inside the rubble of the monastery. The Chinese wanted to capture him alive. Insisting that he would surrender only to the Chinese commanding general, Yunri concealed a handgun inside the long sleeve of his traditional cloak. When the general approached, Yunri pulled out the revolver and emptied its cylinder, killing the commander and another senior officer before being shot dead by the Chinese.

Growing resistance in Eastern Tibet represented the kind of "troublesome problems for International Communism" that NSC 5412/2 was intended to exploit. The major drawback was that the Dalai Lama opposed the use of violence. It would take time for the CIA to devise a plan to get around this problem. Meanwhile, the Agency had its orders from President Eisenhower. As CIA officer Roger McCarthy put it in an interview years later with Mikel Dunham for the book *Buddha's Warriors*, "The U.S. objective was to destabilize China . . . the Dalai Lama's position—whatever that may have been—was no longer an issue."

Chapter 2

The Tennis Champion
of Darjeeling

B y 1956, Gyalo Thondup, the Dalai Lama's second oldest brother, was one of the CIA's best Tibetan assets. In 1951, the year after the Chinese invasion, Gyalo and his brother, Jigme Thubten Norbu, made contact with the CIA. Using a front group called the Committee for a Free Asia, the Agency arranged for Norbu, the Dalai Lama's eldest brother, to come to the United States. Norbu and an assistant flew from India on the midnight Pan Am flight to London and then on to New York. Norbu's cover story for the U.S. trip was to seek medical treatment for rheumatism and then to explore teaching opportunities at the University of California at Berkeley.

But Norbu's real agenda was in Washington, DC, where on July 12, 1951, he met with State Department and CIA officials. Assistant Secretary of State Dean Rusk, who headed Far Eastern affairs, made Norbu an offer that had full backing from President Harry Truman. Rusk said that if the Dalai Lama went into asylum in Sri Lanka, the United States would provide financial support. Norbu was also told the United States would provide military aid, to the extent feasible, given the difficult geographic barriers. The offer was a take-it-or-leave-it proposition conditional on the Dalai Lama leaving Tibet. The Truman Administration wanted the Dalai Lama out of China's grasp so that he could become an international symbol of opposition to communism.

Norbu and Gyalo tried to persuade the Dalai Lama to accept the American offer. Together, the older brothers had coordinated a plan with U.S. Ambassador Loy Henderson in New Delhi for the Dalai Lama and a retinue of 200 high officials and family members to cross into India from the border town of Yatung. If that scheme was blocked, there was a back-up plan to have Heinrich Harrer and a Scottish journalist named George Patterson secretly whisk Tenzin Gyatso and a small party across the mountains under cover of night.

Neither plan was consummated. The Dalai Lama felt that his duty as Tibet's leader was to try to preserve his people's freedom by negotiating with the Chinese. Gyalo decided to help. After a six-month stay in the United States, he returned to Lhasa with an ambitious program for political and economic reforms.

Part of the Chinese rationale for invading Tibet was to develop the backward country. Gyalo believed that if the Dalai Lama made reforms, they would deprive the Chinese of any justification for imposing Communist rule on Tibet. His proposals ranged from abolishing the system of inherited debts to limiting the amount of land the monasteries and aristocracy could own. When his reforms failed because of opposition from vested interests, Gyalo moved to the Indian border town of Darjeeling to set up a business.

The hill station had been a favorite summer retreat of British colonialists seeking relief from the heat and torpor of India's crowded and humid lowlands. In the mid-1950s, Darjeeling's colonial splendor had changed little since the town's Victorian heyday. Against the backdrop of the Himalayas, a Gothic church steeple rose incongruously. At the town's ridge top summit, there was a paved avenue with a fountain, a bandstand, and benches where passers-by could gather their breath while taking in the splendid mountain views. Grand hotels with shaded verandahs, tidy administrative buildings, and Victorian cottages for the colonial elite composed the town's genteel upper streets. Lower down the hillside, the scene took on a more local character, with bazaars, merchants' shops, and villas for the Indian gentry.

Gyalo began exporting tea and White Horse whiskey into Tibet, peddling them to PLA troops. Occasionally, the traders who carried the merchandise by yak and horseback from Darjeeling adulterated the liquor by urinating in the bottles before selling them to the soldiers.

Business was brisk, thanks in part to the People's Republic of China. Mao's strategy to win over the Tibetans during the early years of the occupation was to flood the country with money. Communist party officials and soldiers curried favor with Tibetans by using silver dollar-sized coins to pay lavish rents on buildings from the aristocracy, for supplies, and in the bazaars. Gyalo prospered. He joined Darjeeling's Gymkhana Club, where he became the local tennis star.

His network of merchants was more than a livelihood. It was a valuable intelligence pipeline. Because Tibet was so isolated in the 1950s, there was little way of knowing what was happening inside the country except by word of mouth. As traders returned to Darjeeling from their travels, they gave Gyalo reports on the size and location of PLA bases and how the Chinese soldiers were getting along with the locals.

By the summer of 1956, word of the revolts in Kham and Amdo reached Darjeeling. Some accounts were too sketchy to be useful, but Gyalo collected them patiently, patching together the details. When he was confident of his facts, he sent letters to Indian and American intelligence officials and to newspaper reporters alerting them to the dramatic turn of events inside Tibet.

DESMOND FITZGERALD TAKES CHARGE

Fighting in Eastern Tibet was the news that Desmond FitzGerald had been waiting for. As head of the CIA's Far East Division, he was the chief architect of covert operations against China. The 5412 Special Group was responsible for approving the plans, but FitzGerald was responsible for creating them. Gyalo's reports were his first solid indication that there was an active resistance movement inside Tibet for the CIA to support.

Harvard-educated, handsome and articulate, FitzGerald ran in the same Massachusetts social circles as the Kennedys. In another walk of life, he might have been a rat pack bon vivant. He was urbane, liked quality tailoring, and was impressed by restaurants with fine touches like using a spray atomizer to add vermouth to his martini. But FitzGerald was no fop. He was a battle-hardened World War II veteran who, while assigned to the Office of Strategic Services (OSS), took part in General Joe Stilwell's campaign to liberate Burma.

It was in the Burmese jungles that FitzGerald found his life's calling. He learned the power of local resistance movements to oppose numerically superior and better-armed military troops in the fight against the Japanese. FitzGerald quickly absorbed classic guerrilla warfare lessons, such as the importance of a local understanding of the terrain and the ability of guerrilla fighters to strike hard and then blend into the population. His World War II combat experience formed the basis for a lifetime of high-risk covert wars that spanned the globe from Quemoy and Korea to Cambodia and Cuba, and now Tibet.

After World War II, FitzGerald returned to the United States to practice law in New York City, but civilian life didn't keep hold of him for long. Frank Wisner, a friend who had joined the newly created CIA, recruited FitzGerald into the Agency.

During his tenure, FitzGerald would prove effective, yet provoke contradictory opinions in people. In his memoirs, John Kenneth Galbraith, who was President John F. Kennedy's ambassador to India, called FitzGerald "the most sanguinary, imaginative, and personable architect of covert operations in CIA history" and "also, the most irresponsible." It was FitzGerald who came up with the idea of using an exploding conch shell to assassinate Cuban leader Fidel Castro while he was scuba diving.

John Kenneth Knaus, whose CIA career spanned four decades, described FitzGerald in his book *Orphans of the Cold War: America and the Tibetan Struggle for Survival*, as "a responsible man who questioned the moral issues and objectives of the operations conceived and conducted by his division."

There might be divergent views over whether FitzGerald was a reckless swashbuckler or a highly ethical intelligence operative. But on one thing there was agreement, FitzGerald was a force to be reckoned with inside the CIA. He was respected by CIA Director Allen Dulles for his ability to manage complex and daring intelligence operations. During his career, FitzGerald organized three different plots to assassinate Fidel Castro and oversaw the start of the CIA's largest paramilitary undertaking ever, the secret war in Laos, which lasted from 1959 until 1973. Like other operatives of his era, FitzGerald covered his bureaucratic tracks by not writing voluminous memos or leaving behind long paper trails.

"The rugged Tibetans," Knaus wrote, "appealed to both FitzGerald's romantic spirit and his belief that insurgencies initiated by local people fighting for their own land and beliefs were the only effective way to challenge Chinese Communist expansion in Asia."

But, while Gyalo's reports were tantalizing they were unverified. Before FitzGerald drew up plans that would commit the United States to supporting a covert war in Tibet, he needed to know more about the fledgling resistance.

FITZGERALD GOES INTO ACTION

The Crown Prince of Sikkim, a small Himalayan kingdom bordering India and Tibet, traveled to Lhasa in the summer of 1956 and met with the Dalai Lama. He carried with him a formal invitation from the Indian government for Tenzin Gyatso to attend the annual Buddhist Jayanti celebrations in November. The events would be particularly festive. It was the 2500th anniversary of the birth of Buddha.

Tenzin Gyatso was eager to participate, for religious reasons as well as for affairs of state. Spiritually, the Dalai Lama is a Bodhisattva, an enlightened being whose own salvation has been postponed for the sake of enlightening other human beings. Bodhisattvas choose to reincarnate in human form to help others attain liberation. The Dalai Lama is considered to be the incarnation of Avalokiteshvara, the Bodhisattva of Compassion, who is also known as Chenrezig and is the patron deity of Tibet. His attendance at the Buddhist Jayanti commemoration would be rejoiced not only by practicing Buddhists in India but by Buddhists around the world. It would also give him an opportunity to personally meet with Indian Prime Minister Jawaharlal Nehru and appeal to him to put pressure on China to ease the repression in Eastern Tibet.

Initially, the Chinese occupying forces turned down the Dalai Lama's request to attend the celebrations. To his surprise, a few weeks before the Jayanti events were to begin the Chinese reversed their decision and granted him permission to go to India. In the interval, there had been an uprising in Hungary that was brutally crushed by the Soviet Union's Red Army. The USSR was widely condemned by the international community. The Chinese may have feared that blocking the Dalai Lama from the Buddhist celebrations would spark similar global criticism.

Desmond FitzGerald knew an opportunity when he saw one. The presence of the Dalai Lama and his retinue in India, where he and his entourage would be relatively free from oversight by the Chinese, afforded the CIA the opportunity it needed to make its approach.

During the summer, the 5412 Special Group had decided in principle to support the Tibetan resistance. The question was how. Some U.S. officials, including Air Force General Curtis LeMay, proposed using air strikes against Chinese positions. But overt acts of war weren't within the parameters of NSC 5412/2. Covert wars, however, were. The issue was whether the Tibetans were ready and willing to accept covert aid.

With the Dalai Lama in India, Gyalo would have excellent access to his younger brother and other ranking Tibetan officials. FitzGerald sent a "Flash" cable to CIA officer John Hoskins, who was based in Calcutta. Hoskins was told to make direct contact with Gyalo. The Flash designation meant the matter was of the highest priority.

FitzGerald's cable sent Hoskins packing for the mountain town of Darjeeling. In the 1950s, India was not an easy country for CIA operations. Although, in terms of technology, India's intelligence service was resource poor, it was rich in manpower. It cost only a few rupees to keep counterintelligence agents on the streets all day, shadowing foreign "diplomats" and the potential targets the diplomats hoped to recruit. The amount of manpower that India's security service could devote to tailing CIA officers was exceeded only in places like Moscow, where literally dozens of Soviet counterintelligence staff might be assigned to follow one CIA case officer.

Discretion was critical. The CIA had no way of knowing how the Indian government would react if it learned that the Agency was plotting with the Tibetans to start a covert war on India's northern borders. Gyalo had met with Bhola Nath Mullik, the head of India's Intelligence Bureau, in Darjeeling a few years earlier. The contact virtually assured that local Indian intelligence agents would be watchful.

To gain access to his target, Hoskins finagled his way into a tennis doubles match at the Gymkhana Club. In a private moment he introduced himself as a CIA officer and asked Gyalo to be the conduit between the Agency and the Dalai Lama during his stay in India. Gyalo was receptive to Hoskins's overtures, and the two agreed to meet again in Calcutta where it would be easier to evade the ever-watchful Indian Intelligence Bureau. Hoskins advised Gyalo to use clandestine precautions to avoid detection for future meetings.

On November 25, 1956, the Dalai Lama and an entourage of fifty officials arrived in New Delhi. It was the beginning of a four-month stay in India. His older brothers, Gyalo and Norbu, had met him at the border. Norbu had not seen Tenzin Gyatso for five years. Nearly four years had gone by since Gyalo moved from Lhasa to Darjeeling. The siblings had much catching up to do.

DIPLOMATIC MERRY-GO-ROUND

A whirlwind of diplomatic activity took place during the final months of 1956. Within days of his arrival in New Delhi, the Dalai Lama met with Prime Minister Nehru. The Indian leader was sympathetic to the plight of the Tibetans, but urged the young Buddhist leader to try to work constructively with China.

China's Premier Zhou En-lai was the next to land in New Delhi. It was the first leg of a six-country Asian goodwill tour. In keeping with diplomatic protocol, the Dalai Lama was on hand alongside Nehru to greet Zhou at the airport. During his brief stopover in New Delhi, Zhou met separately with Nehru and Tenzin Gyatso. Nehru urged Zhou not to force the Tibetans to adopt socialist reforms, such as communal farming, or to interfere with the Buddhist monasteries. Zhou cautioned Nehru on the consequences for Indian-Chinese relations if India were to grant asylum to the Dalai Lama. In his meeting with the Dalai Lama, Zhou stressed that he must return to Tibet after the Buddhist festivities concluded. The Chinese leader knew that the Dalai Lama had almost gone into exile in 1951. He was probably aware that his brothers were meeting with U.S. officials.

At the end of December, Nehru was scheduled to meet Eisenhower at the White House. Before leaving for Washington, the Indian prime minister again met privately with the Dalai Lama. The Tibetan leader urged him to press Eisenhower to recognize Tibet's claim to independence. This time Nehru was supportive, despite the pressure from China. Apparently, Zhou's implied threats if India gave asylum to the young leader had stiffened Nehru's resolve.

Tibet was not the main item on the agenda at the White House summit. Bilateral relations with India were foremost. As part of its Cold War strategy, the United States was eager to woo Nehru and prevent the Soviet

Union from making diplomatic inroads with India. America also had a close relationship with Pakistan, India's neighboring arch rival, and Eisenhower needed to bring the ties with both countries into balance.

With the 5412 Special Group exploring the feasibility of a covert program to aid Tibet, there were matters to be discussed with Nehru. The Indian leader could not be asked to approve an undertaking that China would find provocative. It would undermine the spirit of the agreement Nehru had signed with China only two years earlier, the Five Principles of Peaceful Co-Existence. Nor would Eisenhower risk compromising the CIA's plans by revealing details to a foreign leader.

But Eisenhower wanted Nehru's tacit cooperation, in broad terms, with U.S. plans to increase support for the Dalai Lama's government. In 1951, during the Truman presidency, Secretary of State Dean Acheson had tried to broker a deal with the Dalai Lama whereby the United States would aid the Tibetan cause financially, diplomatically, and militarily. It was conditional on Tenzin Gyatso going into exile in a friendly country, where he could become an international symbol of resistance to communism. Five years later, the Eisenhower Administration adhered to the same goal. Urging Nehru to offer the Dalai Lama asylum, Eisenhower outlined the commitment the United States was prepared to make to the Tibetans. Nehru didn't budge on asylum, but he didn't object to the broader American effort.

This was the outcome Eisenhower wanted.

Only a month before, in early November, the CIA's aid to the liberation movement in Hungary had ended disastrously when some 200,000 Russian troops backed by 4,000 armored tanks swarmed into Budapest. Initially, Hungarian resistance fighters fought the Soviets, despite being badly outnumbered and at a severe disadvantage in terms of firepower.

When the CIA proposed using aircraft to drop ammunition and supplies to the beleaguered Hungarians, Eisenhower refused because the flights would have crossed over Warsaw Pact territory and been provocative to the Soviet Union, perhaps to the point of triggering a war between the United States and the USSR. Hungary, Eisenhower thought at the time, "was as inaccessible to us as Tibet."

As he met with Nehru, Eisenhower knew Tibet's guerrillas would face a similar outcome without air support. The CIA had almost solved the problem of airspace. Pakistan had consented to allow the use of a World War II era landing strip on its territory. Supply flights could originate in Okinawa and use stopovers at bases in East Pakistan. The flights would only cross very briefly over India on their final leg into Tibet.

There was still the risk that an American plane bound for Tibet might crash in Indian territory and create a diplomatic incident. What Eisenhower needed was India's agreement to turn a blind eye to minor airspace violations. Nehru assented. India would, of course, publicly deny any knowledge of the secret operation if it were exposed and lodge an appropriate diplomatic protest at America's violation of its airspace.

When Nehru returned from his summit with Eisenhower, Zhou En-lai was just concluding his Asian trip. On the way back to Beijing, he stopped in New Delhi. The Premier and the Prime Minister met again. To Nehru's surprise, Zhou announced that Chairman Mao had decided to suspend his campaign to bring socialist reforms to Eastern Tibet for at least several years. Mao, Zhou said, was prepared to wait as long as 50 years to change Tibet's political and economic system, if necessary.

For the time being, China had backed down. Nehru and the Dalai Lama met again in early 1957. When the subject of asylum arose, Nehru was firm. He told the Dalai Lama to return to Tibet. Tenzin Gyatso agreed but, first, he planned to visit the border town of Kalimpong. When the revolts in Eastern Tibet collapsed, many Khampas had sought refuge there, and Tenzin Gyatso wanted to see them. Zhou En-lai had warned the Dalai Lama to stay away from Kalimpong. The town was a hotbed of political intrigue. Nehru was unhappy, but did nothing to deter his guest from going.

Chapter 3

The Dharma Beatniks
and the Island of the Dead

The White House and the CIA weren't the only ones taking an interest in Buddhism in the 1950s. By an odd instance of cultural synchronicity, not only American warriors, but also American poets were embracing Buddhism. The Beat Generation of writers had awakened to the appeal of Zen Buddhism about the same time as President Eisenhower signed 5412/2, especially an obscure New Jersey author named Jack Kerouac.

In 1956, a Mongolian Buddhist monk named Geshe Wangyal opened the first Tibetan Buddhist center in the West in an old garage in Howell Township, New Jersey. Wangyal was not only the first Tibetan Buddhist scholar to move to the United States, he was also the first intermediary between the CIA and the Dalai Lama's family. Fearing for her son's safety under Chinese rule, Diki Tsering, the Dalai Lama's mother, had asked for Geshe's help in 1951 when they were both in Kalimpong, India. Geshe contacted the American consulate in Calcutta, where he met CIA officer Robert Linn. In the hope that Linn might help persuade Tenzin Gyatso to take refuge in India, Wangyal introduced Linn to the family.

Geshe Wangyal's arrival in New York harbor aboard the S.S. *Liberté* was featured in the *New York World Telegram* with a photo and a caption heralding the arrival of the "Buddhist Minister." In 1951, the United States gave asylum to 800 Mongolians who had been living in refugee camps in Europe since the end of World War II. The Mongolians, who were among the millions of people displaced by the war, came from the region of Kalmykia on the north Caspian Sea, inside the borders of the Soviet Union.

The Kalmyks formed a unique ethnic group and had practiced Tibetan Buddhism for centuries. In 1264 Kublai Khan, the grandson of Genghis Khan, was enthroned as the first emperor of the Mongol Dynasty to rule over China. Kublai Khan was a convert to Tibetan Buddhism. Another Mongol ruler, Prince Altan Khan, bestowed the title of Dalai Lama on a high Buddhist lama of the Gelug sect named Sonam Gyatso. The title "Dalai Lama" is Mongolian. It means "Ocean of Wisdom." The result was an alliance between the Mongol court and the Gelug. Altan Khan extended the Gelug his protection and invited them to establish monasteries in his kingdom to convert the Mongol people to Buddhism.

The Kalmyk Mongol immigrants settled in Freewood Acres, New Jersey. Geshe Wangyal joined them as the community's first spiritual adviser. Not long after his arrival, he reunited with the Dalai Lama's oldest brother, Norbu, who was teaching classes in Tibetan at Columbia University. Geshe also started teaching at Columbia. His local visibility and the university affiliation put him at the epicenter of the literary and cultural ferment that spawned the Beatnik scene. Poets and writers like Allen Ginsberg, Anne Waldman, William Burroughs, and Jack Kerouac were just beginning to flourish.

Zen's arrival on the West Coast was the initial catalyst for the Beatniks' attraction to Buddhism. For many of the Beat Generation writers, but especially Ginsberg and Waldman, Zen served as a pathway to Tibetan Buddhism.

As a virtual unknown, Kerouac was hardly in a position in the mid-1950s to promote the popular spread of Buddhism in the United States. His first novel, *The Town and the City*, had been published in 1950. It received decent reviews but sold poorly. As a result, he couldn't get another book published. Over the next three years, Kerouac wrote four other novels in addition to *On the Road*, the book that would eventually establish him as a literary star and popular culture phenomenon. But even with this prolific output and the unrelenting efforts of his agent, Sterling Lord, he couldn't find a publisher. Fed up with trying to break into New York publishing circles, Kerouac immersed himself in Buddhism.

He began writing an epic tome called *Some of the Dharma*. It would ultimately swell to more than 400 pages of intricate typography and riffs labeled by Kerouac with such idiosyncratic names as "Ecstasy" or "TIC" and "Flash." (Oddly enough, for both the CIA and Jack Kerouac, the word "Flash" was part of a private language. To Kerouac, Flash meant "short sleepdreams or drouse daydreams of an enlightened nature describable in a few words." To the CIA, "Flash" meant a cable of the highest priority.) This epistle to Buddhism was not published in full until almost 30 years after Kerouac's death in 1969 at the age of 47.

Kerouac corresponded often with Ginsberg about the book's progress. In one letter in the spring of 1954, he wrote about his "discovery and espousal of sweet Buddha." In May of that year, he told Ginsberg he had typed a "100-page account of Buddhism for you, gleaned from my notes." He gave Ginsberg a reading list of books and offered to be his guru, or teacher, in studying Buddhism.

The following year, 1955, Kerouac began working on a book called *Buddha Tells Us*. Kerouac considered it "by far the most important thing" he had ever written. He almost got it into print, but the publishers—Crowley, Giroux, and Sterling—wanted him to guarantee the book would sell at least 600 copies before they accepted it. He couldn't. It was a time of trials for Kerouac. His mother was a devout Catholic and his sister, with whom he lived most of the time he was working on his Buddhist books, disapproved of his rejection of their childhood faith for exotic Eastern beliefs.

After the rejection of *Buddha Tells Us*, Kerouac moved to San Francisco, where City Lights Books was publishing work by the Beatniks, to join Ginsberg. The city was home to many Zen Buddhists, including the poet Philip Whalen, who later became a Zen Buddhist priest. Whalen and Kerouac enthusiastically exchanged views on Buddhism.

When City Lights published Ginsberg's incendiary poem *Howl* in 1956, the poet lauded Kerouac in a flattering dedication that called him the "new Buddha of American prose." Ginsberg cited Kerouac's extraordinary output of eleven books over a five-year period, including *Some of the Dharma*. He noted plaintively, for readers who might understandably have been mystified as to where Kerouac's books could be found, that "all these books are published in Heaven."

Ginsberg's paean of praise helped conjure Kerouac's worldly fame, for in 1956, Sterling Lord finally succeeded in selling *On the Road* to

Viking. The book was published in September 1957. *The New York Times* gave it an approving review, and Kerouac's literary career went into orbit. In 1958 *The Dharma Bums* made its way into print.

The attraction between the Beat Buddhists, as they came to be called, and Tibetan Buddhists was mutual. In 1959, Lama Anagarika Govinda placed poets on a high spiritual plane in his book, *Foundations of Tibetan Mysticism*:

> The seer, the poet, and singer, the spiritually creative, the psychically receptive and sensitive, the saint: they all know about the essentiality of form and sound, in the visible and the tangible. They do not despise what appears small or insignificant, because they can see the great in the small. Through them the word becomes *mantra*, and the sounds and signs of which it is formed, become the vehicles of mysterious forces . . . the tangible becomes a creative tool of the spirit, and life becomes a deep stream, flowing from eternity to eternity.

America's literary avant-garde and the vanguard of the presidency—the CIA—were embracing Tibetan Buddhism simultaneously, although each in their own measure and with distinctly different motives and means. The Beat Buddhists gave prominence to words and awareness, the CIA, to intelligence training and weapons. This synchronicity between establishment and counterculture was a rare convergence, one that would shape the fate of Tibetan Buddhism in America.

FITZGERALD FORMS THE TIBET TASK FORCE

After the summit between Eisenhower and Nehru in 1956, the 5412 Special Group was ready to ramp up operations inside Tibet. Desmond FitzGerald needed a point man to coordinate the fledgling program. The officer designated for the job of heading what would soon become the CIA's Tibet Task Force was John Reagan. A task force is formed when the Agency needs to focus on a specific mission or operation. Those officers assigned to a new task force come from divisions and specializations throughout the CIA, according to the program's needs.

During the Korean War, Reagan had been assigned to FitzGerald's paramilitary operations in Korea. A graduate of Boston College, Reagan epitomized FitzGerald's preference for CIA officers who combined intellectual prowess with the ability to handle themselves in tough situations. According to his Agency colleagues, FitzGerald once described his ideal CIA officer as "a Harvard Ph.D. who could handle himself in a bar fight."

To get an operation going, FitzGerald needed trained people on the ground inside Tibet who could work with local leaders and report back to the CIA. The problem was that the CIA had no such agents. Reagan had to find suitable recruits, train them, and then get them into Tibet.

Duane Clarridge, a junior case officer, was assigned to work for Reagan as his gofer. Clarridge felt a sense of urgency on the Tibet desk. The tempo of operations increased significantly following the summit. Among the changes the Agency made was the establishment of a permanent CIA base in Nepal. Before, the CIA covered the country by occasionally sending an officer to do the rounds in Katmandu by making inquiries.

Being assigned to the Near East Division fulfilled a desire Clarridge developed as a graduate student at Columbia University, where he studied under renowned Altaic scholar Karl H. Menges. Professor Menges kindled Clarridge's interest in Nepal and Tibet. One of Clarridge's gofer duties was to help figure out how to infiltrate Tibetans back into their country over the Himalayas after they were trained by the CIA.

In February, 1957, Reagan tasked Hoskins, the CIA officer who had met with Gyalo Thondup in Darjeeling the previous summer, with recruiting a handful of young Tibetans for clandestine training. Hoskins turned to Gyalo for help.

THE KALIMPONG CONNECTION

Gyalo scoured the community of Tibetans who had taken refuge in Kalimpong for candidates. A hill station similar to Darjeeling, the town was the epicenter of trade between India and Tibet and home to a Tibetan trade office. For generations, Tibetan merchants made the trek through the Himalayas to Kalimpong and back, their beasts laden with export goods. Historically, more than half of the volume of commerce between the two countries happened here. On its streets and in its market, Tibetan traders, Indian merchants, and assorted middlemen would grip hands, cloaked under privacy of the long, roomy Tibetan sleeve, and exchange signals with one another using their fingers to indicate offer and counteroffer. When a mutually agreeable price was settled for a major purchase, blessings were bestowed by the seller on the buyer and, in the case of live goods like horses, on the animals as well.

Kalimpong also beckoned European merchants, who brought goods from firms like the East India Company to exchange for valuable commodities, such as wool from sheep and, especially, the valued downy undercoat of the Tibetan goat, similar to the better-known cashmere from the Kashmir region. Borax, salt, herbs, musk, yak tails to be made into whisks and brooms, and even deer antlers believed by Chinese healers to have medicinal properties were traded in Kalimpong.

The Europeans then left behind in Kalimpong, as elsewhere, children of mixed parentage. So prolific were these births that a charity known as St. Andrew's Colonial Homes sprang up in Kalimpong, dedicated to rearing and educating the children who were otherwise at risk of falling into the chasm between two cultures.

A group of Khampas from Eastern Tibet that included the sons of traditional Tibetan nobles had moved to Kalimpong to evade the Chinese after the revolts of 1956. Descended from nomadic tribesmen, the Khampas were taller than other Asians and had features similar to Native Americans. They described themselves as *ten dzong ma mi*—Warriors of the Fortress of Faith—and saw their role as protectors of the Tibetan theocracy. Gyalo sounded out local leaders in Kalimpong about the character and qualities of leading candidates, including relatives of an important resistance leader named Gompo Tashi Andrugtsang.

Gompo Tashi was a 51-year-old merchant from Litang in the province of Kham. The town was famed across Eastern Tibet for its annual horse festival, a display of martial skills and horsemanship that hearkens back to the days of the Mongols. As a trader, Tashi traveled widely across Tibet. Angered by the Chinese bombing of the Litang monastery in the summer of 1956, he began talking to local leaders about organizing a movement as he journeyed along his trading routes. The result was the existence of a nucleus of cells of resistance well before the CIA became involved.

Thubten Woyden Phala was one of the Dalai Lama's closest advisers. His title was Lord Chamberlain, and he handled confidential matters of government between the Dalai Lama and his ministers, the Kalons, of the Tibetan Cabinet (the *Kashag*). Phala was sometimes called the "keeper of the secrets." Among his secrets was an ancient Tibetan code book used for communicating confidential matters. Phala had given a code from this text to the Dalai Lama's brother, Norbu, to transmit the contents of his meetings with CIA and State Department officials in Washington in 1951.

Gompo Tashi kept Phala informed of his progress with the burgeoning Tibetan resistance, but it wasn't a simple task. Like all guerrilla movements, the Tibetans had schisms and jealousies that could complicate any effective resistance to the Chinese. In Eastern Tibet, local chieftains were a hereditary class that looked down on merchants, even wealthy ones like Gompo Tashi, as social inferiors. Moreover, the people of Eastern Tibet had been the first to feel Chinese oppression directly, which gave them a sense of ownership of the resistance struggle. If anyone should lead it, they felt with some justification, the hereditary chieftains should. Yet it was Gompo Tashi who stitched together a national resistance movement, based largely in Central Tibet.

These internal frictions were of little concern to the young Khampas whose families had sent them to India to get beyond the reach of the Chinese. Spirited, resolute, and full of bravado, they were itching to fight.

During the Dalai Lama's stay in India, a group of them met with him to urge open resistance to the Chinese. They were disappointed when he advised patience and nonviolence, but nonetheless continued to dog his entourage throughout the Buddhist Jayanti events. Twenty-seven Khampa youths followed the Dalai Lama to the Indian town of Bodh Gaya, where his brother, Norbu, was also present. He approached the men and asked if he could take their photographs—not as a group, but individually.

The photographs were used to identify the men. It was a first step in selecting recruits for CIA training. The candidates were subjected to scrutiny to weed out those who might be unsuitable because of character traits, personality, or questionable associations—including with the Chinese.

Gyalo and CIA officer Hoskins narrowed the list to six candidates. The CIA planned to give the six men espionage training and then parachute them back into Tibet. Their job would be to establish direct, secure radio communications between CIA headquarters and the Tibetan government in Lhasa and the resistance. They were to assess the military needs of the guerrillas and coordinate the delivery of supplies by aircraft.

Twenty-seven-year-old Wangdu Gyalotsang was the first of the group to sign on. A nephew of Gompo Tashi Andrugtsang, he was in an ideal position to evaluate the state of the Tibetan resistance. Wangdu gathered the other five recruits for a 9:00 PM roadside rendezvous outside Kalimpong. Gyalo Thondup arrived on schedule in his jeep. The men rode south until they reached the border with East Pakistan and then got out at a tea plantation. They crossed the border on foot and were met by a group of Pakistani soldiers and one of Thubten Norbu's servants. They transferred to another covered jeep and drove to a safe house where a CIA officer named Edward McAllister was waiting. After tea and biscuits, McAllister ushered them into yet another jeep for a five-hour road trip that ended at a train station, where Pakistani soldiers escorted them into the first-class section of a train. Outside Dacca, they offloaded and were hustled onto a truck, which took them to a second safehouse near an airfield named Kurmitola that was used by the U.S. Air Force Strategic Air Command.

John Reagan had flown to East Pakistan to meet the Khampa trainees for the next leg of their clandestine journey. The men boarded a C-118 aircraft, the military version of the DC-6. The airplane's windows had been blacked out and thick curtains isolated the crew from their passengers. From Pakistan, the C-118 headed to Thailand for a fuel stop. They then flew to Okinawa, to a small CIA base at Kadena where the Khampas were given physical exams by CIA-vetted doctors.

At Kadena, Thubten Norbu joined the group for the final leg of their journey. He had taken time off from his teaching at Columbia University to help translate for the CIA instructors. None of the Tibetans knew their ultimate destination. They had only been told that the Americans had promised to help them fight the Chinese, and that was enough to gain their trust.

Meanwhile, the Dalai Lama started his journey back to Lhasa from New Delhi. In Kalimpong, he had time to talk with Gyalo. His brother reassured him that the United States was poised to help the Tibetans in their struggle for freedom. Gyalo believed (and still believes) that the Americans had promised to support Tibet's claim to independence. One aspect of American aid was withheld from the Dalai Lama. Gyalo told Phala about the CIA's plans to provide covert military aid, but he didn't tell his brother.

SAIPAN'S SCHOOL FOR SPIES

Out in the Pacific Ocean, far from prying eyes, the CIA had a secret $28 million training base on the island of Saipan, located at the southern end of the Northern Marianas island chain. Designed for instruction in everything from underwater demolition to small arms and explosives training and CIA tradecraft in codes, espionage, counterintelligence, and communications, the Station was a full-fledged school for spies. It had separate compounds, physically isolated from one another, to permit the CIA to work simultaneously with separate teams of agents without compromising the identity of one group to another.

Saipan was the scene of bloody fighting between the United States and Japan during World War II in 1944. Some 70,000 American troops laid siege to the island. The Japanese fought to the end and almost 30,000 died in the fighting. Hundreds more perished by throwing themselves off cliffs at the northern end of the island, including women and children who feared the American invaders. Bleached bones still stood out against the dark volcanic stone at the base of the cliffs.

The Saipan Training Station, as it was known inside the CIA, was as secure as a clandestine facility could be. This was a time before satellite surveillance, and aerial reconnaissance was limited to risky overflights by aircraft like the U-2. The Station's cover name was the Naval Technical Training Unit. The Tibetan trainees had their own name for Saipan. They called it *Dursa*, or Island of the Dead.

CIA officer Roger E. McCarthy headed the training team on Saipan. McCarthy was known only as "Mr. Roger" to the Tibetans. He and his fellow CIA trainers had been allotted four-and-a-half months to school their six recruits. They quickly gave them American nicknames—(Athar) Tom, (Lhotse) Lou, (Dedrup) Dan, (Tsewang) Sam, (Dreshe) Dick and (Wangdu) Walt—and went to work.

Had they known of it, an incident in Wangdu's youth might have concerned his CIA recruiters and given them a better idea of the complexities of training these men to fight. One day, Wangdu had ridden his horse into a village where the local chief's protocol dictated that no one should wear a hat in his presence. When Wandgu refused to take his hat off in front of the chief, a bodyguard removed it by knocking it off his head. Wangdu drew a pistol and shot the man in the head, killing him.

Had McCarthy known the story, he might have realized that Wangdu's impulse to shoot when confronted by the bodyguard displayed the hot-bloodedness typical of Khampas. While their bravery was a virtue, the lack of discipline was a definite disadvantage in battle.

CIA small arms training ran the gamut from handguns and rifles to light machine guns, 60mm mortars, and 57mm recoilless rifles. Other training included learning how to ambush, work in five-man fire teams, use fragmentation and incendiary grenades, improvise munitions, and fight hand-to-hand.

Curiously, not all the weapons the CIA trained the Tibetans to use were likely to be useful for guerrilla war against the Chinese. A military analysis by General S.L.A. Marshall of the performance of U.S. weapons and tactics against the PLA in the Korean War had concluded that the 57mm recoilless rifle was ineffective for long-range use in destroying Chinese bunkers. Typically constructed of heavy logs and earthwork, the bunkers could only be taken out with a direct hit. At ranges of 1,000 yards—the safe distance for a guerrilla to fire against an enemy machine gun bunker—it was a waste to use the 57mm rounds when only the heavier 75mm recoilless sufficed for the job.

In contrast, the 57mm recoilless was useful for direct assaults on Chinese bunkers at close range. But these tactics were used in a standard infantry assault, not guerrilla fighting. Given that the CIA wanted to teach the Tibetans to use classic guerrilla hit-and-run tactics, it seems odd that the recruits weren't trained and equipped from the start with the 75mms. Marshall's 1952 study on combat effectiveness in Korea won him a promotion to general and was adopted into U.S. Army training doctrine. By 1957, the CIA's paramilitary operators ought to have been aware of Marshall's work concerning the most effective weapons to use against the People's Liberation Army.

Teaching the Khampas the use of modern weapons and explosives and clandestine operations techniques would be the easy part. The difficult part of the mission would involve coordinating air drops of tons of weapons and supplies that the United States intended to provide the Tibetan guerrillas. This required precise, secret communication between CIA teams inside the country and Headquarters. This posed a problem. CIA pilots depended upon exact timing and directional instructions for the success of their missions. Not only the language, but the very thinking of the Tibetans lacked intimacy with modern technology. To most of the trainees, concepts like the twenty-four-hour clock were utterly foreign.

The Khampa trainees were well-educated by Tibetan standards. As with other children of the Tibetan nobility, most of the trainees' schooling began with learning the Tibetan alphabet and basic arithmetic. By seventeen, students were expected to master the *Nyeng-nga*, a classic text with hidden meanings. Much of the instruction was—and is, given by tutors instead of in formal classrooms. If the son of a noble enters either the monastery or Tibetan civil service, there is additional, specialized training. Still, they were not up to the level of American public education in the 1950s.

GESHE WANGYAL JOINS THE TEAM

One of the first challenges facing the Agency instructors was to devise a code that could accommodate the Tibetan language. For Norbu, this was a challenge. The Tibetan language has the potential to be notoriously ambiguous. There was a need to invent words to convey unfamiliar concepts. None of the CIA trainers had anticipated this problem but, fortunately, Norbu knew where he could find help.

Geshe Wangyal took a temporary leave from Columbia University, where he was teaching Mongolian and Tibetan language classes. He traveled to Saipan to work directly with the recruits and their CIA trainers to tackle the language problems. Wangyal helped devise a code book and translated espionage jargon into language the Tibetan trainees could easily understand.

The men were taught how to communicate by Morse code and the use of one-time pads for coding and decoding messages. They were trained on RS-1 radio sets, with their hand-cranked generators as a power source. The Khampas also learned CIA tradecraft, from how to collect and verify information and write reports to making disguises. It was a comprehensive training program that took most CIA trainees a full year to complete. The Tibetans were expected to finish their course in about a third of that time.

Once their espionage and guerrilla warfare training on Saipan ended, the Khampas still had to master parachute jumps to get safely back into Tibet. They practiced jumping from a parachute tower built on the island and were instructed on how to move through the mountain terrain under the cover of darkness.

Once they learned the basic skills, it was time to put them to the test. The trainees were taken to Okinawa, where there was suitable terrain for real jumps. Using a World War II-vintage B-17, the same aircraft that would be used to infiltrate them back into Tibet, the men parachuted out of a "Joe Hole" in the belly of the plane. This technique had been used by the Office of Strategic Services (OSS), the CIA's predecessor, to insert agents into occupied Europe during World War II. Each trainee was given three jumps to become familiar with the aircraft and a specially modified T-10 parachute.

Choosing the location for the drop zone had been difficult. Tibet was so remote the CIA had no current topographical maps and had to use photographs taken during Younghusband's 1904 invasion. One of them showed a broad embankment on the Tsangpo River that looked promising. Although the photo was more than 50 years old, it was the best the CIA planners had.

In October, under the light of a full moon, Tom and Lou—a.k.a. Athar and Lhotse—were flown south of Lhasa and parachuted onto the sandbar. They were equipped with two sets of radios, British Lee-Enfield .303 rifles, and 9mm Sten machine guns, code books, miscellaneous supplies, a pamphlet from the Dalai Lama, and cyanide pills. Their mission was to make contact with Gompo Tashi and help organize resistance cells.

Wangdu's team was scheduled for infiltration into Eastern Tibet in October, but cloudy weather caused a delay. In November, when the moon was again full, Wangdu and his team were parachuted into Kham. They landed near a force of resistance fighters, called the *Chushi Gangdruk*, on the heels of a skirmish with the Chinese and were almost mistaken for enemy paratroopers. When it was realized these were Tibetans parachuting from the sky, the *Chushi Gangdruk* fighters were elated. The name meant "Four Rivers, Six Ranges" and referred to the mountains and rivers that cut across Kham. Wangdu radioed back to the CIA that his team had met a friendly reception.

John Reagan had been waiting anxiously for the reports. With just two teams and six trainees in total, the CIA covered the capital city of Lhasa in Central Tibet and the border region of Eastern Tibet. It had been 22 months since Eisenhower issued NSC Directive 5412/2. The CIA was about to engage in the most ambitious, and bloodiest, covert war it had yet undertaken.

Chapter 4

All Tsampa Eaters
Must Stand Together

By November, 1956, Geshe Wangyal was moonlighting steadily for the CIA, translating radio transmissions that reported the location and size of Chinese troop concentrations, the strength of the resistance, and news of fresh attacks on Chinese truck convoys. Then, the reports from Wangdu's team in Eastern Tibet ceased. At CIA headquarters, they assumed the worst—that the team had been killed or captured. Tom and Lou, however, continued to relay reports on resistance groups springing up across the country. The radio transmissions were followed by requests for aircraft to drop guns and ammunition.

Large-scale support from the CIA was out of the question so long as the resistance remained divided along regional and tribal lines. In covert warfare operations, it is basic tradecraft that a cohesive command structure must exist before the intelligence service provides any significant aid. The promise of arms and ammunition is used to unify splintered or disorganized guerrilla movements. The threat to withhold those weapons and aid is used to maintain discipline once a unified resistance movement comes into being.

FitzGerald had been badly burned by operations on the mainland of China, where supposedly 500,000 guerrillas were merely waiting for weapons and assistance to rise up against Chairman Mao. In fact, no such underground resistance existed. It was a fable spun by con artists eager to scam the CIA out of money, and it succeeded. In Tibet, the United States needed to be reassured that there was a resistance worthy of greater support.

Irving "Frank" Holober took over as chief of the Tibet Task Force in the summer of 1957 when John Reagan moved on to a new assignment. Holober decided that the best way to determine whether the resistance was real was to have an in-person debriefing with one of the Saipan agents. The meeting was set for Calcutta, where the CIA had a base and safehouses. Tom crossed the border on horseback and rendezvoused with Gyalo in Darjeeling. CIA officer John Hoskins took Tom and Lhamo Tsering, an assistant of Gyalo's who was there to translate, to a safehouse where Holober was waiting, loaded with questions. At the end of the week he was satisfied with what he had learned. Holober returned to Washington ready to support an increased flow of arms into Tibet.

THE NATIONAL VOLUNTEER DEFENSE ARMY

Gompo Tashi Andrugstang was the CIA's man-on-the-ground for unifying the Tibetan resistance. In early 1958, he convened a secret get-together of 24 key guerrilla leaders from across the country at his home in Lhasa. He urged them to unite, saying that "all *tsampa* eaters must stand together," referring to the Tibetan barley-grain staple. The leaders, mainly from the Eastern regions of Kham and Amdo, knew that Gompo Tashi had something more than *tsampa* to unify the resistance. He had the backing of Gyalo Thondup, the principal liaison between the Tibetans and the CIA. Tashi also had the tacit approval of Phala, the Lord Chamberlain. According to CIA officer Knaus, Phala approved not only of the creation of the resistance but also the use of violence. Phala was a monk, but so were approximately half of the Tibetan resistance fighters.

The majority of resistance leaders agreed to form a national movement. Because the *Chushi Gangdruk* was named for the four rivers and six mountains of Eastern Tibet, it was felt that a new name would help overcome regional rivalries. The group called itself the National Volunteer Defense Army (NVDA.) In front of Gompo Tashi's meditation shrine, with its photograph of the Dalai Lama, the members made a covenant to stand united against the Chinese. On June 16, 1958, on the shores of the Drigu Tso Lake, the leaders and NVDA fighters posed for a propaganda photo. Tom shot the film, and it was carried by courier across the mountains to Gyalo in Darjeeling.

THE DALAI LAMA REFUSES
TO SANCTION VIOLENCE

Even though Holober gave his support, a new requirement was imposed by the 5412 Special Group before launching a full-scale covert war. President Eisenhower's men wanted an explicit request from the Dalai Lama for military assistance. The CIA relayed this news to its teams inside Tibet. Tom and Lou received the messages from headquarters on two different occasions, but no official request came. The Dalai Lama would not budge from his policy of nonviolent opposition to the Chinese.

The 5412 Special Group was faced with a choice. The Group's members could withhold aid until the Dalai Lama changed his policy, but that meant foregoing the opportunity to carry out President Eisenhower's explicit directive to harass the Chinese. Or they could go forward with an expanded covert program without any official request from Tenzin Gyatso.

FitzGerald argued for going forward. His reasons were personal as well as professional. In moments of deep reflection, FitzGerald was somber to the point of melancholy over the fate of modern humanity. World War II made him abhor mass movements like Nazism that subordinated the individual to the service of the state. Whether Marxist or Fascist, he loathed collectivism. Reports from inside Maoist China about reeducation camps, propaganda blaring over loudspeakers, and *thamzing* public criticism sessions played into his gloomiest nightmares for the future.

Thamzing galled FitzGerald. Entire towns and villages were required to assemble in a public place to witness the humiliation of political adversaries of Mao's new China. Anyone labeled a "class enemy" or a "reactionary" or an "imperialist" was hauled onstage and forced to confess their errors and crimes before the crowd. Hecklers, some of them legitimate and others acting at the behest of party authorities, charged the accused with fresh offenses as soon as they began a public confession. In this way the *thamzing* session could go on for hours, even days. The prisoners were usually beaten before the sessions began, and then tormented throughout with kicks and blows, and sometimes stomped to death.

Thamzing was a combination of political theater and political torture, the goal of which was to intimidate the population into rejecting opponents of the regime and accepting the legitimacy of China's Communist party.

In a pessimistic letter to his 14-year-old daughter, Frances, FitzGerald expressed his fears that the world would one day be dominated by mass movements that crushed the spirit of the individual. He wrote of "nations of blind warrior ants" and the dehumanization of mankind he had seen in his own lifetime, questioning whether there was anything he, or any-one else, could do to prevent the triumph of totalitarianism and leave her a better world. Yet in his optimistic moments, which far outweighed the pessimistic ones, FitzGerald believed fervently that the actions of one individual could make a difference.

This was such a time. In 1958, it was far from certain that Chairman Mao's grip on China, especially along the regions of its far-flung frontier, was firm. There was always the chance that a determined resistance on China's periphery might cause the regime to retrench. The fighting between Chinese forces and the Tibetans was fearsome. Monks were being annihilated in monasteries, women and children slaughtered in villages. Nor were the Tibetans giving quarter. Captives were often slain. In one instance in 1958, some 200 PLA prisoners were sent back to the Chinese lines—with their noses cut off as a warning to others. The more costly it could be made to occupy Tibet, the greater the prospect that Mao might give up trying to control the unruly, independent-minded inhabitants.

FitzGerald's views were persuasive. Despite the lack of an official request from the Tibetan government, the 5412 Special Group decided it was time to send the resistance fighters the weapons they had been told would come.

THE SECRET HIMALAYAN AIRLIFT

The wheels set in motion in Washington meant wheels up for a unique contingent of flyboys half a world away. It was time to deliver on the promises made and that meant delivering tons of weapons and ammunition to the Tibetan resistance by parachute. Flight crews would have to cross the Himalayas, find their drop zones, and return safely without being detected by the Chinese or crash landing along the way and compromising the clandestine operation.

The CIA had a small proprietary airline it had secretly bought in August 1950, from General Claire Chennault and Whiting Willauer for the grand sum of $950,000. Chennault and Willauer started the airline in China shortly after the end of World War II. Operating under the names of Civil Air Transport and Western Enterprises, the CIA utilized the airline for a range of covert operations in Korea and China.

Based on Taiwan, the fleet included the B-17 which carried the Saipan trainees back to Tibet. Known as the "Flying Fortress," it was designed as a bomber. The B-17 was fine for dropping small teams or solitary agents, called "singletons," inside hostile territory. But it was the wrong airplane for transporting and delivering military supplies over long distances, especially deep into the Himalayas.

Getting weapons to the Tibetan fighters called for a different kind of aircraft. The C-118 "Liftmaster" was a four-engine workhorse that could fly at altitudes up to 20,000 feet. The Air Force's 313th Air Division at Okinawa had C-118s in its Detachment 2 that were available to the CIA for special operations. Military teams had perfected the delicate art of loading the Liftmaster with bundled supplies that could be dropped and parachuted to the ground without destabilizing the craft. With a skilled pilot, navigator, and load masters, the aircraft was suitable for carrying weapons over long distances and air-dropping them precisely.

The C-118 started its journey on the island of Okinawa, where a 12,000 lb. load of Lee-Enfield .303 rifles, 57mm recoilless rifles, .30-caliber machine guns, 60mm mortars, 2.36 bazookas, and grenades and ammunition were put on pallets and placed in the rear of the aircraft. From Okinawa, the plane flew to Kurmitola, in East Pakistan, for refueling. En route, the aircraft bore United States Air Force (USAF) decals. The removable insignia were taken off in Pakistan. From Kurmitola onwards, the plane had to be stripped of anything linking it to the United States.

After the C-118 rumbled off the airstrip at Kurmitola, it flew over the low-lying, green terrain of East Pakistan. The land rose gradually in height, until the plane crossed the wide expanse of the Brahmaputra River, far downrange from its headwaters in Tibet, where it was known as the Tsangpo River. Now the terrain climbed dramatically, with rock-strewn bare peaks that towered above the airplane. Loaded with weapons and supplies, the C-118 lacked the power to fly over the peaks of the Himalayas. Instead, the aircraft had to navigate through the mountain passes.

They were over unfamiliar terrain, and any error could plunge them into a mountainside where, if they survived, their capture could create an international incident. It was widely known within the teams that capture could also mean a long confinement. The CIA had lost one clandestine flight over China in which an operative was captured alive. He spent 25 years in a Chinese prison before finally being released.

The first drop zone approved for the aerial supply operation was in Kham in Eastern Tibet. Jim Keck was the mission navigator. As do many men in battle, Keck kept a lucky talisman with him—a *Playboy* centerfold. He taped the pin-up girl over his navigation post inside the plane. After each successful mission, the crew would tap the centerfold on her derrière and say, "Thanks."

They needed luck. They could only partially rely on radar. Therefore, the missions were scheduled to coincide with a full moon, so the pilots would have sufficient visibility to stay on course and avoid hitting the peaks towering above and around them. A full moon, of course, also meant that they were visible from the ground and therefore vulnerable to Chinese small arms fire from the surrounding mountains.

As they neared the designated drop zone, the plane was blanketed by layers of clouds. The pilot kept the aircraft in a turn while trying to break through the clouds, looking for the signal fires demarcating the zone. The C-118's radar was reliable only with the plane flying level. Eventually they did break out of the cloud cover, and Keck saw several mountain peaks looming higher than the aircraft. The plane leveled out, and he took a radar fix on their location. They had flown past the drop zone, but with the new heading they were able to circle back and find the five signal fires that marked the spot.

The men waiting on the ground knew what to expect. The CIA radio operators alerted them in advance to the contents of each load and the precise number of bundles that would be dropped. This way they knew how much they had to recover, and how many pack animals it would take to move the supplies away from the zone. The CIA packaged the weapons and ammo so they could easily be divided into 80- or 85-pound parcels. Then, with the weight evenly distributed, they were loaded onto each side of the pack animals, making it easier to negotiate the mountainous terrain and trails of dirt and rock.

From the ground, the guerrilla reception teams confirmed recovery of the weapons and munitions and reported losses from breakage. The first aerial supply drop was a success. The flight had taken 13 hours to complete. Later, the radio operators sent feedback about the effectiveness of the mortar shells. Left over from World War II, many were duds. Using the batch numbers of the faulty rounds, the CIA logistics team made sure no other mortar rounds from the same numbered lots were loaded on the C-118s. Cargo space and weight capacity was too precious to waste, given that resupply flights could only take place during the full moon cycle.

Not every drop during 1958 went smoothly. On one flight, there were problems with the static line that was used to automatically open the parachutes as bundles dropped from the rear of the aircraft. It ripped loose from its mount, and the plane had to make several passes over the drop zone to compensate for the faulty line. The drop was sloppy, with the load spread so widely over the ground that it covered several miles, causing extra work for the ground teams and risking lost supplies. By the time of the next flight, the mount for the static line had been redesigned. As the plane approached its target, the "kickers," who handled the load, successfully knocked the stops out and gave the pallets a gravity-assist kick to get them rolling out the back of the C-118. Underneath the canopies of billowing parachutes, the weapons and supplies fell smoothly into the target area.

THE AIR COMMANDOS JOIN THE FIGHT

The 5412 Special Group had ambitious plans for the Tibetan resistance, plans that would culminate in a national uprising. Even with the loan of the Air Force C-118s, equipping the resistance with sufficient weapons and ammunition overwhelmed the CIA's proprietary airline. To resolve the problem, CIA Deputy Director Charles Cabell called Air Force General Curtis LeMay. Cabell explained that he wanted to use Air Force C-130s to make the drops.

General Cabell, who came to the CIA from the military, knew that he was calling on a former colleague he hoped would be sympathetic to his request. Using the C-130s in a covert war was a risky proposition. The C-118 had a civilian counterpart, the DC-6, widely in use across the world. That gave the CIA a slight veneer of deniability in the event a C-118 went down on a clandestine mission. But the C-130 was a U.S. military aircraft. If a plane crashed inside Tibet, the U.S. government would be clearly implicated. General Cabell, however, knew that the superior capabilities of the C-130 and the larger payload it could carry in a single flight offset some of the risk. Fewer flights meant fewer chances for planes to stray off course into a mountain peak or crash land because of mechanical failure. Overall, the C-130 could deliver more punch with fewer missions than the C-118.

General LeMay agreed. He was an enthusiastic supporter of the Tibetan cause. But LeMay had one condition. Oversight of the C-130 operations would be under the command of an Air Force officer seconded to the CIA specifically for the purpose of supporting the growing requirements of the Agency's covert operations in Asia.

Enter the Air Commandos. While Desmond FitzGerald had been honing his covert armies in Asia, Major Heinrich "Heinie" Aderholt was taking the first steps toward building what would grow into a formidable U.S. Air Force special operations capability. Aderholt took command of Detachment 2 of the 1045th Observation, Evaluation, and Training Group, based on Okinawa. He and his air commandos had a dual assignment, overseeing the use of the C-130s in Tibet and supplying General Vang Pao in a brand new Desmond FitzGerald operation, the CIA's fledgling secret war in Laos.

Instead of Kurmitola, the forward base for the Tibetan supply operation was shifted to Takhli, Thailand. The Takhli base was growing in importance as a Civil Air Transport/Air America hub for the support of covert operations across Southeast Asia. By centralizing facilities at one principal base, Aderholt increased the efficiency of the growing number of Asian covert air operations. C-130s specially equipped with long-range fuel tanks were flown to Takhli, where the Air Force insignias were removed and the planes turned over to Civil Air Transport (CAT) flight crews.

Many of the CAT pilots and crew members were Eastern European émigrés who had signed on with the CIA, but some were also "smoke jumpers"—firefighters who parachuted into wildfire blazes—from the American West. The smoke jumpers had been specially recruited because of their skill at ridge-hugging flying and skydiving in mountainous terrain. Because many came from Montana, the smoke jumpers were nicknamed the "Missoula Mafia." Jerrold Barker Daniels typified the smoke jumpers who joined forces with the CIA. Jerry had been both a chess champion and a state wrestling champion in high school. After graduation, he joined the jumpers, making his first dive a few weeks after his 17th birthday in 1958. After a season of fighting blazes, he was recruited by the CIA and became a "kicker" on one of the first C-130 missions to Tibet. Daniels went on to work with the CIA in Laos and served with the Hmong tribes until their defeat at the end of the Vietnam War, after which he and a buddy went on an extensive hunting trip in Montana's Bob Marshall Wilderness. Like others on the CAT crews, Jerry Daniels worked as a contractor, earning $350 per flight, and $500 if the mission was especially dangerous.

Before the C-130s were loaded the resistance was informed by radio of the quantity of supplies that would be dropped. This enabled them to assemble the men and animals needed to retrieve the load. The preflight radio reports from the resistance advised the CIA of the precise location of drop zones, nearby landmarks, and any Chinese troops or bases in the vicinity. In turn, the CIA sent information about the recognition signals that would be exchanged between aircraft and ground crews. While the C-130s were airborne during the mission, the resistance teams radioed updated weather reports from the ground to the aircraft.

With Aderholt's aircraft on the job, the tempo of operations picked up. Instead of a single C-118 flight carrying a payload of 12,000 lbs. per full moon, the C-130s could make up to five drops in each full moon phase. Payloads ranged between 15,000 to 24,000 lbs per aircraft, depending on how far the planes had to fly to reach the drop zone. On many missions, a single C-130 took the lead, followed by two more on its tail, enabling the teams to drop between 50,000 and 75,000 lbs. of supplies per night.

The throb of the C-130 Hercules's powerful turboprop engines reverberated against the stone-covered mountainsides as the aircraft neared the drop zone. On the ground below, the Tibetans had piled mounds of dried animal dung and lit them on fire to mark the site. Wood was scarce on the Tibetan plateau but manure from livestock was plentiful and it burnt well enough to serve as signal lights for the low-flying aircraft overhead.

On the ground, hundreds of men waited anxiously by their mounts and pack animals. They were most vulnerable to ambush by the Chinese in the long minutes after the parachutes and their pallets of bundled weapons, ammunition, explosives, and money hit the ground. This is when the men scurried to collect the parcels, which were sometimes scattered over a wide area, lash them to the animals, and get away from the drop zone undetected. Even at night, the full moon and open terrain made them easy targets.

From the cockpit of the C-130, the landscape below seemed bathed in a silvery light. A few breaths from an oxygen mask as the plane neared its target served to rejuvenate the pilot's senses and made the landscape below glow brightly. The quick hit of oxygen was a trick used by military pilots when night flying, fatigued, or just hung over. The full moon created surprisingly strong shadows, almost as pronounced as those cast in sunlight. Promontories and peaks and even rocky features dotting the terrain were clearly visible. In Tibet at that time, there was no electrical lighting from houses or towns, no beams from automobile headlights, no ambient light at all save from the moon and stars.

The pilot and navigator had no trouble locating the drop zone. The dung fires shone brilliantly, their pattern—sometimes a geometric shape, sometimes a letter "L" or "T"—meant to safeguard against the random possibility that a scattered group of campfires among nomads or bandits or even a Chinese patrol might inadvertently be mistaken for the drop site.

In the rear of the aircraft the kickers, often recruits drawn from the "Missoula Mafia" of smoke jumpers, readied themselves by donning oxygen masks. They opened the aircraft's cargo doors to a blast of bracing cold air. The pilot eased off the throttle and lowered the wing flaps and the plane's nose pitched slightly upward to make it easier for the kickers to slide their payload out the back of the plane.

The pallets rolled out into the open air, the ripcords yanked open by the static line, snapping the parachutes open. In the moonlight, the floating bundles cast fleeting shadows over the land for the Tibetans waiting on the ground to trace. When the last bundle had been retrieved and its contents inventoried for damage a radioman sent a coded transmission back to the CIA confirming receipt of the air drop.

The CIA also got serious about the arms it was delivering to the Tibetan resistance. The antiquated British Lee-Enfield, bolt-action .303 rifles were replaced by the American semiautomatic M-1 Garand, the only combat rifle in the U.S. arsenal that was heavily favored by S.L.A. Marshall in his review of the effectiveness of U.S. infantry weapons in Korea. The 57mm recoilless rifle was dropped and replaced by the 75mm recoilless. 80mm mortars were added to the 60mm variety the CIA had originally supplied, as were heavier bazookas. Anyone analyzing the payloads between early 1958 and the end of that same year, when Aderholt's C-130s were in full flight over Tibet, could tell that the 5412 Special Group was getting ready for a showdown.

CAMP HALE, THE CIA'S SCHOOL
FOR GUERRILLA WARFARE

More Tibetans needed to be trained in classic guerrilla fighting techniques before the resistance would be ready for its showdown with China. Saipan was no longer ideal. As the number of Tibetan trainees grew, a bigger facility was needed. CIA officer John Greaney had the job of finding a new facility for a guerrilla warfare school. The ideal location would have a climate similar to Tibet, with mountains and altitudes like those where the guerrillas would fight.

Near Leadville, Colorado, the U.S. Army had control over the remains of an abandoned World War II base named Camp Hale. During the war it had been used to train the 10th Mountain Division for combat in Europe's Alpine environment. Camp Hale had not been used in a decade. All but a few of its buildings had been dismantled.

Greaney surveyed the situation to determine whether Camp Hale would fit the CIA's requirements for clandestine training. Tibetans could be flown secretly to Peterson Air Force Base at Colorado Springs. From there, they would be loaded onto buses with blacked-out windows and driven up the front range of the Rockies under cover of darkness through the mountains to the isolated base. After they completed training, they would return in the same manner.

Camp Hale was suitable, except for one hitch. The only buildings that remained standing at the derelict base were near a public road. The Tibetans would be too exposed to curious onlookers. The solution was to erect new buildings in a remote corner of the base, screened off by a wall.

Camp Hale came under the jurisdiction of the U.S. Army at Fort Carson, and the military was eager to help the CIA with the hush-hush guerrilla warfare camp. Even with the Army's cooperation, it would take time to complete construction. Winter was looming in the Rockies, and the pace of work depended on the weather.

CAMP PEARY FILLS THE GAP

Although Camp Hale would be ideal for the fully expanded program, the need for new trainees was urgent. In the interim, the CIA had to fall back on its own spy school at Camp Peary, Virginia, known as "The Farm." Here CIA officers learned skills ranging from cloak-and-dagger tradecraft to small arms and explosives training, parachuting, border and barrier crossing, clandestine communications, escape and evasion techniques, and how to withstand hostile interrogations.

As with the Saipan trainees, Gyalo Thondup was primarily responsible for recruiting this next group of young men eager to fight the Chinese. The Tibetans weren't told where they were being taken for training. The clandestine flights that ferried weapons to Tibet now began carrying clandestine cargo back to the United States—human cargo. After what must have seemed like an interminably long journey— although most accounts depict the Tibetans as high spirited and adventurous, playing traditional betting games like *sho* to while away the tedium of flight inside the aircraft cabin with its darkened windows—eight Tibetans arrived at Camp Peary in the winter of 1958.

Tom Fosmire, a junior officer on the Tibet Task Force, was responsible for overseeing an accelerated course schedule that required the men to train seven days a week. The curriculum was heavy on paramilitary skills. The CIA planned to familiarize the eight men with guerilla combat techniques, so that they could impart their skills to others. The concept was to deploy them alongside the resistance groups Gompo Tashi was organizing, where the trainees would, in effect, train the NVDA fighters. If it worked, the combat effectiveness and military discipline of the resistance would improve. In modern military terms, these trainers were force multipliers.

One of their CIA instructors was Anthony Poshepny, a.k.a. Tony Poe. He was a Marine Corps veteran of the Pacific Theater, just in his mid-thirties when he was assigned to get the Tibetans ready for combat. Poshepny would have a long career in CIA covert operations, including a stint in the CIA's secret war in Laos. Some say Poshepny was the inspiration for Colonel Kurtz, the character played by Marlon Brando in the film *Apocalypse Now*, a paramilitary officer who goes off the deep end and is targeted for assassination by his own team. Poshepny's antics were definitely dramatic. Twice he sent severed human heads to enemy villages as a warning. On one occasion, he showed up for a meeting with the American ambassador in Vientiane roaring drunk, with a machete in one hand and a rifle in the other. Poe and other CIA employees like him in the Agency's paramilitary operations were called "knuckledraggers," a term that likened them to gorillas and carried a connotation of savagery.

Not all of the instructors were knuckledraggers. John Kenneth Knaus, one of the Agency's China experts, was asked to brief the Tibetan trainees at the Farm. His arrival coincided with *Losar*, the Tibetan New Year celebration.

Knaus had planned to give a formal presentation on the Sino-Soviet rift. The subject was a particular preoccupation of the CIA in the late 1950s. Analysts were uncertain about whether the Soviets and Chinese were secretly cooperating with one another. They couldn't figure out whether the alleged fissure was nothing more than a deception, misinformation designed to lull the United States into complacency, or whether it was in fact the first evidence of a significant breach in "monolithic" communism. James Jesus Angleton, the CIA's counterintelligence czar, was convinced that the rift was a deception operation. Angleton's belief that China and the Soviet Union were cooperating fully to advance the interests of international communism was a world view which fit neatly within the premises of National Security Directive 5412/2.

Knaus's audience included Lobsang Samtem, another of the Dalai Lama's brothers. Lobsang introduced Knaus to the group of young trainees. Instead of talking about China and the USSR, Knaus decided to improvise about how the Tibetan resistance formed part of the free world's opposition to communism. When he was done the group invited him to join in their New Year's celebration featuring beer and *mo-mos*, a Tibetan variant on the dumpling that comes steamed or fried and filled with meat or vegetables.

During the course of the day, Knaus noticed a gap in the teaching curriculum. No one was explaining to the Tibetans why guerrilla warfare, with its hit-and-run harassment of the PLA, was the most effective way to oppose the Chinese. Knaus decided to develop the outlines of a political program the trainees could use to impress this on their fellow resistance fighters.

Knaus had hit upon a crucial weakness in the CIA's plans for Tibet. Early reports of resistance fighting showed that the Tibetans were eager to mount direct, sustained assaults on the Chinese. It was normal for hundreds, sometimes thousands, of Tibetan fighters to assemble *en masse* to go after the PLA. This made them easy targets for artillery strikes and attacks from the air, both areas in which China held the advantage. It also made them vulnerable to becoming entrapped by flanking movements in set-piece infantry battles, where the PLA also had an important advantage in radio communications. With their superior radio contact, it was relatively simple for them to maneuver against the Tibetans in a pitched battle.

For the Tibetan resistance to stand any chance of long-term survival, the CIA trainees had to persuade the NVDA leadership to use guerrilla tactics. It was critical to their prospects for success in harassing the Chinese to leave Tibet.

DUMRA, THE GARDEN SPOT

By Memorial Day, construction was complete at Camp Hale. The eight Tibetan trainees were flown from Virginia's tidewater country to Colorado and the Rocky Mountain heartland. The contrast could not have been greater. Virginia in the spring was a landscape of verdant canopy, stands of hardwoods broken by lush farmland. Colorado's famed "fourteeners," bare mountain peaks soaring far above treeline at 14,000 feet and higher, hearkened of Tibet. In early spring, the high passes and peaks were still lined with snow, another reminder of home for the men. In the mountain valley where Camp Hale sat, even the plants underfoot smelled like home. The Tibetans christened Camp Hale "Dumra," the garden spot.

At Dumra they were joined by 17 new recruits freshly arrived from India. Tom Fosmire's training program now included dividing the Tibetans into rival teams with one side staging mock ambushes and the other trying to evade them. Tony Poe was supposed to teach mule handling to the Tibetans, but the animals were uncooperative. Fortunately, the Khampas were born muleteers. Like horse whisperers, they spoke to the stubborn animals for hours and soon were able to handle them with ease.

A minor glitch threatened to compromise the security of the secret operation at Camp Hale. During a training run, an instructor accidentally struck a telephone line with a rocket. The damage made it difficult to conceal that something unusual was happening at the abandoned

World War II camp. The Defense Department came to the rescue by concocting a cover story about secret nuclear experiments at the base and holding a news conference to make sure the media reported it. At the time, it was believed that anything nuclear would keep even the most curious gawkers away, but just in case, a detachment of military police were assigned to patrol Camp Hale's boundaries.

Not only Tibetans, but Americans too were receiving specialized training in Colorado. CAT flight crews were sent to Peterson Air Force Base to work alongside USAF crews to learn to handle the C-130.

In September, the first contingent of Camp Hale graduates was parachuted to Lake Nam Tso, north of Lhasa, from a C-130. The mission was flawless. The C-130 dropped its agents and their weaponry over the mountain lake. The war in Tibet had entered a new phase. The stakes were escalating. Despite the cover stories and veneer of plausible deniability, the use of the C-130s and the heavier weapons made the effort more identifiable as a CIA operation. Balancing the risks of public exposure against the risks of losing the Dalai Lama, the 5412 Special Group had concluded that a more aggressive campaign was warranted. If the CIA could not get the Dalai Lama out of Tibet soon, he might become a prisoner of the Chinese.

The Dalai Lama's Escape Route
Map By: Eric Olason.www.ericolason.com

Chapter 5

The Dalai Lama's Great Escape

At the beginning of the Tibetan year of the Earth-Pig, 1959 in the Western calendar, Lord Chamberlain Phala and Gompo Tashi Andrugtsang had urgent business. CIA officer Roger McCarthy, the new head of the Tibet Task Force, needed a contingency plan for bringing the Dalai Lama safely across the Himalayas to India.

Since 1951, the United States had urged the Dalai Lama to leave Tibet and go into exile. But in 1951, and again five years later at the end of the Buddhist Jayanti celebrations in 1956, Tenzin Gyatso had chosen to return to Lhasa. McCarthy was worried about his safety. The United States had airdropped tons of weapons and ammunition to the resistance, and fighting was growing across Tibet. Frank Holober was departing as head of the Task Force, and McCarthy was about to assume full responsibility for the operation. McCarthy feared that it was only a matter of time before the Chinese retaliated against the Dalai Lama, possibly by taking him prisoner or even killing him. He knew the time to get the Dalai Lama out of Tibet was nearing.

Phala and Gompo Tashi were in the best position to plan an escape. They knew the countryside intimately. Travel would have to be by horseback. A journey would take several weeks to complete at this time of year, when passes were still snowbound. Gompo Tashi would coordinate an escort of Khampa warriors to serve as bodyguards. Still more resistance fighters would be deployed to block strategic passes to prevent the Chinese from pursuing and capturing the Dalai Lama.

Once the details were set, the CIA was notified of the proposed escape route in coded radio transmissions. This way the Agency could be prepared if it became necessary to drop supplies from the air once the plan was underway. But for the time being, it remained a contingency plan. The Dalai Lama was still not ready to leave Lhasa.

Fighting escalated in late January. NVDA fighters overran an entire Chinese garrison at Tsethang, a strategic crossroads town only 35 miles from Lhasa. In February, the guerrillas began attacking PLA supply lines across Central Tibet. The Chinese responded by sending more troops and aircraft into Tibet.

General Tan Guensen, China's political commissar in Lhasa, demanded that the Dalai Lama order Tibet's army to quash the guerrilla revolt. Although Tenzin Gyatso had not sanctioned Gompo Tashi's resistance movement, he would not send Tibetan troops against it. His refusal infuriated the Chinese general. In answer, the Chinese officials stripped the Dalai Lama's brothers, Gyalo and Norbu, of their citizenship. This gesture of retaliation for their role with the resistance was futile. Neither man intended to return to occupied Tibet.

On March 1, shortly before the Dalai Lama was due to take important monastic exams that would confer the equivalent of a doctor of divinity degree on him, General Tan had two orderlies hand deliver an invitation. A visiting Chinese dance troupe was scheduled to perform in mid-March at the Military Area Command, the Chinese military garrison on Lhasa's outskirts. General Tan wanted the Dalai Lama to be his guest. The usual way to issue such invitations was through the Tibetan government, not directly to His Holiness. Although surprised by the breech of protocol, Tenzin Gyatso wrote and accepted the offer without specifying the date on which he would attend.

The final exams were held in the Tsuglakhang, the 1300-year-old edifice that is Lhasa's central cathedral. Before an audience of 20,000 monks, the 24-year-old Dalai Lama debated Buddhist theology with 80 Tibetan scholars. The examinations took from eight in the morning until ten at night, with only two breaks for tea and refreshment. Having satisfied the scholars and abbots of Tibet's top monasteries, Tenzin Gyatso was pronounced validated as the reincarnation of Chenrezig, the country's sacred protector.

A regal procession accompanied the Dalai Lama's March 5 return to the Norbulingka, the summer palace whose name means "garden of jewels," or Jewel Park. The occasion should have been celebratory, but the atmosphere in Lhasa was tense. Refugees from the fighting crowded the city. They were joined by 25,000 Buddhist monks, who had made pilgrimages from monasteries across Tibet.

General Tan pressed the Dalai Lama to attend the dance performance, and the date was set for March 10. Normally, a bodyguard of 25 men would accompany him and his route would be lined with Tibetan soldiers. On March 9, one of Tan's officers called the head of the Dalai Lama's bodyguard to a meeting, where he told him that Tenzin Gyatso could bring only two guards—unarmed.

Word of the unusual Chinese demand spread quickly. Rumors of a plot to kidnap the Dalai Lama raced through the streets. Adding to the intrigue were three Chinese aircraft that had flown into Lhasa and were parked on the runway, quite possibly to transport the Dalai Lama to Beijing as a prisoner.

THE TIBETAN NATIONAL UPRISING

On March 10 fighting flared around the country. Guerrillas cut roads and supply lines and launched scores of attacks on Chinese military posts and bases throughout Tibet. Monks, Tibetan soldiers, pilgrims, and ordinary people thronged to the gates of the Jewel Park, refusing to let the Dalai Lama be kidnapped by the Chinese. Thirty-thousand strong, they surrounded the Norbulingka and made a cordon of human flesh around Tenzin Gyatso.

Diki Tsering, the Dalai Lama's mother, was at Changseshar, the cluster of houses where Tenzin Gyatso's extended family resided in Lhasa. Diki's elderly mother resided in one of the houses at the compound, and she was there visiting her. Diki was embroidering when a friend from the province of Amdo interrupted to tell her that across the country—but especially in the East—Tibetans had taken up arms against the Chinese.

It was the beginning of the Tibetan National Uprising. Events had reached the boiling point. Phala knew it was time to act. A car was sent to bring Diki to the Norbulingka, but the unfortunate driver had donned a Chinese uniform to make the trip. The mob set on him, and he was badly stoned and beaten before someone recognized him and saved his life.

The Chinese also knew it was vital to reach the Dalai Lama's mother. An armed group a dozen strong—eight men and four women—barged into Changseshar looking for her. An intrepid housekeeper blocked them from entering her rooms by telling them she was ill and shoving them until they left.

The next foray to bring Diki safely to the Norbulingka was made by her son-in-law and daughter, armed with a permit from the Army to escort her through the multitude. They hustled her away from Changseshar without even giving her time to pack. She had no idea that it was the last time she would ever see her mother.

This effort succeeded, and Diki Tsering found temporary sanctuary in the Norbulingka. Shortly after she was reunited with her son in the palace, the Dalai Lama sought the guidance of his protector divinity, the Nechung oracle, who also protected the Tibetan government. Lobsang Jigme was no ordinary Buddhist monk. He was also a *kuten*, the physical body into which the oracle is channeled. The *kuten* can be a man or a woman, and literally is the bridge between the natural and spiritual realm. The *kuten's* body is the physical basis that Dorje Drakden, the Nechung oracle, enters. His Holiness consulted Nechung several times throughout the year about specific questions that would arise and it was not uncommon for the Dalai Lama to ask the oracle about how to handle the Chinese. In his autobiography, the Dalai Lama refers to his consultations with the oracle as an "ancient method of intelligence gathering."

Wearing an ornate robe of golden silk brocade, blazoned with red, blue, green, and yellow designs of ancient origin, the *kuten's* appearance during a formal ceremony is formidable. On the *kuten's* chest is a circular mirror, bejeweled with amethyst and turquoise. An armature, supporting four flags and three victory banners, is fastened to the costume.

To the chanting of prayers and invocations, accompanied by cymbals, horns, and drumming, Lobsang Jigme began to enter the trance. Attendants helped him to a small stool in front of the Dalai Lama's throne. As a second cycle of chanting began, Lobsang's trance deepened and the attendants strapped a heavy helmet, weighing approximately 40 pounds, to his head.

Lobsang's face started to contort, his cheeks swelling and his eyes bulging, as Nechung crossed from the spiritual world into the *kuten*. He began to tremble and hiss loudly as the deity took possession of his body. His breathing altered, and then stopped briefly. At this point the attendants knotted the helmet tightly to his chin, so tightly as to make normal respiration impossible. Lobsang's possession by the deity was now complete. As he did often, the Dalai Lama probed the oracle. The Nechung advised Tenzin Gyatso to remain in the Norbulingka.

The palace offered only the illusion of safety, however. Between March 11 and March 16, General Tan and the Dalai Lama exchanged a series of notes, culminating in the General offering the Dalai Lama refuge in his military headquarters. Ostensibly, this was because the crowd around the Norbulingka was dominated by "reactionaries" who might become dangerous. General Tan sent word through an emissary that the Chinese would shell the crowd with artillery if the Dalai Lama was not permitted to pass. Moreover, Tan advised the Dalai Lama to take shelter in specific rooms away from the perimeter of the Norbulingka, purportedly to reduce the risk of being hit by a stray shell if firing commenced on the crowd. If heeded, the advice would also make the Dalai Lama an easy target for the Chinese artillery.

Phala ordered that the preliminary steps in the escape plan be put into effect. On March 15, a caravan of horses, supposedly hauling manure, crossed the Tsangpo River. Their packs actually carried supplies for the Dalai Lama's trek across the Himalayas. The horses were stabled on the opposite banks of the Tsangpo, awaiting Phala's next step. At the same time, Khampa resistance fighters commandeered coracles, the traditional yak-skin covered boats, and kept them ready. As an added step, they rounded up and hid all the other boats they could find to hamper the Chinese from crossing the river in pursuit. With the horses and boats in place, the Dalai Lama could leave at any time.

On the afternoon of March 17, two mortar rounds exploded outside the Norbulingka's north gate. Some accounts say they struck a pool on the grounds, other versions contend the shells crashed harmlessly into a marsh and caused no damage. They were probably fired by the Chinese as warning shots.

That same day, the Dalai Lama turned again to the Nechung oracle and asked if he should leave Lhasa. Again, Lobsang went into a trance. This time, the oracle suddenly shouted "Go! Go! Tonight!" He lurched forward, grabbed pen and paper, and wrote explicit instructions for the Dalai Lama's escape from Tibet. The instructions Lobsang wrote were meticulous, down to each stop in the small mountain villages on the route the Dalai Lama should take.

Whether it was an act of cosmic intervention, or a CIA trick to convince the Dalai Lama to choose exile, the oracle's instructions were the same as the contingency plan Phala had crafted months earlier and relayed to Roger McCarthy. The Agency knew that in 1951 and again in 1956, Tenzin Gyatso had heeded the oracle's advice in choosing to stay in Lhasa instead of taking up the offer of asylum.

FAREWELL TO LHASA

Phala's plan called for the Dalai Lama, his mother, youngest brother, elder sister, her husband, 18 senior government and religious officials, and their guards to depart the Norbulingka in secrecy. They were to move in three separate groups to minimize chances of detection by the Chinese. The throngs of Tibetans surrounding the palace also posed a risk. Despite the protective intent, if the crowds recognized the Dalai Lama, the clamor would surely alert the Chinese and abort the escape.

At 8:45 on the night of the 17th, Diki Tsering, her daughter, and youngest son were among the first group to leave the Norbulingka. Slipping out a side gate, the Dalai Lama's mother carried a toy rifle strapped over her shoulder; both were dressed as Tibetan soldiers. After getting through the crowd unrecognized, the next challenge involved passing Chinese administrative headquarters. Although lights were on in the offices, as they headed toward the Tsangpo, no one took notice.

Before his departure from the Norbulingka, the Dalai Lama left a white silk scarf on the altar of a shrine in the palace chapel as a gesture of farewell. In Tibetan Buddhism, the Dalai Lama is a Great Adept of the Kalachakra Tantra. He is a Master of the Wheel of Time and has a hand in shaping destiny. He was in the next wave to leave. Cloaked in an army tunic and carrying a rifle so he could pass as an ordinary soldier, the Dalai Lama left his home in Tibet. Others in the group included Phala, the Lord Chancellor, two soldiers, and the brother-in-law who headed the Dalai Lama's bodyguard. They told the Tibetan Army guards outside the palace compound that they were making an inspection tour of the perimeter. This got them through the crowd without attracting undue notice.

The third group to depart consisted of the Dalai Lama's tutors, advisers, and key government ministers. Traveling in a military truck, they were covered by a tarpaulin, hoping to be taken as just another Army vehicle moving through the city.

The plan called for the three groups to rendezvous on the banks of the Tsangpo and cross the river together. The single movement of coracles might pass unnoticed, but there was a greater likelihood that three separate groups of boats would be spotted. Instead, Diki Tsering's group, confused about the details of the plan, crossed first. When they reached the opposite shore, some 30 well-armed Khampa freedom fighters were waiting by their horses to receive them.

Diki watched anxiously for the coracle carrying her son to cross. She prayed that the Chinese would not hear the racket and implored those around her not to make any more noise than was absolutely necessary. Then the Dalai Lama appeared through the darkness. Between his retinue and the Khampa escorts, there were almost 100 people and horses. To Diki, the sound of their hooves as they galloped over the gravel riverbanks was deafening.

According to CIA officer McCarthy, Phala dispatched two other groups of Tibetans, disguised as merchants, monks, and pilgrims. Sooner or later the Chinese would wake up to the fact that the Dalai Lama was missing. Heading in different directions toward the border, these groups were decoys. Their purpose was to confuse the PLA so they would not know which group to follow to find the Dalai Lama. The intention was to force the Chinese to disperse, tracking multiple horse caravans across the Himalayan vastness.

Other NVDA fighters were mobilized to guard the escape route itself. This protective measure covered the escape party's flanks and blocked key passes along the route to India. They rode unseen by the Dalai Lama and his entourage, so that the Chinese could not break through to capture, or kill him. The chase was on.

THE CIA LEARNS THE ESCAPE
PLAN IS IN PROGRESS

Couriers gave the news of the Dalai Lama's escape to two of the Saipan-trained guerrillas. Athar and Lhotse, a.k.a. Tom and Lou, used a hand-cranked RS-1 crystal-operated transmitter to inform the CIA of the successful exit from Lhasa. They then made plans to link up with the traveling party, so that progress or emergency reports could be relayed to Washington.

The Dalai Lama and his entourage stayed on the move until about three on the morning of March 18. The next hurdle in their journey was the 16,000 foot Che-La pass that separated Lhasa valley from the Tsangpo valley.

After resting for a few hours, refreshing themselves with tea and *tsampa*, the group continued the mission. Reaching the Che-La pass shortly after daybreak, the Dalai Lama looked back on the ancient city of Lhasa one last time. Colonel Younghusband had taken the same route out of Lhasa in 1904 and wrote in his memoirs about casting his eyes back on the city from a similar vantage. Glancing at the towering Potala in the evening twilight, Younghusband had been overcome by an almost inexplicable sense of elation. It was overpowering and transforming, and he vowed then and there to abandon his military career. No sooner had he mustered his columns of British troops back to India than he resigned his commission and gave the rest of his life over to a blend of Buddhist and Hindu mysticism. So compelling was this vision that Younghusband had this last sight of Lhasa carved in stone above his grave in an English churchyard.

The Dalai Lama's party rode on toward the town of Chidisho under cloudy skies. They were welcome because any Chinese aircraft would be hampered in spotting the group. But the group's passage did not go unnoticed.

One observer was an elderly Khampa named Tashi Norbu, who rode toward them out of a shroud of mist on a magnificent white horse. Having special significance in Tibet, the animals are thought to possess knowledge that humans cannot attain. It is believed that horses can save a life or tell when the time has come to die and, are therefore revered as gifts.

Tashi Norbu approached the group and offered to exchange his horse for the Dalai Lama's pony. The old man said he feared that without a strong mount to carry him across the mountains, the Dalai Lama's escape might fail. The trade made, Norbu disappeared again. The travelers saw the encounter as a favorable omen.

Tom and Lou also rode toward the traveling party. Tom, escorted by resistance fighters, left first with one of the four RS-1 radio sets that had been provided by the CIA. Lou followed with a second group of guerrillas. They were more heavily laden with weapons from an air-drop that included Sten 9mm submachine guns, bazookas, and the 57mm recoilless rifle. Packed among the weapons was a film camera from the CIA to record the Dalai Lama's exodus for movie newsreel and television audiences worldwide.

Tom's rendezvous with the Dalai Lama was on March 25 at the Chongye valley. The Dalai Lama had been traveling for eight days. It was then that the first coded radio report on his progress was sent from Tibet. The broadcast was received at a CIA listening post on Okinawa and then relayed to CIA headquarters in Washington, DC. There, CIA Director Allen Dulles and Desmond FitzGerald awaited news of the Dalai Lama's journey.

Working from a CIA safehouse on Wisconsin Avenue in Georgetown, Geshe Wangyal translated the radio reports. The ultimate recipient of the message was the White House National Security Council (NSC). It was CIA Director Dulles's job to keep the NSC and President Eisenhower briefed on the Dalai Lama's trek. On March 26, Dulles told Eisenhower, "We have every reason to hope that the Dalai Lama will get out of Tibet soon." The entourage was still about 60 miles from India. One last major mountain range separated them from safety. With the CIA-trained radio operators on the scene, Eisenhower received daily updates on the Dalai Lama's movements.

Jim Keck, an airman for the CIA's proprietary airline, had a knack for being in on the turning points in the Tibetan operation. He had navigated the first air drop of weapons to the resistance. As the Dalai Lama and his retinue trekked through the mountains, Keck got a bird's eye view from his C-130 as it passed over the column of refugees.

The group of men, women, and horses that trudged through the Himalayas underneath Keck's wings was protected on its flanks by fighters from the *Chushi Gangdruk*. They were paying a high toll in blood and lives to keep the Chinese pursuers at bay. Events inside Tibet were not going well. Fierce fighting engulfed Lhasa after the Chinese discovered that they had been fooled by the Tibetans' ruse and realized the Dalai Lama had eluded them.

Across the country, the national uprising was being met by a show of strength from the People's Liberation Army. Now that the PLA commanders had less incentive than ever to show restraint toward the

Tibetans, the slaughter intensified in a cascading cycle of revenge and reprisal. Neither side was inclined to take prisoners.

Two days after Tom's rendezvous with the entourage at Chongye, the Dalai Lama received the news that China had dissolved Tibet's government. He had already learned that when his departure was discovered, crowds around the Norbulingka were shelled with artillery. Thousands had been killed in the capital after days of fierce fighting.

Because China had formally abrogated its agreement to respect the Tibetan government's limited autonomy, the Dalai Lama was left with few alternatives. On March 27, he and his ministers reached the stronghold of Lhuntse Dzong. The town was an important base for the Tibetan resistance. In the town's hilltop fort, he formally repudiated the 17-Point Agreement that China had forced Tibet to accept in 1951. The agreement conceded Chinese control over Tibet's defense and foreign policy, but left management of religious and domestic affairs in the hands of the Tibetan government. It also allowed Tibet to maintain a token army. But the Chinese had reneged on the agreement, albeit incrementally, since 1956, when Chairman Mao began to impose communism in Eastern Tibet.

Before a crowd of more than one thousand people, accompanied by full Buddhist rites, the Dalai Lama ceremoniously declared the formation of the Tibetan government-in-exile. This was the event the CIA had anticipated in dispatching a film camera to the resistance fighters. The momentous occasion was captured on film for use in rallying world opinion to the Tibetan cause. But before that could happen, the travelers would have to get safely across the border into India with the film footage intact.

India had agreed in advance to grant asylum to the Dalai Lama. Gyalo met with Prime Minister Nehru in New Delhi a few days after the start of the March 10 uprising and had been given his personal assurance that the Dalai Lama would be welcome when he reached India. But Nehru didn't want to extend an asylum offer until the Dalai Lama formally requested it. If India unilaterally offered asylum, it might provoke China. Instead, the radio operators broadcast the Dalai Lama's formal request. It reached Washington after midnight on March 28.

Desmond FitzGerald had Wangyal translate the message. Normal bureaucratic procedures called for informing the NSC and the State Department. But FitzGerald didn't have to go through channels on such a high-priority presidential initiative. He simply routed the request from CIA headquarters directly to the U.S. Embassy in New Delhi. Nehru's official acceptance was cabled back by 6 AM, just in time for the news to be incorporated into Eisenhower's daily intelligence brief.

Then on March 31, the radio team reported that the Dalai Lama had crossed into India. His journey had taken 18 days.

THE SEEDS OF THE TIBETAN DIASPORA ARE SOWN

A 19-year-old monk, far from Lhasa, named Chögyam Trungpa, also faced the question of leaving Tibet. Chögyam was the reincarnation of the Tenth Trungpa Tulku, the supreme abbot of the Surmang monasteries and a high lama of the Kagyu lineage, one of the four schools of Tibetan Buddhism.

In its effort to suppress the uprising, the Chinese Army had seized monasteries throughout Eastern Tibet. One of them was Düdtsi-Til, the key monastery in Trungpa Tulku's order. It was the burial place of the Tenth Trungpa Tulku.

The PLA pillaged the monastery and desecrated the tomb, exhuming the body and leaving it in the open. The library was ransacked and ancient Buddhist texts were wantonly destroyed. To Tibetans, this was a particularly painful affront, for a mere fragment of writing from a sacred text, down to the tiniest scrap of paper, is revered and treated preciously. Texts that are no longer needed, having been copied and replaced, are often sent to caves to be allowed to disintegrate naturally. The Chinese, however, left the torn pages to be eaten as fodder by their pack animals and trampled under hoof. After occupying the monastery for almost a month, the Chinese decamped, leaving destruction behind.

Chögyam, the Eleventh Trungpa Tulku, headed for a mountain cave to meditate. The cave he chose was on Mt. Kulha Ngang-ya. An earlier Buddhist master, Lama Montrug, discovered the cave and used it for the rest of his life. With two chambers, a natural window, and a running stream nearby, the cave was idyllic.

For more than a week, Chögyam, an attendant, and a nun from a nearby monastery meditated. After leaving the nun behind, the men moved to another cave on Mt. Kiyo Rinchen-pungpa, three hours away by horse. Here the Eleventh Trungpa Tulku passed his time in solitude, reading a 1000-page long Tibetan text, seeking answers, oblivious to events unfolding in Lhasa.

On April 11, Chögyam awakened to the sound of a horse neighing. A monk had been sent to warn him that he might no longer be safe. There were Chinese in the vicinity. The monk told him that the PLA had completely taken the city of Lhasa after days of fighting. Chinese loudspeakers in Chamdo were blaring that the Dalai Lama had been abducted by reactionary forces. The propaganda claimed that the fighting in Lhasa had been provoked by the guerrillas and that the PLA had been forced to fire artillery at the Norbulingka but only minor damage had been done.

In fact, the Chinese shelling had begun shortly after midnight on March 19. The Tibetans answered with their own artillery and rose up en masse against the Chinese troops. The fighting in Lhasa continued for six days and nights, according to eyewitness Tsipon Shuguba, a Tibetan nobleman who was inside the Norbulingka Palace when the artillery barrage began. Independent reports said thousands were killed in Lhasa. Diki Tsering heard later from a household employee that so many shots were fired the man felt like he was walking on "fields of dried peas" because of the enormous volume of empty bullet casings littering the streets.

A return to Chamdo seemed out of the question. Chögyam Trungpa made plans for his departure from Tibet and set the date for April 23. The uprising was little more than a month old, but already it had run into severe setbacks. Gompo Tashi had met with his field commanders to rally them for a counterattack, but found the group dispirited. The ranks of fighters were badly depleted by the showdown with the Chinese. Refugees began streaming out of Tibet.

Chapter 6

Eisenhower Expands the Covert War

On April 1, after CIA Director Allen Dulles confirmed that the Dalai Lama was safely out of Tibet, he sent a memo to Eisenhower. It summarized the Tibetan Operation to date and included Dulles's assessment about what seemed like a contradiction — Buddhist warriors.

"The Tibetans," Dulles wrote, "particularly the Khampas, Goloks, and other tribes of East Tibet, are a fierce, brave and warlike people. Battle, in defense of their religion and the Dalai Lama, is looked upon as a means of achieving merit toward their next reincarnation."

CIA Director Dulles intended to give these warriors plenty of achievements for future lives. His memo to Eisenhower concluded by informing the president that with the Dalai Lama now in exile, fresh plans for Tibet's resistance were being drawn up.

To Dulles, it was essential for the United States to fight back against International Communism in Tibet. The year 1959 had already delivered a setback to the United States in the Cold War, when Fidel Castro ousted Cuban dictator Fulgencio Batista in January and took over Cuba.

But before April was over, conditions inside Tibet had badly deteriorated. A month of fighting between the Chinese and Tibetan resistance in the south along the Dalai Lama's route into exile had virtually decimated the guerrillas. Captured Chinese documents tallied the Tibetan death toll at 87,000. Pockets of resistance were short on food, supplies, and hope. Many guerrillas were fleeing toward India, carrying with them the same weapons that Jim Keck and his colleagues at Civil Air Transport had labored to air drop into Tibet. On the ground, the backbone of the rebellion had been smashed.

CIA veterans insist that the setback resulted from a failure of discipline. The Tibetans were supposed to limit their engagements with the Chinese to classic guerrilla warfare hit-and-run attacks, not launch major attacks against the PLA. As one CIA veteran put it, the attacks were to have been little more than "pinpricks." But the Tibetan National Uprising was far from a pinprick. It featured coordinated assaults on a national scale that erupted into full-fledged fighting to protect the Dalai Lama from capture. The official records of CIA involvement in Tibet remain classified, but the likelihood that the uprising was coordinated and instigated by the CIA for the purpose of fulfilling the longstanding U.S. objective of getting the Dalai Lama out of Tibet cannot be ignored. This had been a consistent feature of U.S. policy since 1951. It took eight years, but now it was a *fait accompli.*

A simpler explanation accounts for the discrepancy between how the CIA and the Tibetans viewed the resistance. The Tibetans were for independence and wanted to expel the Chinese from their land. The CIA, following NSC 5412/2, wanted to make trouble for the PLA and discredit International Communism. Put bluntly, the Eisenhower Administration was using the Tibetans for its own purposes, which were far more limited than the goals of the resistance. The two objectives were compatible, but not identical.

Not everyone favored secret aid to the Tibetans. Air Force General Curtis LeMay proposed in a Cabinet meeting to openly use the U.S. Air Force to bomb the PLA. It was not such a preposterous suggestion in 1959. With poor roads and no rail access, the logistical task of maintaining PLA forces inside Tibet meant long, exposed supply lines. Air power could cut off supplies to the Chinese, while guerrilla forces hit at their outposts and bases. Overt military aid to Tibet might have succeeded in forcing the Chinese back. But LeMay was overruled. Eisenhower wanted covert opposition to the USSR and China, not military action that risked triggering a World War III.

If ever there was a moment for the 5412 Special Group to reflect on the limits of what it could realistically accomplish by supporting the

NVDA resistance, this was it. The Tibetans had paid a huge price for what amounted to a Cold War propaganda coup. Mao was more firmly in control of Tibet than before the National Uprising.

Despite the setbacks, President Eisenhower approved an expansion of the program. Code-named ST BARNUM and ST BAILEY, Eisenhower's program authorized covert assistance in waging guerrilla warfare inside Tibet on a larger scale than ever before.

The CIA had most of the elements it needed for a protracted covert operation. Camp Hale generated newly trained fighters and the C-130 airlifts kept them supplied. In one of his last official acts on Tibetan ground, the Dalai Lama had made Gompo Tashi a general in Tibet's military. While still in the Himalayas in transit to India, Tenzin Gyatso issued an order that was the equivalent of a battlefield promotion for Gompo Tashi. The order cemented his authority and gave the NVDA resistance fighters the same legal status as Tibetan soldiers.

Most importantly, to the men of the 5412 Special Group, the Dalai Lama was now in India. This was a crucial detail. Until now, the Dalai Lama had been a virtual pawn in the dangerous Cold War chess match being played out on the rooftop of the world. So long as the Dalai Lama remained within reach of the Chinese in Lhasa, the danger was very real that any exposure of the CIA operation could result in the Chinese taking direct action against him. With the Dalai Lama safely beyond the reach of the Chinese and the long game of trying to reach a *modus vivendi* with Beijing temporarily at an end, however, the CIA was free to step up operations against the Chinese.

But, for Desmond FitzGerald, there was still a missing element.

HOWARD BANE, THE CIA'S ULTIMATE "STREET MAN"

FitzGerald lacked his own "street man" on the ground in India to handle the Tibetan operation. At the time of the 1959 Tibetan National Uprising, FitzGerald was in charge of the CIA's Far East Division. Under the geographical divisions by which the CIA operated, FitzGerald's Far East Division really shouldn't have been involved in operations in India. Those fell under the control of the Near East Division.

But a worldwide exception had been created for operations targeting the Chinese. Under this exception, CIA officers from FitzGerald's Division could be posted anywhere in the world, as long as their targets were Chinese. Far East Division clandestine officers might work out of an Embassy in Africa, for example, or India, even though those CIA stations reported to different geographical division chiefs. This meant that the officers assigned to Chinese operations reported through the CIA Station Chief, who came from a different geographic division than the subordinate case officer. The arrangement had the potential to create bureaucratic friction beyond the normal pull and tug that often existed between CIA officers in the field and those manning desks back at headquarters.

FitzGerald's street man was Howard Thomas Bane, a 32-year-old CIA officer. Bane had worked in one of the Korean War operations FitzGerald ran from the CIA's Taiwan base that involved rescuing downed American fliers. During the Korean War, he was stationed at Inchon under cover as an Army captain, even though he was in fact still a Navy enlisted man, but working for the CIA.

Bane joined the Navy at the age of 17 because he wanted to be a naval gunner. Instead, the Navy taught him to scuba dive and plant underwater demolitions. His early CIA assignments included training agents and paramilitaries at secret facilities on the islands of Paengyong, Cho Do, and YoDo in Wonsan Harbor.

Flying on military aircraft, Bane took a team of Korean agents to the CIA base on Saipan. He said it was "miserable" in the plane's unheated cabin. On Saipan, the sunken Japanese ships from World War II made ideal targets for teaching underwater demolition techniques.

Bane hadn't been fond of wreck diving since having a bad accident when his air hose was cut on a piece of jagged wreckage. During the training he expected to snag his gear on ragged metal at any time. He found the atmosphere down in the sunken ships "eery." Bones scattered throughout the submerged vessels were reminders that these were watery tombs, and Saipan's caves were still filled with skeletons of Japanese fighters charred by flame throwers during the furious battle for the island. Despite the lack of heat in the passenger cabin, he was glad to get back on the airplane when the training was complete and return to Korea.

In many ways, FitzGerald and Bane were a study in contrasts. FitzGerald was a cosmopolitan and wealthy Irish-American who hailed from Boston and counted Robert Kennedy among his personal friends. Howard Bane's father was an illiterate coal miner from West Virginia. They epitomized the social and economic diversity of the early CIA, which was composed of OSS veterans from World War II, émigrés from Eastern Europe, Ivy Leaguers, and men and women from humble backgrounds.

As a teenager, Bane worked part-time jobs at the local post office and town library. The library job allowed him to indulge his passion for books. They fed his thirst for knowledge about history, geography, and foreign cultures, igniting a longing for exotic travel and adventures. Authors who made an impression on him included Peter Abelard, T. S. Elliot, Eugene O'Neill, Jean Jacques Rousseau, and an early hero, T. E. Lawrence. For the rest of his life, Bane was an avid reader, giving and soliciting book recommendations and compiling entire reading lists for his friends. When Bane graduated from George Washington University, he was among the first in his extended family to get a college degree.

Despite being an odd couple in most respects, FitzGerald and Bane had one thing in common—disdain for bureaucracy. Like FitzGerald, during his four-decade career with the CIA Bane developed a reputation for taking the initiative and preferring light supervision by headquarters. Duane Clarridge, who served with Bane in India during the heyday of the Tibetan Operation, wrote in his 1997 memoir *A Spy for All Seasons* that Howard "had no patience for management of which he was not a part."

THE CIA'S DELHI STATION TAKES CHARGE

In 1959, Bane was sent to New Delhi with cover as a State Department Foreign Service Officer in the Political Section assigned to Refugee Affairs. Despite his young age, he was already a veteran spymaster. His recent posting in Thailand had been especially productive. In three years, he had recruited 33 high-quality agents.

The CIA Station Chief in New Delhi was Harry Rositzke, an intellectually gifted former professor. Rositzke had a reputation as a gruff perfectionist when it came to espionage. He was a demanding boss who ran his Station meetings leaving no detail untouched in terms of spotting, developing, and recruiting the agents his case officers handled. Bane reported through Rositzke to headquarters, but both knew well enough that Bane's real boss was FitzGerald.

The situation was further complicated by the relationship between India and the United States. The Indians were willing to give asylum to the Dalai Lama, provided the American government paid the bulk of the costs associated with supporting the exiled Tibetans. In this sense, there was tacit cooperation between the two countries. But the level of cooperation was never deep. When he arrived in New Delhi in 1957, Rositzke established a liaison relationship with the Indian intelligence service. Although there were meetings between the CIA officers and their Indian counterparts, an insider recalls that the exchanges rarely amounted to more than "chit chat."

When the two intelligence agencies weren't feigning cooperation at the liaison meetings, they spied on each other aggressively. Bane was not only expected to run the Tibet operation in India, giving it a new political and intelligence dimension in addition to the paramilitary operations, he was also expected to recruit spies from among India's military and political elite. In this regard, Bane's activities fell directly under Rositzke's jurisdiction.

For his part, Rositzke tried early on to assert his authority over Bane with the matter of housing. Bane had a young wife and a growing family. Anita, whom he married in April 1953, had managed well with difficult housing conditions on earlier assignments. But now, Howard wanted to make it up to her. He found a house with grounds and a walled garden in a neighborhood called Friend's Colony just outside of central Delhi that seemed perfect.

Rositzke, however, withheld his approval.

The cause of the friction lay, in part, in the complex arrangements made for giving CIA officers diplomatic cover. Soon after the CIA was established in 1947, the State Department agreed to provide protection to CIA employees as diplomats. This had the advantage of giving officers immunity from prosecution if they were caught spying. But the State Department had its conditions. One was that the CIA employees had to be older than 28 years of age. The age cut-off was set after some still-classified misbehavior by junior officers created a diplomatic incident. The State Department told the CIA it would no longer agree to diplomatic cover for spies younger than 28.

Even when the CIA officers met the age requirement for diplomatic cover, the quality of housing an officer was assigned fell under further restrictions. Bane, of course, was past the cut-off age, but CIA tradecraft called for concealing the true rank of its officers by arranging "below grade" Foreign Service cover assignments. This meant that the CIA officers masqueraded as lower ranked Foreign Service officers than their true ranking in the intelligence agency. A practical consequence of these interdepartmental procedures was that CIA officers and their families ended up assigned to housing that was beneath their status.

Rositzke felt the house Bane wanted at 5 Friend's Colony Road was too good for his cover position and would alert others, including Indian counterintelligence, that there was something noteworthy about the Refugee Affairs officer. In fact, the house was not ostentatious. To the rear, it was bounded by a railway line that ran from Delhi to Bombay. Its location in a quiet neighborhood was actually less conspicuous than other alternatives.

But Rositzke rolled out a new objection.

"You won't get many bicycle riders to come all the way out there," the Station Chief said, referring to the junior government officials and clerks who rode bicycles to work and were often the targets of CIA recruitment efforts in India.

"I don't recruit bicycle riders," Bane shot back.

It was true. Bane was prolific in recruiting spies. He distinguished himself in Thailand for his ability to get close to a target and pitch an agent, recruiting generals, security officials, and rising politicians. He likened it to seduction and went to great lengths to develop an approach to his targets. In India, he took up golf, hunting, and glider flying to befriend a senior military official whom he successfully recruited. Some of his pitches were unorthodox. When cables came back from CIA headquarters approving his more creative maneuverings, the response was often, "Give it a go, Bane." The line appeared so frequently in station cable traffic that it became his nickname among CIA insiders.

One of Bane's unique recruitment attempts involved a Soviet Ambassador in Africa. Bane had been trying to develop the Ambassador into someone who would spy for the United States but had not yet made his pitch. The CIA had just pulled off a coup in the country where a number of Soviet "advisers" were killed. The Ambassador, complaining of chest pains, took refuge in his official residence. Bane learned that the man was having heart trouble. EKG machines were rare in the country, but the American Embassy had one. Bane had one of the medical staff give him a crash course in how to use an electrocardiograph, then grabbed the machine and left for the Ambassador's residence.

As he drove into the compound, he took note of a number of men working in the gardens. Bane was sure they were KGB. Some doubtless were friends or colleagues of the Soviet advisers who had been slain. In the tense atmosphere of the coup, anything might happen, but he pressed on anyway. To his delight, the Soviet Ambassador accepted his offer of the EKG test. Bane used this brief private access to the ambassador to ask if he would spy for the United States, making the needles on the EKG jump. The diplomat turned him down, but didn't unmask Bane to the KGB agents surrounding the building.

Bane, however, wouldn't give up on the house at 5 Friend's Colony Road. After a few months in which he and his family lived in temporary housing, Rositzke finally relented. Bane moved Anita and their three children into the house with the walled garden. It was on a pleasant untrafficked street, bounded by deep gutters to carry away the monsoon rains, with two narrow lanes divided by a planted median. Overhanging trees gave shade, and twin black lamps were perched atop stout pillars from which a sturdy iron gate was mounted. Bane had the address emblazoned on one of the pillars to announce to guests that they had found the right place. Getting the house he wanted was a minor bureaucratic victory, and it heralded things to come.

Stationing Howard Bane in India elevated the CIA's access to the Tibetans. In characterizing the CIA Tibet operation, one insider says that before Bane's arrival in India, there was no "field" in the operation—spies in the streets and political action inside the country. But not everyone was pleased with Bane's assignment. Roger McCarthy, head of the Tibet Task Force back at headquarters, felt a strong sense of ownership of the operation. He had been in on it from the start, helping train the first Tibetan agents on Saipan, and intended to keep control.

There was plenty to do. The Dalai Lama's asylum in India stirred controversy. Initial plans to establish a Tibetan government-in-exile in India had to be shelved because of opposition from China and some Indian politicians. By early May 1959, the debate over Tibet was prominent in India's Parliament. The Chinese issued proclamations denouncing the Dalai Lama as a counterrevolutionary and insisting that Tibet was legitimately a part of China. They singled out Kalimpong as the center of the Tibetan resistance and tried to put pressure on Prime Minister Nehru to curtail the movement. Sympathetic Indian journalists and politicians with ties to the Communist party parroted the charges. Nehru, predictably, denied that the Tibetan resistance drew its support from India.

An All-India Convention on Tibet was held in Calcutta at the end of May.

"Tibet is being gobbled up by the Chinese dragon," noted Indian politician and freedom fighter Jaiprakash Narayan warned. He continued, "A vast scheme of colonization by China was set on foot, so that large parts of Tibet should cease to be Tibetan and become Chinese."

One of the CIA's jobs was to backstop the Indian politicians who believed in the justness of the Tibetan cause. In some cases this meant subsidizing the publication of pro-Tibet speeches and arguments made by supportive Indian politicians. To ensure their wide availability, the CIA paid for the printing and distribution of pro-Tibet books and pamphlets. One of these books, according to Howard Bane, was *Dalai Lama and India*, published in 1959 by Hind Book House. Journalists also received money to publish articles supporting Tibet or criticizing China.

This propaganda war, in which both sides engaged freely, was in keeping with the CIA's mandate under NSC Directive 5412/2. As noted, Eisenhower's intent was not merely to harass the Chinese through guerrilla warfare, but to discredit the prestige of International Communism. With the world divided between the East Bloc, the West, and the non-aligned nations, the Cold War struggle for public opinion was viewed as critically important by both sides.

In June, McCarthy went to India to meet with Gompo Tashi in Darjeeling. McCarthy wanted a candid assessment of the resistance's condition after the battering it had taken from the Chinese. After three days of detailed talks, the Task Force chief was satisfied that enough remnants of resistance remained to justify continuing the operation.

McCarthy also met with Tom and Lou, the two CIA trainees who had provided radio support between CIA headquarters and the Dalai Lama. With the expansion of the training program that Eisenhower had approved, McCarthy realized that Tom and Lou were more valuable as instructors at Camp Hale. He made arrangements for them to return to Colorado.

At CIA headquarters, some of the Far East Division brass were skeptical about Station Chief Rositzke's commitment to the Tibet operation. They believed Rositzke, a Near East Division officer, feared he would be left to clean up the mess if something went awry with the operation and it blew up in their faces, but that he would reap little in the way of rewards if the operation was successful. This divisional rivalry existed more in the minds of headquarters staff than it did in the field.

HOWARD BANE AND GYALO THONDUP TEAM UP

Bane's principal Tibetan agent was Gyalo Thondup, to whom he was known as "Mr. Howard." Other CIA officers who had briefly handled Gyalo had not been overawed. Gyalo sometimes came across as passive. Bane's take on the Dalai Lama's sober-minded older brother was exactly the opposite. Bane had great respect for him. He considered Gyalo intelligent, articulate, and a valuable agent.

The difference in viewpoints can be explained by the fact that Bane was a spymaster—a case officer who thrived on the recruitment and handling of agents. He valued the production of good intelligence above sometimes questionable covert action, misadventures like encouraging the Hungarian Revolt and then leaving the Hungarians at the mercy of the Soviet Union. This was a value shared with Rositzke, and over time it bonded them. Not that Bane shied from covert action; over the course of his career he received the CIA's first and second highest awards, the Distinguished Intelligence Medal and the Intelligence Medal of Merit for still-classified covert actions. Bane could see from the start that even if the Tibetan resistance faltered in liberating Tibet, it still had the capacity to deliver timely intelligence to the CIA.

When it came to Tibet's independence, Gyalo pressed Bane, and it was perhaps the one point on which he and Mr. Howard may not have found full agreement. The CIA officers involved in the Tibetan operation insist they never told the Tibetans that the United States backed independence for their country. The very prospect of independence put the United States in a quandary, given American support for the Chinese Nationalists on Taiwan, who shared at least one thing in common with the Chinese Communists—the view that Tibet belonged to China. Gyalo maintains with equal vigor that American officials didn't promise support for Tibet's autonomy, or human rights under Communist Chinese rule, but full-throated, unequivocal independence.

Men engaged in secret, dangerous undertakings bond deeply, even cynical, jaded operatives. The 5412 Special Group may have understood the limits of U.S. support to the Tibetans, especially to the guerrillas. But when the CIA's street men, paramilitary trainers, knuckledraggers, smoke jumpers, and derring-do pilots who flew the moonlit midnight missions across the Himalayas gave their bond, it was doubtlessly sincere. Men don't fight for legalistic abstractions. They fight for causes like independence, and the Tibetans were convinced their CIA allies shared the same goal.

Now that he was settled into the house at Friend's Colony, Bane lost little time in organizing the Wednesday Club, afternoon get-togethers over a long and liquid lunch hosted at the home of one of the half-dozen or so case officers invited to attend. The get-togethers filled what would otherwise have been a void in the week. Recruiting agents was a matter of meeting people, "developing" them as a potential agent if they had information or access that was of value, and then finally pitching them to spy for America. In cities with lots of restaurants or bars the socializing necessary to advance this process can be done during the day, but in New Delhi, in the late 1950s, it was strictly a nocturnal affair. With the heat of the day dissipated, social functions were held, and people came out to see and be seen, especially at the diplomatic events and receptions common to all capital cities.

Duane Clarridge, whose career in the CIA included being Chief of the Latin America Division, Chief of the European Division, and Chief of the Counter-Terrorist Center, was one of the attendees at the Wednesday Club lunches. At the time, he was early in his CIA career and fresh off a posting in Nepal. The topic of conversation always turned to tradecraft—how to develop targets for recruitment, how to pitch spies, how to handle them once they were yours, the nuances of gaining operational control over an agent, and, of course, war stories from previous posts. Clarridge understood that the Wednesday Club was Bane's way of creating an alternative power base outside the CIA station, a fact that hardly escaped Rositzke's notice.

So long as they didn't interfere with the Station's productivity, Rositzke didn't object to the Wednesday afternoon brainstorming sessions. The site for the meetings rotated and soon became competitive, with the spouses and their Indian kitchen help vying to outdo one another with the best food and the best table settings of china and silver.

One of Bane's recruits was an Indian journalist who often interviewed India's future prime minister, Indira Gandhi. Bane developed the relationship, and the journalist's private access yielded good information for the CIA about India's inside politics and foreign affairs. Bane learned from the journalist that Gandhi liked oral sex from her lover. In the sexually repressed atmosphere of the 1950s, some of the group wondered whether this meant Gandhi was a closet lesbian.

Another Indian recruit was a senior military officer who had flown with the British Royal Air Force in World War II. The officer became one of Howard's best agents. When he delivered blueprints of Soviet aircraft and detailed contracts between the Indian government and USSR on military purchases, Howard had to awaken Anita to type copies so that the documents could be returned before morning. So that the Indian officer wouldn't need to take unnecessary risks carrying sensitive documents to a clandestine rendezvous, the CIA station trained the agent in clandestine photography.

Years later, the same agent was posted to Europe. The CIA had kept him on the payroll, but no case officer was assigned to him. Bane went to see him, almost as a courtesy call. Virtually the first words out of his mouth were "Howard, where have you guys been? I've been waiting to hear from you." In his diplomatic safe the agent had thirty-six rolls of undeveloped film. They were copies of documents the pro-Soviet Indian Defense Minister had asked the agent to safeguard when shuttling between New Delhi and Moscow.

By the end of his tour as Station Chief, Rositzke quietly petitioned Clarridge to see if he could become an honorary member of the Wednesday Club. Clarridge sounded out the others and found them in agreement. At his farewell party, they gave Rositzke an engraved mug with the names of the current members of the club inscribed on it along with his own.

In his memoir, A Spy for All Seasons, Clarridge recalls stopping the conversation at one Wednesday Club session when he described the sensation of successfully pulling off a difficult recruitment of a new spy. Clarridge said it was like an orgasm. Seduction, orgasm, the thrill of illicit knowledge, the breaking of another country's rules, secret purposes and deception, knowing the facts beneath the diplomatic fictions; espionage is heady. Nothing in the business is quite as exhilarating as a full-blown covert operation, especially one involving war.

In December 1960, Ambassador Ellsworth Bunker and Howard Bane traveled north to Dharamsala to meet with the Dalai Lama and the others in his retinue with a need to know. Their purpose was to brief Tenzin Gyatso on the comprehensive program of support that President

Eisenhower had authorized—from aiding refugees and the fledgling government-in-exile to winning recognition for Tibet's cause with the United Nations to the training and infiltration of guerrilla fighters back into Tibet.

Interpreters translated the briefing and questions and answers into Tibetan. The session extended through lunch and lasted three hours. When it was over, Bane asked one of the CIA officers on hand to photograph Bunker and himself with the Dalai Lama. The CIA Station's Polaroid camera elicited the first words in English the Dalai Lama had uttered during their meeting.

"Mr. Howard, you have a Minute Camera!" the Dalai Lama said.

Always keenly fascinated by new technology, Tenzin Gyatso seized on the chance to examine Edward Land's revolutionary camera which made photographic prints in under a minute without any need for a darkroom.

On their way back to New Delhi, Bunker and Bane speculated about who had taught the Dalai Lama his English. They settled on Heinrich Harrer, the German mountaineer who had befriended the Dalai Lama during his seven year stay in Lhasa, as the likeliest person. But they never really knew the answer. Harrer remained something of a cipher to the CIA. Earlier proposals by other CIA officers to approach Harrer about the Dalai Lama had been rebuffed by headquarters because of this uncertainty.

There were others "Mr. Howard" took to meet the Dalai Lama, notably those very few members of Congress who were made aware of the CIA's Tibet operation. For these excursions, Anita made meals that Howard could bring to be eaten picnic style en route during the day-long road trip to Dharamsala. Bane knew that nothing would spoil the positive impression of a meeting with the Tibetan spiritual leader quicker than the intestinal ills that might result from eating unfamiliar Indian food on the road.

FROM REFUGEES TO GUERRILLA FIGHTERS

From a trickle at the beginning, the number of Tibetans following the Dalai Lama to India became a flood. Tens of thousands arrived in India by the end of Tenzin Gyatso's first summer in asylum. As their ranks swelled to more than 80,000, seeing to the welfare of the refugees became one of the Dalai Lama's most urgent concerns.

Handling refugee affairs was Bane's cover job at the U.S. Embassy. Maintaining his cover meant dedicating a portion of each day to work that conformed to his job title. He devoted his efforts to making life better for the refugees by coordinating emergency shelter, food, and medical assistance.

Refugee camps were fertile grounds for finding young men ready to fight the Chinese. Unlike Kalimpong, where Gyalo and his trusted associate Lhamo Tsering drew recruits mainly from the families of Khampa nobles, they now had access to men from all over Tibet. They eagerly sought out trainees from the provinces of Amdo and U-Tsang and tribes like the Goloks, all of whom were underrepresented in the early guerrilla warfare programs. Balancing the classes with fighters from different provinces would help overcome regional rivalries when the teams were parachuted back into Tibet.

The planes ferrying Tibetans to the secret Colorado training camp continued to churn their way across the waters with their tedious turboprop monotone. The Camp Hale schooling continued under the direction of Tom Fosmire and his deputy, Zeke Zilaitis, but it grew in scope and purpose. Earlier training had focused on sending skilled agents into Tibet. The new agenda called for building up paramilitary forces. Instruction was expanded to include operating military vehicles ranging from Jeeps and trucks to tanks. Psychological warfare, field maneuvers, conducting multiple ambushes, and other paramilitary skills were added to the core intelligence curriculum.

The men were taught to form cells of guerrilla fighters, to pass checkpoints in disguise, to fool interrogators by falling back on a cover story just at the moment when their Chinese captors expected them to break under pressure. They were expected to stay on the run for weeks if necessary and elude pursuers while living off the land, sometimes pursued by their own CIA trainers using live ammunition to add realism to the exercises. During their training, the mountains outside Leadville, Colorado echoed with gunfire from small arms and light machine guns and concussive blasts of mortar rounds and plastic explosives. Yet, unbelievably, the program continued to remain secret.

There were close calls. When the phosphorous from a tracer round ignited a small forest fire, the CIA instructors had to call for firefighting crews. But, before they let them on base to put out the blaze, the Tibetans had to be placed under virtual lockdown in their quarters. Some of the firemen saw inscriptions on rocks in an alphabet that was distinctly foreign. What they saw were *mani* stones, incised with Tibetan letters and used for prayers.

Another time, while a group of trainees were being flown out of Peterson Air Force Base, civilian workers at the base caught glimpses of the Tibetans. Word spread around Colorado Springs, and rumors of Orientals and strange goings-on in the Colorado mountains reached *The New York Times*. The paper refrained from publishing a story after the Secretary of Defense asked that nothing be printed.

The CIA added an element of motivation to the program. To give the Tibetans a taste of American military might, trainees who had completed their work in Colorado were sent to the Marine Corps base at Quantico, Virginia. Roger McCarthy escorted the first batch of Tibetans to the Marine training base located southeast of Washington, DC. The two week course at Quantico was capped off by a "Mad Minute" firepower demonstration in which the Marines let loose with everything at their disposal. The barrage lit the sky in a cacophony of explosions that reverberated straight through the entrails. The Tibetans loved it.

Desmond FitzGerald and Gyalo Thondup flew to Camp Hale to personally review the training program in 1960. Gyalo was in the United States to make the rounds in Washington and New York, partly to consult with officials about the multipronged aspects of the Tibetan operation and partly to lobby on behalf of the Tibetan cause. In Colorado, Fitz-Gerald devoured the details of the training program and the tradecraft the Tibetans were absorbing.

From specially erected bleachers, he and Gyalo watched as the latest batch of Camp Hale graduates gave a flawless demonstration of their fighting skills and weapons handling. The martial display culminated in a mock attack on a Chinese post, with the guerrillas unleashing everything they had, from mortar rounds to machine gun fire, in their own version of the "Mad Minute."

When the deafening demonstration ended and the acrid smell of burnt propellant wafted over FitzGerald, Thondup, and the others in the stands, a Tibetan hidden in some brush sprang to his feet brandishing a 9mm submachine gun. This was the element of surprise the CIA was counting on, the only way a guerrilla force could outlast the People's

Liberation Army, with its superior firepower and a virtually bottomless reservoir of manpower. The Chinese were advantaged over the Tibetans in every respect save two: the Tibetans were on ground they knew intimately, and they were battling for the survival of their people and way of life. It was up to the CIA to ensure that this time their fight would end differently.

Chapter 7

Hearts and Minds

War and propaganda are inseparable, and the covert operation in Tibet was no exception. From the start, the Chinese government had heavily propagandized its own population, claiming that the PLA had liberated Tibet's peasant farmers and nomads from abusive monks and an aristocracy that treated them like feudal serfs. Since the early 1950s, party cadres had fanned out to extol the reforms of Chairman Mao, loudspeakers blared the miracles of socialist development and agrarian reform and praised the five-year plans. Leaflets, posters, and newspapers trumpeted the party line. Communist bureaucrats hewed to the Central Committee's dictates in their speeches and official remarks. Not even a dinner toast could be made that didn't conform to Beijing's official *pronunciamientos* and party *diktats*. Those who questioned or opposed the party's version of reality were branded counter-revolutionaries, fascists, bandits, lackeys, and running dogs of the imperialists.

Beyond China's borders, the public dimly grasped this Orwellian reality. China was a closed society until the Dalai Lama's escape shattered the boundaries of the propaganda war. His arrival in India escalated the war of words, expanding the territory across which it would be waged by transforming it into a global tug-of-war for hearts and minds.

CHINA TOUTS CREATION
OF A "DEMOCRATIC TIBET"

China lost no time mobilizing for this new phase of the battle for public opinion. One of the weapons in its arsenal was an American journalist named Anna Louise Strong. In the parlance of the 1950s, Strong would have been branded a Communist "fellow-traveler." She was a Marxist and a chronicler of the Russian Revolution. Like the crusading journalist John Reed, whose *Ten Days That Shook the World* is arguably the most compelling rendering of a regime in the final throes of dissolution ever written, she too moved to Moscow after the fall of the Tsar. Strong shared Reed's passion for socialist revolution, but lacked his talent. Her work had the appearance of reporting, but was in fact propaganda.

Strong was in her seventies when China put out the call for right-minded journalists to travel to Tibet and document the Chinese version of events that had just taken place. She was invited to go on a press junket with 18 other journalists from 11 countries, who had been gathered in Beijing for the journey. The majority came from the East Bloc and covered the news for radio, television, and print.

Because of the rigors of the junket, with flights at altitudes of 21,000 feet and ground travel at elevations of 15,000, she had to pass a medical check-up to qualify for the trip. After an electrocardiogram and blood pressure readings, a Chinese doctor gave his qualified approval. "Passed for Tibet," his certification read, "if special care is taken and special arrangements made against over-exertion." Strong thought the doctor didn't want to be held responsible if she died in the attempt to get the Tibet story.

Hoping it would take Chinese officials a week or more to make final arrangements for the press tour, Strong headed for the beach. She had just put the finishing touches on another propaganda book, *Tibetan Interviews*, and badly wanted some time off before making the arduous trip to Lhasa. She was only there one day when the phone call came telling her to report to Beijing. At the introductory trip briefing, Chinese party officials made clear that this was no routine junket. Their message, Strong later wrote, was to "take it seriously."

Armed with a camera and Hermes Baby typewriter, she joined the other journalists, mostly male and decades younger. The only other woman was Eva Siao, a young photographer for East German television. Four Soviet-built Ilyushin aircraft had been laid on by the Chinese government to take "the first foreigners of any kind" to report on "democratic Tibet." Although daunted by the age difference and wondering how she would keep up with the interview schedules of the younger members, Strong couldn't resist joining the entourage. To prove her stamina, she danced with the Governor and the Party Secretary of the Province of Chinghai, at a dinner party thrown for the group the night before their departure for Lhasa.

The reporters were divided among the planes. Strong was on the second Ilyushin to fly that morning, accompanied by Secretary General Tang-Li of the *People's Daily*, a reporter from Britain's *Daily Worker*, and a Russian correspondent from *Pravda*. Strong wanted to know if the trip was riskier than the World War II flights over the Burma Hump. A minor official confirmed that it was more difficult because of the higher altitude. He then mentioned, offhandedly, that there were already plans to build a railroad between Beijing and Lhasa "in the next few years" to make travel easier.

As was expected of her, Strong brazenly touted the party line. One gets the sense in her 1960 book, *When Serfs Stood Up in Tibet*, that Strong was literally taking dictation from the party's ideologues. She uncritically repeated the claims of a Chinese official, the head of the Propaganda Department in Tibet, as if it was gospel: "A million serfs have stood . . . building a democratic Tibet which will become a socialist Tibet. All the clamors of the imperialists are useless. The wheel of history turns always forward and not back. We shall build here a happy tomorrow."

To help spin the wheel of history, Strong didn't hesitate to fabricate. She wrote that after the March 1959 fighting ended, "a dungeon was found under the Potala containing poisonous scorpions into which prisoners had been thrown for quicker killing." She claimed the dungeon was kept secret until the Dalai Lama's exodus, but was now on exhibition to showcase "the horrors of past serfdom." Strong also wrote that "the rebels" used monasteries and "holy places" as toilets and left empty ammunition boxes marked in English and military boots "made in Kalimpong" littering the Potala Palace. She accused the resistance fighters of sheltering in the Potala in order to lob artillery rounds into the Chinese hospital below.

Elsewhere in her book Strong recounts a show trial at which several Buddhist monks are charged with aiding the resistance. They face their accusers publicly while a hostile crowd, goaded by Chinese officials, shouts at them to "Confess! Repent!" Strong characterizes these *thamz-*

ing public criticism sessions as "political discussions" and completely omits that they typically involved brutal beatings.

To the sacrilegious and defamatory, Strong adds the salacious. She accuses the "arch-rebel Thubten Tseren," a Tibetan noble, of being a womanizer and owning a "pearl headdress" worth $10,000, an unimaginable sum for Tibet in 1959. She writes about a Buddhist lama of the Drepung Monastery who "raped over a thousand women in the thirty-five years between his twentieth and his fifty-fifth birthday." As if this were not sufficiently repellent, she goes on to imply that he also sodomized young boys who had entered the monastery as novice monks.

And so it went for 300 pages, replete with now-vintage propaganda photos of smiling Tibetans warmly interacting with their Chinese occupiers. The old order—superstitious, exploitive, corrupt, venal—had been swept away by the new, in which virtuous party officials would oversee the transformation of Tibet. Peasants freed from the tyranny of their masters, would join the newly emergent working class in a just and harmonious society.

"Tibet's working class, recently non-existent, now numbers 25,000," Strong wrote as evidence of socialist progress, "including many young men from poor families who have left the biological and productive sterility of enforced lama-hood."

"Tibet, having burned out the age-old serfdom that sapped its vitals and the imperialist intrigues that backed that cannibal system," Strong editorialized, "is more an expression of its people's virtues, passion, and potentialities than ever before in history. At the same time it is more inseparably merged in the common crucible of revolution in multi-national China."

When Serfs Stood Up in Tibet was China's opening salvo in trying to seize the high ground in the struggle for international public opinion. But in this war, China had a major disadvantage. Books like Strong's, printed by the Chinese government in Beijing, simply lacked credibility. The publishing house was an organ of the state, and its publications were viewed as little more than one-sided propaganda.

WESTERN MEDIA FOCUS
ON CHINESE AGGRESSION

Tibet had long been a source of fascination to the independent media in the West. *LIFE* magazine, with its mass circulation, large format, photo essays, and enviable reporting, first featured an article on the

Fourteenth Dalai Lama in the October 9, 1939, issue. Tenzin Gyatso was only four years old. The story, which appeared on page 81, announced his recognition as the reincarnation of Tibet's Thirteenth Dalai Lama. The same edition of the magazine featured a profile of Marlene Dietrich, the actress and singer, and an overly optimistic account of how Holland and Belgium were prepared to withstand military challenges from Nazi Germany.

When China invaded Tibet in 1951, *LIFE* devoted its cover and a 25 photo spread to the Dalai Lama's temporary refuge in Yatung, on India's border. When Tenzin Gyatso went into exile, the April 20, 1959 issue of *TIME* magazine pictured a determined-looking Dalai Lama on its cover, along with a red banner labeling his exploit "The Escape that Rocked the Reds."

ST BAILEY AND THE CIA'S PROPAGANDA CAMPAIGN

In hindsight, the asymmetry between the credibility of the free press and the lack of credibility of the Communist-controlled media might make it seem that there was no need for the Eisenhower Administration to try to influence news coverage of Tibet. But CIA Director Allen Dulles and Desmond FitzGerald were taking no chances.

National Security Directive 5412/2 was clear: damaging the prestige of International Communism ranked alongside running covert wars in terms of importance. The war of words had equal priority with the war of weapons. When FitzGerald got hold of some drawings done by one of the Tibetan trainees at Camp Hale depicting Chinese soldiers abusing Tibetans, he passed them up to Dulles. The CIA Director, in turn, gave them to C.D. Jackson, publisher of *LIFE International*, suggesting he use them in the magazine.

Jackson didn't need urging. He was a conservative and an anticommunist who had served under Eisenhower in psychological warfare during World War II. Jackson later worked for Eisenhower's election campaign.

LIFE International's publication of the anti-Chinese sketches was part of a CIA covert program known as ST BAILEY, the CIA's cryptonym for the political action and propaganda component of the Tibetan operation. Within the Agency, only the Clandestine Service uses cryptonyms. They are assigned by the Records Integration Division whenever a new operation is launched or a new agent recruited. These cover names are then used in internal CIA documents to safeguard the security of an operation. If it becomes compromised, whether by foreign intelligence, someone losing a briefcase or laptop, or simply forgetting to lock up documents in a safe overnight, the cryptonym makes it harder to understand what is being referenced.

The first two letters, ST, indicate the country involved, in this case China. BAILEY was the cover name assigned for CIA political action in India and with other countries, at the United Nations, with human rights organizations, and on the propaganda front. The cover for the Tibet Task Force, whose members were primarily concerned with covert military action and intelligence collection, was ST CIRCUS. A third part of the operation was ST BARNUM, the cover for the airlift of agents, military supplies, and support equipment into Tibet. Along with these names the files contained many more cryptonyms assigned to the Tibet operation; names of agents, Tibetan trainees, side operations, and programs—more than a thousand. True name lists were kept separate from the cryptonyms and were used to help CIA personnel make sure they had it right when referring to one of them. It was a serious security violation to lock up a true name list and a cryptonym list in the same safe. If someone cracked the safe and stole the documents, an entire covert operation would be blown. Emergency measures would be immediately taken to ensure the safety of agents and put cover stories into place to minimize the damage.

There was a reason that ST BAILEY was (and still is) highly classified. In the wake of the Dalai Lama's departure from Tibet, the Eisenhower White House decided to adopt a policy called "strategic silence." Officially, U.S. government spokespersons were to refrain from criticizing China too strongly. The Administration didn't want to appear to be exploiting Tibet's troubles. America's closest allies were officially informed that President Eisenhower didn't want to make Tibet's plight a Cold War problem, and so the United States was muting its response. This restraint did not apply to the CIA, where Eisenhower's orders to "create and exploit" problems for China remained in full force.

ELEANOR ROOSEVELT AND THE CIA

In intelligence parlance, former first lady Eleanor Roosevelt was "unwitting" to her role in ST BAILEY. Although she featured prominently in the CIA's propaganda war against China, she was never aware that she was being used by the Agency.

After her husband, Franklin Delano Roosevelt, died in office during wartime, President Harry Truman turned to Eleanor Roosevelt to become America's first delegate to the newly established United Nations in 1945. Roosevelt was instrumental in the General Assembly's passage of the Universal Declaration of Human Rights. When her tenure at the UN ended, she became a radio personality, returned to writing a syndicated newspaper column, as well as a column in *McCall's* magazine, and embraced the new medium of television.

In trying to settle on the major theme of the propaganda war, there had been a debate between the United States and Tibetan leaders. The Dalai Lama wanted to emphasize Tibet's claim to independence. The Eisenhower White House wanted to focus on the struggle for human rights in the battle for public opinion.

Largely in deference to the protests of Generalissimo Chiang Kai-Shek and his Nationalist Party on Taiwan, which also claimed Tibet as part of China, the Eisenhower Administration had never completely embraced independence for Tibet. The U.S. policy was that the Nationalists were the legitimate government of China, and the Communist party and Chairman Mao illegitimate usurpers. Emphasizing human rights instead of independence meant the United States wouldn't have to choose between its Chinese Nationalist allies and Tibet.

Reluctantly, the Tibetans agreed to make human rights violations the principal focus of the public relations campaign. The Eisenhower Administration wanted UN support for Tibet and urged the Dalai Lama to appeal personally to Secretary General Dag Hammerskjold. At a meeting in New Delhi, Prime Minister Nehru counseled the Dalai Lama not to appeal to the UN, warning that it would only strengthen China's resolve. He also warned that it would be hard to prove human rights violations based on refugee accounts and that a similar UN resolution on South Africa had not made any positive impact in that country. Neither UN forces nor those of other nations were any more likely to fight on Tibet's behalf, Nehru argued, than they had done for Hungary in 1956 when the Soviets invaded.

Despite two days of dialog in New Delhi, the Dalai Lama was unable to change Nehru's mind. The Prime Minister simply didn't want to further aggravate China. Despite the lack of support from India, the Dalai

Lama decided to proceed in lobbying the UN for a resolution condemning China. His principal messenger for this effort was Gyalo Thondup.

One of the reasons Howard Bane valued Gyalo was his urbanity.
Dressed in a Western suit, he was the perfect spokesperson for the cause.
The Dalai Lama's brother was not only persuasive in articulating Tibet's
case, he also made a strong personal impression. Gyalo arrived in New
York at the beginning of October 1959, for a prolonged stay that would
include lobbying UN delegations and making Tibet's case to the
American and international press. The Waldorf Astoria Hotel on Park
Avenue became headquarters for the trip.

To ensure Gyalo's access to the American media, the CIA retained a
public relations firm. But it turned out to be unnecessary. Robert Murphy,
a veteran diplomat who ranked third at the State Department, signed up
a former ambassador named Ernest Gross to help present the Tibetan
case before the UN. Gross was deputy U.S. representative to the UN in
1950, when the Tibetans turned to the UN for sanctions against China's
aggression. But the UN had not acted on the plea, largely due to opposition from India.

Ernest Gross was the right man to build international support for
Tibet. In addition to his diplomatic contacts, Gross had good access to
the reporters and editors whose beat included the UN. Moreover, he had
even better access to the Secretary General, as he had served as counsel
to Hammerskjold.

At first, Gross clashed with Gyalo over strategy. Reflecting the Dalai
Lama's preference, Gyalo tried one more time to persuade the Americans
to press the UN to support Tibetan independence. Gross, reflecting the
near-unanimous view of the Eisenhower Administration, preferred a resolution condemning China's denial of human rights. Gross pushed hard for
the human rights resolution, and Gyalo pushed back equally hard. In the
end, Gross persuaded him that there were better odds of winning a resolution on human rights. After achieving passage of a resolution on this
issue, it would be easier, although still difficult, to get a second resolution
supporting sovereignty. Gyalo conceded, but not without misgivings.

The two men scored an immediate success. In the second week of
October, the UN General Assembly voted to debate "The Question of
Tibet." That same week, Gross introduced Gyalo to Eleanor Roosevelt.
She asked him whether it was true that the Tibetan people had such a

low standard of living that it gave the Chinese an excuse to intervene in the name of reform. Gyalo countered the argument.

"He told me the Dalai Lama had already planned to move on four different fronts," Roosevelt wrote in her column, "to bring some changes into the old agriculture system of the country and to improve the standard of living for the people."

For good measure, Gyalo added that Communist officials in Tibet gave formal approval to the Dalai Lama's reform agenda. But when they started increasing the number of Chinese troops inside the country, Gyalo told the former First Lady, the Tibetan people began to fear for the Dalai Lama's safety. The result was the Tibetan National Uprising. The people loved the Dalai Lama, Gyalo told Eleanor Roosevelt, and she reported it in her column of October 16.

Tibet was not a new topic for the former First Lady. In April of 1959, while the Dalai Lama was still trekking across the Himalayas to safety, she wrote that "it seems incredible to me that Communist China can calmly announce to the Asian world that it has crushed Tibetan strong-holds close to the capital of Lhasa and wiped out the bulk of the rebellion. . . . Didn't Communist China promise freedom to these people?"

All together, Eleanor Roosevelt wrote about Tibet five times in 1959 in her column, "My Day." As she had shown through the three terms of the Roosevelt Administration, the Great Depression, and World War II, once an injustice or a cause caught her attention, Eleanor Roosevelt was tenacious.

"The action in Tibet should alert the Asian-African world to the true aim of communism everywhere," she wrote from her Hyde Park home. "Until the communists give up their avowed intention of achieving a communist world without regard to the methods used, there is little chance that we can settle down to disarmament agreements and peaceful co-existence . . . behavior such as we have seen in Tibet does not give us much hope."

Eleanor Roosevelt was unaware of the Eisenhower Administration's involvement with the Tibetan resistance or the CIA's role in arming the Tibetans. "Nobody," she wrote confidently, but erroneously, "incited this rebellion."

Roosevelt was not the only influential journalist to take up the Tibetan cause. There were others like Lowell Thomas, Jr., who had traveled to

Tibet with his father in 1949 as a young man. In 1959 he published a book about the Tibetan resistance, *The Silent War in Tibet*, in part using information supplied to him by the CIA.

Syndicated cartoonist Bill Mauldin, who discovered his talent for combining commentary with cartoons when he served in the Army's 45th Infantry Division in World War II, had a fondness for underdogs. His creation of two ordinary GIs named Willie and Joe and their wartime trials and exploits made him famous. They also made Mauldin the target of General Patton, who thought the characters—often bearded, rumpled, and disgruntled—were bad for morale. But Mauldin's ordinary heroes were a hit with the public, and they made him famous and rich. By the late 1950s, Mauldin's penchant for the little guy led him to sympathize with Tibet. Even though his own political leanings had grown increasingly left wing, Mauldin penned a number of cartoons depicting the Chinese as brutal oppressors and the Tibetans as fearless in defense of their homeland.

With a popular First Lady and a famous cartoonist on their side, the Tibetans made quick strides in capturing the support of the American public.

On October 21, the UN voted 45–9 to approve a resolution supporting the "fundamental human rights and freedoms" of the Tibetan people and expressed grave concern that they were being "forcibly denied." The resolution also took note of Tibet's autonomy and cultural and religious heritage. But it was a half victory, as 26 countries abstained from voting, including democracies like Great Britain.

Eleanor Roosevelt wanted the Chinese to appear before the UN to explain their actions in Tibet, even if it, ultimately, meant extending UN membership to China.

"Having to justify one's actions before a world body must be a salutary thing," she wrote, ". . . membership might mean that they would think more carefully about their future actions."

China did not appear before the UN that year, but the Chinese did justify their actions to Eleanor Roosevelt. Anna Louise Strong sent a long letter to Roosevelt explaining the Chinese viewpoint. She stayed up late reading it.

In a December 1959 column, Roosevelt gave her reply.

"Here is a woman who lived in Russia many years, was finally imprisoned as a spy and, when released, came here for protection. Yet as soon as it was safe for her to do so, she returned to the Communists. . . .She has always found excuses for the Communists, and in this letter she explains why they entered Tibet to 'free the people' . . . I am not at all convinced by what she writes."

If anything, Strong's letter to Eleanor Roosevelt seems to have been counterproductive. When China claimed in 1960 that Mt. Everest fell exclusively within its borders instead of jointly with Nepal, Roosevelt wrote that taking over Tibet had emboldened the Chinese to try to grab more territory. In a column later that year, with the UN scheduled to take up a second, more toughly worded resolution on Tibet in the near future, she called the Chinese action "a flagrant case of usurpation by a foreign nation" and called for talks between China and the Tibetans to restore their human rights.

Working with the American and foreign press and at the UN to make the case for Tibet was one front of the CIA's efforts in the propaganda war. Putting the best case forward, as was done through the press contacts and diplomacy, is little different than politicians spinning a story in their favor. The CIA's efforts in this regard resembled a standard public relations or public diplomacy campaign.

BLACK PROPAGANDA AND THE INTERNATIONAL COMMISSION OF JURISTS

There was a second, more unsavory front in the CIA's war of words. There was also black propaganda—the fabrication of atrocities and abuses by the enemy—and its dissemination through credible sources.

The Agency had "assets" in important human rights organizations, individuals who were sympathetic to the United States or had been recruited as agents of the CIA. One of these organizations was the widely respected International Commission of Jurists. In June 1959, the Geneva-based Commission issued a toughly worded statement decrying China's "violation of fundamental human rights" and use of violence against the Tibetans. The statement charged that China's "acts constitute the crime of genocide under the Genocide Convention of the United Nations of 1948."

It was the prelude of things to come. CIA Tibet Task Force head Roger McCarthy collected reports of Chinese atrocities—political executions, reprisal killings, rapes—in debriefings of Tibetans. These were real war crimes and human rights abuses. To these reports, the CIA propagandists added fabrications that were particularly repellant, mingling the details of real abuses with sensational tales designed to vilify China.

The fabrications included stories of the Chinese forcing Buddhist monks to publicly rape nuns at gunpoint, of children made to shoot their parents, of villagers being forced to watch as dozens of landowners were publicly burnt to death, of men being castrated publicly, parents being executed by having nails driven through their eyes for refusing to send their children to Chinese schools, and grisly executions by roasting people over open fires or crucifixion or being dismembered and disemboweled while still alive. Still others were said to be killed by being dragged behind horses or thrown out of airplanes. Reports of gang rape were widespread, as were massacres of entire villages.

The methodology for making the fabrications credible was simple. Knowing that it already had assets in place who were sympathetic to the Agency, the CIA handlers took small delegations of Tibetans to meet with members of the International Commission of Jurists to report the war crimes and genocidal actions of the Chinese. The CIA's assets on the Commission were then told to work the process internally to see that the most sensational charges made their way into the body of the final report.

It would be wrong, of course, to think that there were no war crimes or human rights abuses committed in Tibet. Real atrocities were committed by both sides in the fighting. PLA soldiers who surrendered or were wounded were often beheaded by the resistance fighters, in part because guerrilla movements are ill equipped, logistically, to handle large numbers of prisoners. In some instances, to instill terror, Chinese captives were deliberately mutilated by having their noses or ears and fingers cut off before being sent back to their military bases.

PLA atrocities were particularly brutal in the aftermath of the March 1959 National Uprising. Tibetan civilians suffered terribly not only in the fighting but in reprisals. Imprisonment, beatings, and killings were commonplace. In parts of Tibet the resistance fighters were nomads, and women and children often moved with the fighters as their camps shifted. The PLA didn't distinguish between innocent civilians and armed men in attacking the resistance. Many monasteries, too, came under attack, causing significant cultural destruction. The monasteries were often centers of political resistance and sometimes used to cache supplies and weapons, and this made them military targets.

In 1959 and again in early 1960 the International Commission of Jurists issued reports that included the sensationalistic atrocities. According to Howard Bane, one of the books that resulted from ST BAILEY's propaganda operation was *The Question of Tibet and the Rule of Law* published by the International Commission of Jurists in Geneva, Switzerland, in 1959. The CIA fabrications rapidly became accepted as fact in the heated debates over China's occupation of Tibet at the UN and other international forums. It was a black propaganda coup for the CIA.

At a time when the CIA was trying to reconstitute an active resistance inside Tibet and foster international support for the Dalai Lama and his people, little was taken for granted. FitzGerald knew that the success of the operation depended not only on the efforts of officers like Bane and McCarthy, but also on public opinion and political developments in India and the United States.

1960 was a presidential election year. Eisenhower confidently told CIA Director Dulles and FitzGerald that the Tibet operation would continue unabated if Richard Nixon won the campaign. But he couldn't say with certainty what would happen if Senator John F. Kennedy, Jr., won in November.

Chapter 8

America's Secret Bay of Pigs

In April 1960, the CIA suffered its first American casualty of the war in Tibet. A small shack at the airstrip in Kurmitola served as one of the relay posts for the radio traffic from Tibet. It was a vital link in the chain between the resistance and the C-130 airlifts. Without outside support, the Tibetan guerrillas could not survive. The radiomen who kept the communications bridge open were their lifeline.

The temperature was 105 degrees when Stephen Kasarda, Jr., a 30-year-old CIA communications officer, stripped to his shorts and shoes to climb the commo building's steeply pitched metal roof. Kasarda wanted to improve the location of the antennas. The metal roof was hot from the sun, but also from an improperly grounded wire. As soon as he got on the roof, Kasarda was electrocuted. He had only been at Kurmitola for a few weeks on what was supposed to be a temporary duty assignment.

There were no public announcements of Kasarda's death. He was posthumously awarded the Intelligence Medal of Merit, but 47 years later, in 2007, the CIA publicly acknowledged that he had died working on a clandestine mission. A star, for his name, was added to the 86 others on the Memorial Wall at CIA headquarters commemorating Americans who have died serving the Agency. The very first star on the Wall was for Douglas Mackiernan, a CIA officer who had been serving under cover as a vice consul in China. As Mao Zedong's revolutionary army swept toward Mackiernan's post, he decided to pack up his operation and, along with several others, seek refuge in Tibet, only to be shot at the border and then beheaded. The border guards had no idea he was an American spy. They shot him simply because he was a foreigner, and they were under orders to bar foreigners from entering Tibet.

Kasarda's electrocution marked the beginning of a run of bad luck for ST BARNUM. That same month one of the first air drops went badly awry because of weather and nearly ended in catastrophe. Two C-130s were manifested for a mission during the April full moon. On their way in, they ran into strong headwinds that put them behind schedule and ate into their fuel supply. As they neared the drop zone, a heavy cloud cover obscured the signal fires. Unsure of where to offload the supplies, they had no choice but to scrub the mission and circle back. The first C-130 headed to Thailand. Near dawn, with its long-range fuel tanks perilously close to empty, it reached the base. A thick haze of fog hugged the ground, and they couldn't find the runway. With engines balking and threatening to stall, the crew was headed toward trouble.

Heinie Aderholt was on the ground below, listening to the C-130 engine sputtering somewhere in the haze overhead, when the idea to fire off an emergency flare struck him. Using radio to alert the crew to watch for the burst of a red flare, Aderholt went to the landing strip to fire it off. Normally, flare guns are used by downed air crews to signal rescue aircraft overhead. Aderholt reversed the concept, using the flare to show the hapless C-130 crew where to pierce the gloom and guide them to the airfield below. It was typical of Aderholt's genius for improvisation.

The second C-130 opted to head toward Kurmitola because it was closer than Thailand. The plane was wheels down and well into the landing when a torrential downpour blinded them. The pilot circled around to try again. As he made his approach, a bolt of lightning from the thunderstorm illuminated the area. The plane had been heading toward a village instead of the runway. The pilot corrected course and managed to touch down before running out of fuel.

The biggest setback to ST BARNUM came a few weeks later. It had nothing to do with operations in Tibet. On May 1, 1960, America's ultrasecret surveillance plane, the U-2, was shot down over the Soviet Union. Initially, the United States denied that any spy flight had taken place.

CIA headquarters immediately sent a "Flash" cable to stations and bases worldwide suspending intelligence overflights. The May 1 suspension was an operational precaution; the United States was not certain that Powers' U-2 had actually been downed over the Soviet Union until May 2. Five days more went by before the Soviets announced that the pilot, Capt. Francis Gary Powers, had been captured alive. The operational precaution was necessary because until the fate of the plane was certain and the method by which the USSR had been able to shoot down the supposedly invulnerable craft was known, it was simply too risky to put other assets like the C-130s in the air.

When he got word of the Flash cable, Major Aderholt literally raced to the flight line. A C-130 was about to depart for Tibet to drop weapons and ammunition to a large formation of resistance fighters engaged in a major fight with the Chinese. The lightly armed guerrillas were waging a desperate battle against PLA infantry units advancing behind armored tanks.

Grimly, Aderholt ordered the loaded C-130 to halt the mission. The grounded airplane on the tarmac was quite literally the resistance fighters' salvation. Their radio messages called urgently for help. With the flight suspended, the Tibet Task Force back in Washington had no other option than to decipher the radio traffic with a growing sense of frustration. Finally, there were no more transmissions. The Chinese had overrun the guerrillas.

EISENHOWER SUSPENDS THE C-130 MISSIONS

A few days later, Powers was paraded in front of television and newsreel cameras by his Soviet captors. They showed off pieces of the aircraft indicating that it was made in the United States and displayed Powers' cyanide pill, provided by the CIA for him to commit suicide in the event of capture.

It was a propaganda coup for the Soviet Union and an embarrassing intelligence setback for the United States. No one felt it more keenly than President Eisenhower. From the U-2 program's start four years earlier, Eisenhower personally approved each spy plane mission, often carefully reviewing charts plotting the surveillance plane's flight plan before signing off on a mission.

From a diplomatic standpoint, the timing was catastrophic. Eisenhower was on the verge of leaving Washington for a summit in Paris. For months he had built the groundwork with French and British allies on a proposal calling for a comprehensive ban on the testing of nuclear weapons.

The summit was Eisenhower's best chance at improving prospects for world peace. Premier Nikita Khrushchev had given informal indications that the Soviet Union might embrace a test ban. Eisenhower thought of it as a first step toward curbing the nuclear arms race between the West and the Soviet Bloc, and he hoped to follow it with an "open skies" proposal to allow monitoring from the air. The Open Skies concept was intended as a confidence-building measure to provide evidence to policymakers in Moscow and Washington that neither side was preparing an imminent first strike against the other. His second term as president was drawing to a close and the initiatives might have been his crowning diplomatic achievement. Any prospects for a breakthrough with Khrushchev at the Paris summit were wrecked by the diplomatic fallout over the U-2 incident.

In mid-May, Eisenhower decided that covert aerial flights over foreign nations' airspace posed too great a risk. Knowing that the United States was fairly close to fielding intelligence-gathering satellites that would diminish the need for surveillance by aircraft, he established a general prohibition of secret overflights. On a case-by-case basis, exceptions were allowed, but only after careful evaluation and in limited circumstances. Eisenhower's ban included the C-130 flights over Tibet.

THE TIBET TASK FORCE HITS BOTTLENECKS

Meanwhile, at Camp Hale, the CIA continued to churn out guerrillas. More than a hundred Tibetans trained in an expanded program that included motor vehicles and tanks. The CIA might not be able to provide tanks to the Tibetans, but at least it could train them in the vulnerabilities of armored vehicles and give the guerrillas the knowledge to use captured vehicles if they were lucky enough to lay hands on them.

The prohibition on overflights, coupled with the growth in the training program, posed a logistics bottleneck. With the aerial lifeline suspended, the CIA had to find new ways to supply the resistance with weapons and ammunition and infiltrate trainees back into Tibet. To help puzzle out the problem, Tom Fosmire left Camp Hale in the fall of 1960 to take a job at headquarters with Roger McCarthy on the Tibet Task Force.

Then in November, Senator John Kennedy defeated Vice President Richard Nixon in the 1960 presidential election. The election meant that the government went into transition mode, a period of suspended animation in the federal bureaucracy. It would be two-and-a-half months before President-elect Kennedy was sworn in as president, and longer still before his senior appointees were confirmed by the Senate and serving at their desks.

In mid-November, CIA Director Dulles briefed Kennedy on the Agency's most sensitive intelligence programs. One of the top items on the CIA agenda was an audacious program to back a team of exiles planning to return to Cuba and overthrow Fidel Castro's Marxist regime. Eisenhower had approved the operation, which called for the exiles to make an amphibious landing at a remote stretch of beach along the Bay of Pigs. Dulles also briefed Kennedy on the CIA's growing clandestine war in Laos, a Desmond FitzGerald operation. It was December before Dulles got around to briefing Kennedy on Tibet. The President-elect gave the operation his backing.

Kennedy's designee as Secretary of State, Dean Rusk, was enthusiastic about the operation when briefed about it as an incoming Cabinet officer. As a mid-level official at the State Department in 1951, Rusk met with the Dalai Lama's brother, Thubten Jigme Norbu, to extend America's offer of support.

THE SECRET BASE AT MUSTANG

While the CIA's Tibet Task Force concentrated on rebuilding resistance forces inside Tibet, Gompo Tashi wanted to build a base of operations for the resistance in an adjacent country. Gyalo Thondup gave the idea his backing. In the spring of 1960, he, Tashi, and Lhamo Tsering met with Howard Bane to discuss the proposal.

Bane and other CIA officers listened with interest. He knew that the Tibetan resistance faced two great shortcomings. First was that the Chinese now controlled all the territory inside Tibet, denying the resistance any safe haven in which to regroup before striking out against the PLA. The second shortcoming was tactical. Instead of the hit-and-run attacks necessary for successful resistance operations, the Tibetans kept getting drawn into direct battles with the PLA. This was in part a natural consequence of the lack of any safe haven where Tibetan fighters could retreat to after a successful hit-and-run raid.

Tashi proposed using the tiny Kingdom of Mustang, a remote and mountainous territory of several hundred square miles which he had visited as a trader, as the location for the base. Politically, Mustang was receptive. Its King was a Buddhist of Tibetan ancestry who was sympathetic to the cause. Geographically, the country was ideal. The Dhaulagiri and Annapurna mountain ranges formed natural boundaries that left the country protected on several flanks. To the south Mustang bordered Nepal. To the north lay Tibet. Lo Mantang, the capital, was a mere twenty miles from the Tibet border. Beyond that, some three hundred and fifty miles more, lay Lhasa.

The advantages were clear. A guerrilla base in Mustang could be supplied without the risky moonlight flights. By slipping through the mountains, resistance fighters could infiltrate to raid Tibet and return to Mustang's safe haven, where the Chinese were unlikely to pursue them. Gompo Tashi felt that he could easily gather a force of some 2000 men, most of them veteran *Chushi Gangdruk* fighters who had followed the Dalai Lama into exile after the failed National Uprising. Many were now at work camps scattered around the Himalayas from India to Sikkim, laboring on road crews.

Bane reported the meeting to CIA headquarters. The Tibet Task Force cabled back an objection. It was not politically feasible without first getting approval from the Nepalese, which at present was impossible because it risked revealing the CIA's hand in the Tibetan operation. McCarthy apparently thought the suspension of C-130 flights would be temporary. He was focused on rebuilding the resistance inside Tibet, not in a third country.

Undaunted, Bane and Gyalo brainstormed alternatives. Mustang could be used as a staging ground. Groups of several hundred guerrillas at a time could assemble there and infiltrate Tibet to locate lightly patrolled territory from which to operate permanently. Once one group had successfully established itself inside Tibet, a second wave of guerrillas could be assembled in Mustang, trained and equipped, and follow to establish an additional location. Eventually, there would be multiple guerrilla bases inside Tibet, with Mustang as the springboard. McCarthy's objective of rebuilding and rearming the resistance could be accomplished, using the adjacent guerrilla base instead of relying on the C-130 flights.

McCarthy grudgingly accepted the compromise, but he set strict conditions. One was that the use of Mustang to infiltrate Tibet had to remain absolutely secret. Provided this condition was met, the Task Force would send trained teams from Camp Hale to aid the newly formed guerrilla groups. Weapons would be air-dropped to the new fighters once the suspension on overflights was lifted. McCarthy was still relying on a resumption of the C-130 missions.

Gompo Tashi chose Baba Gyen Yeshe, a monk who had fought with the resistance in Central Tibet, to set up the logistics to support the resistance fighters during their transit through Mustang. In June, he and two CIA-trained radio operators arrived in the tiny Kingdom. Tashi chose another man, Lobsang Champa, to become the commander of the Mustang contingent of resistance fighters after they were set up inside Tibet. Champa and 25 other recruits were sent to Colorado for training.

Almost immediately, plans for the Mustang base ran into problems. Secrecy was compromised when resistance fighters working on road crews in India and Nepal got word to go to the new base. They dropped their picks and shovels and boasted to their fellows about returning to Tibet to fight the Chinese. As word spread through the refugee camps men flocked to Mustang, volunteering to join up.

McCarthy's requirement to maintain secrecy was shattered. CIA headquarters repeatedly instructed Baba Gyen Yeshe to turn the volunteers away from Mustang, but it was useless. The little Kingdom was soon overrun with men eager to fight. The Task Force had little choice but to accept the fact that a resistance base in Mustang was a *fait accompli.* The idea of using the base as a covert transit point went out the window. The presence of the resistance in Mustang was one of the most widely known "secrets" in the Himalayas.

Gyalo Thondup and Gompo Tashi had achieved the result they wanted. Howard Bane took ownership of the resistance, whom he thereafter referred to as "my Khampas." The action had shifted from headquarters to the field. McCarthy realized that a coup d'état of sorts had taken place. Instead of a transit point, Mustang was now a base of operations.

Soon after Kennedy was sworn in as president, he approved C-130 missions to begin supplying the Mustang guerrillas. The first drop took place on March 15, just across the border from Mustang, so that it was technically in Tibet. This preserved the diplomatic fiction that the

United States was not arming the resistance inside Mustang, but no one objected when Baba Yeshe's men carted the weapons and supplies across the border and back to their base.

AMBASSADOR GALBRAITH OPPOSES
THE "INSANE ENTERPRISE"

There was one member of the Kennedy foreign policy team who was skeptical about supporting a guerrilla war in Tibet. John Kenneth Galbraith, Jr., was Kennedy's nominee for the post of U.S. Ambassador to India. At the end of March 1961, Galbraith received his first classified briefing on the CIA operation. He made no secret of the fact that he thought the entire operation was an "insane enterprise."

Galbraith doubted the value of the Tibetan operation. He was unpersuaded that the guerrilla movement would ever dislodge the Chinese, while fully convinced that it would prolong the bloodshed and suffering of the Tibetan people. The incoming ambassador thought the base at Mustang was particularly ill advised. Galbraith began lobbying for an end to the CIA operation, but his concerns were overshadowed by other world developments.

At dawn on April 17 in Cuba, the CIA launched the Bay of Pigs invasion. It was a fiasco. The plan called for preemptive strikes to cripple the Cuban air force. Aderholt, who had just received a long overdue promotion to Lieutenant Colonel in March, was detailed back to Washington from his duties on the Tibetan airlift to provide temporary support to the Cuban invasion. At the last minute, President Kennedy decided not to authorize the air strikes. Without air support from the United States, the men on the beach were sitting ducks. Those who were not killed on the spot were rounded up and taken prisoner by the Cubans. CIA officer David Atlee Phillips, who had been involved in planning propaganda aspects of the affair, went into the backyard of his Georgetown home when he learned the fate of the Cuban exiles and threw up. Lt. Col. Aderholt was soon back on Okinawa working on the C-130 missions over Tibet.

With the new weapons from the March 15 air drop, Baba Yeshe started operations inside Tibet. Small groups of guerrillas began ambushing Chinese posts along the Lhasa-Xinjiang highway, the major artery linking the PLA with China. Bane called the raids "pinpricks," but Gyalo reassured him that the Chinese had diverted an entire division to guard the highway.

The pinpricks sometimes yielded important intelligence. On one raid, Baba Yeshe's men captured Chinese documents that explained why the PLA had not pursued the resistance fighters inside Mustang. Short on supplies and equipment, the PLA enlisted men were disgruntled. Officers complained in dispatches that the Tibetans, whom they believed to be better trained in marksmanship and better disciplined in a fight, were inflicting heavy casualties. For every one Tibetan bullet that found its mark, the Chinese officers estimated their own troops had to fire 20 rounds.

INFIGHTING ON ALL SIDES

As Baba Yeshe's success grew, he became the *de facto* commander of the Mustang resistance. A different fighter, Lobsang Champa, was designated by the Tibet Task Force to assume command of the rebels after his training at Camp Hale. In the summer of 1961, he arrived in Mustang. Instead of welcoming him as base commander, Yeshe assigned Champa to head a company of 100 men, keeping overall command for himself.

The March 15 air drop was not enough to supply all the fighters at Mustang. Baba Yeshe appealed for more weapons. Through State Department channels, Ambassador Galbraith continued to oppose the program. He succeeded in winning an additional restriction on overflights—that they not take place without the consent of the Indian government. To get around Galbraith's new condition, the CIA charted routes so that the C-130s were never over India for more than a few minutes of flight time.

Problems were now multiplying for the resistance. There was a tug of war between the Tibet Task Force at headquarters and CIA officers in the field over control of the operation, a leadership struggle at Mustang, and infighting between Ambassador Galbraith and the CIA. The tension between Lobsang Champa and Baba Yeshe, combined with Galbraith's opposition, created hesitancy at the level of the 5412 Special Group. The request to drop more weapons for Mustang was discussed, but approval was withheld.

INTELLIGENCE BONANZA GIVES
RESISTANCE A REPRIEVE

Then, in October, one of the pinpricks resulted in an intelligence trove. A Chinese commander's convoy was ambushed by resistance fighters, killing the officer. Inside his vehicle were more than 1000 classified Chinese documents. The most secret paper was titled "Bulletin of Activities of the General Political Department of the People's Liberation Army." It was in the commander's pouch, soaked in his blood when the guerrillas laid hands on it.

The document stunned American intelligence analysts. The portrait of China it revealed was completely at odds with the conventional wisdom prevailing in U.S. intelligence circles. Its contents reported problems with Mao Zedong's "Great Leap Forward" and cited instances of open rebellion by militia units and widespread famine across China. Because of the unrest, the bulletin said, plans to unify China by seizing Taiwan (then known as the island of Formosa) were indefinitely postponed.

Among the many significant pieces of intelligence contained in the pouch, one stood out. China's relationship with the Soviet Union had deteriorated so badly, the bulletin purported, that in the event of nuclear attack by the United States, Moscow would not back Beijing.

This was an explosive piece of intelligence. If true, it shattered one of the bedrocks of National Security Directive 5412/2—the assumption that the shared Marxist ideology between China and the USSR was so cohesive that both nations functioned as one. NSC 5412/2, in fact, lumped China and the USSR together under the heading "International Communism." This theory of monolithic communism had dominated U.S. Cold War thinking, and U.S. analysts assumed the two nations had identical foreign policy objectives. This was the first documentary evidence of the Sino-Soviet rift, and it held the potential to dramatically alter American policy toward China.

Like a Comanche warrior bearing a scalp, CIA Director Dulles took his grisly trophy to a meeting of the 5412 Special Group in the fall of 1961. The bloodstained pouch graphically illustrated the means by which this vital new intelligence had been collected. Better still, one of the Tibetans responsible for capturing the intelligence trove and carrying the priceless documents back to Mustang was a CIA-trained Camp Hale alumnus.

In the face of this proof of the value of the Tibetan guerrillas, Ambassador Galbraith's objections paled. The captured documents gave the Tibetan resistance a reprieve. The 5412 Special Group approved more weapons for Mustang, but only enough to arm half the resistance fighters gathered at the base.

Soon after his dramatic presentation, Allen Dulles retired from the CIA and was replaced by John McCone. Desmond FitzGerald continued to oversee the Tibetan operation, but his time was increasingly taken up by the demands of the CIA's growing clandestine war in Laos.

AMERICA'S HIMALAYAN BAY OF PIGS

Despite the setbacks suffered at the hands of the Chinese, there were still scattered concentrations of resistance fighters deep inside Tibet. Efforts to rearm and regroup the fighters were slowly paying off, but in their eagerness to fight the Tibetans were still being drawn into large-scale battles.

In late 1961, a force of several thousand guerrillas was maneuvered into an engagement that turned out to be a trap. Outflanked, the resistance fighters found their retreat route cut off by encircling Chinese troops. With their ammunition and food dwindling, their only hope was receiving support from the C-130 lifeline in the form of parachute-dropped supplies over the battle zone.

Howard Bane knew that it was a long shot. The likelihood that the Khampas, surrounded by Chinese troops, would be able to fight their way out of the killing field was slender. But without the air drop, there was no hope whatsoever. They would be overrun and captured or, more likely, slaughtered.

Everything the group had done—attacking superior Chinese forces, allowing themselves to be drawn into a protracted fight—went against the CIA training. But that no longer mattered. The men relied on the Agency. A bond of honor existed between the Tibetans and the CIA officers, a tie as strong as blood. When the CIA logistics planners went to work drafting flight plans and readying supplies for the emergency mission, there were a few choice words about the stubborn Tibetans who had gotten themselves into the jam, but there was never any hesitancy to try and bail them out.

On Okinawa, Aderholt's C-130 crews were standing by to start the flight over the Pacific to Takhli, where the CAT pilots would take over the final leg of the hazardous mission. It was one thing to make clandestine drops over remote areas, but quite another to fly directly into a battlefield. Aderholt was prepared to risk the aircraft, and the CAT crews were ready to gamble their lives. All they needed was the go ahead.

That decision rested with Ambassador Galbraith. When he lifted Eisenhower's restriction on overflights, President Kennedy gave Galbraith the power to approve this type of emergency mission. The Tibet Task Force insisted that Galbraith authorize the flights. Bane had the job of getting Galbraith's approval.

Bane went to see Galbraith. The Ambassador cleared out his office so the two men could speak privately about the highly classified matter. Bane outlined the dire situation the Tibetans faced, explaining how the mission would proceed to drop supplies to the embattled fighters.

Galbraith noted acidly that when the airlifted ammunition and rations were used up, the Tibetans would only need more. How long, he asked rhetorically, would the resupply effort have to be kept up before the PLA won the battle? The C-130 missions could only postpone the inevitable, Galbraith said, while risking that a plane would be shot down and expose the whole operation. The Chinese government would protest to the Indian government and the result would be a nasty diplomatic flap.

Bane stood his ground. Even if they were resupplied, the resistance fighters' survival wasn't assured, but they knew the terrain and, with ammunition, they stood a fighting chance of breaking through the Chinese lines. The radio traffic indicated their supplies were almost exhausted. Without the C-130s, they had no chance at all. If relief didn't reach them soon, it would be too late.

Galbraith listened dispassionately, and then dismissed the request.

It was too much for Bane. He knew the resistance field leaders bore most of the responsibility for their predicament, but without help, they were doomed.

He exploded at the Ambassador. In a raised voice, Bane said it was one thing to oppose the policy, but you don't leave men that way, not when they're counting on you. That isn't how you end it, he said. It was dishonorable, like at the Bay of Pigs in Cuba. You don't leave men to die that way. The meeting degenerated into a shouting match until Bane stomped out in disgust.

There was no air drop. The Chinese overran the encircled Tibetans. It was a massacre, not of hundreds, as in Cuba, but of thousands. It was also the CIA's second disaster with paramilitary forces in the space of a mere twelve months. Bane's relationship with Ambassador Galbraith soured. When the CIA assigned him to his next posting, he was glad to go.

The episode remains classified. To this day, the CIA will not release information on the location of the guerrilla battle or radio transcripts, cables, and other documents pertaining to what happened at America's second, and still secret, Bay of Pigs.

After the slaughter, the Tibetan operation went into limbo. There was no longer a sense of urgency. CIA Director John McCone confronted Secretary of State Dean Rusk in November 1962, about the seeming drift in U.S. policy toward Tibet. McCone said his impression of recent meetings of the 5412 Special Group was that it was no longer clear to the participants themselves that the Kennedy Administration "really wished to pursue the original 1958 objective of freeing Tibet of the Chinese Communist occupation."

If McCone was looking for reassurances from Rusk, he got none. The 5412 Special Group began to develop contingency plans for demobilizing the fighters, just in case the Kennedy Administration decided to eliminate the Tibetan program. Although the United States continued to support the Mustang base, active resistance operations—raids into Tibet to attack the PLA—were frozen. Six years had passed since the start of Dorjee Yudon's rebellion. It was becoming clear that guerrilla war wouldn't liberate Tibet.

The Fourteenth Dalai Lama, age four. (*Source:* A. T. Steele, Demton Khang Photographic Archive)

The Fourteenth Dalai Lama at his summer residence, the Norbulingka, Lhasa, Tibet. (*Source:* Demton Khang Photographic Archive)

Family of Tibetan nomads with prayer flags on tent, c. 1934. (*Source:* Sven Hedin Collection, U.S. Library of Congress)

The Fourteenth Dalai Lama, third from right, and his mother, four brothers, and two sisters. (*Source:* Demton Khan Photographic Archive)

The Fourteenth Dalai Lama, left, greets Chairman of the People's Republic of China, Mao Zedong, Beijing, 1955. (*Source:* Demton Khang Photographic Archive)

Geshe Wangyal, the first Tibetan Buddhist lama to settle in the United States, arrives in New York harbor aboard the *S.S. Liberte,* 1955. (*Source: New York World-Telegram,* U.S. Library of Congress)

Escorted by Tibetan resistance fighters, the Dalai Lama escapes to India following the Tibetan National Uprising of 1959. (*Source:* Demton Khang Photographic Archive)

After the failed National Uprising in 1959, Tibetan refugees followed the Dalai Lama into exile in India by the thousands. (*Source: U.S. Library of Congress*)

President Dwight Eisenhower and Indian Prime Minister Nehru and spouses at the Washington, D.C., summit meeting, December 16, 1959. (*Source:* U.S. Library of Congress)

Marxist propagandist Anna Louise Strong, author of *When Serfs Stood Up in Tibet*. She sent Eleanor Roosevelt "pages and pages" justifying China's invasion of Tibet. Moscow, 1937. (*Source: New York World-Telegram*, U.S. Library of Congress)

Thubten Jigme Norbu, the Dalai Lama's eldest brother, pleads the case for Tibet over Radio Free Europe, New York, 1959. (*Source: New York World-Telegram*, U.S. Library of Congress)

Gyalo Thondup, the Dalai Lama' second oldest brother, lobbies former first lady Eleanor Roosevelt to support Tibetan independence. (*Source:* Tommy Weber, *New York World-Telegram*, U.S. Library of Congress)

Left to right, CIA officer Howard Bane, the Dalai Lama, and U.S. Ambassador Ellsworth Bunker following a three-hour meeting in December 1960 at Dharamsala, India. (*Source:* Polaroid photo courtesy of the family of Howard T. Bane)

President John F. Kennedy and CIA Director Allen Dulles, Washington, D.C., 1961. (*Source: U.S. Library of Congress*)

The Dalai Lama visits a school for the children of Tibetan refugees, Bylakuppe, South India, c. 1965. (*Source* : Demton Khang Photographic Archive)

Tibetan students at the Young Lamas School in India, c. 1960. (*Source:* Photographer unknown, Collection of the Shambhala Archives)

Chögyam Trungpa, Sister Palmo, and various Kagyu Sect teachers with Prime Minister Nehru, c. 1960. (*Source:* Photographer unknown, Collection of the Shambhala Archives)

The counterculture embraces Tibetan Buddhism. From left to right, Allen Ginsberg, Timothy Leary, and Ralph Metzner at a "Psychedelic Celebration," Village Theater, New York, c. 1967. (*Source:* New York World-Telegram, U.S. Library of Congress)

Allen Ginsberg and Trungpa Rinpoche, founder of Shambhala and Naropa University, at a poetry reading in Boulder, Colorado, c. 1971. (*Source:* Blair Hansen)

The Dalai Lama, left, and Trungpa Rinpoche, right, discussing Tibetan Buddhist institutions in the United States. (*Source:* Andrea Roth)

Beat Generation poets Anne Waldman, right, and Allen Ginsberg, left, co-founders of Naropa University's Jack Kerouac School of Disembodied Poetics. (*Source:* Collection of the Shambhala Archives)

Lama and retreat master Kalu Rinpoche helped spread the Kagyu School of Tibetan Buddhism in the United States and Europe in the 1970s. This photo was taken in 1988, a year before his death. (*Source:* Don Farber, BuddhistPhotos.com)

Geshe Wangyal, founder of the Tibetan Buddhist Learning Center, revered religious freedom so highly he kept the small flag he received after becoming a U.S. citizen at the center of his mandala. (*Source:* Katrina Thomas)

Tenzin Gyatso, the Fourteenth Dalai Lama, emerged from isolation in India to become one of the world's best-known spiritual leaders. (*Source*: Andrea Roth)

Chancellor Angela Merkel meets with the Dalai Lama in Germany, 2007. (*Source*: Demton Khang Photographic Archive)

Part Two: Resilience

As we've seen, the first part of the movement to free Tibet began as a secret Cold War operation—part guerrilla war, part battle to shape public opinion. The brainchild of the 5412 Special Group, it was spearheaded by the CIA and ultimately backed by four successive presidents—Truman, Eisenhower, Kennedy, and Johnson. But with the guerrilla forces inside Tibet decimated and the fighters in Mustang divided and bickering, the movement to free Tibet had to evolve beyond the narrow base of U.S. government patronage.

The Dalai Lama had not endorsed the covert CIA war because he opposed the use of violence. While American officials worked with his brothers and resistance leaders, the Dalai Lama concentrated on the survival of Tibet's people, culture, and religious institutions during exile. He also broadened his contacts with Westerners, including serious students of Buddhism and counterculture figures, such as the Beatnik poet Allen Ginsberg, who traveled to India seeking spiritual and intellectual enlightenment, often with the aid of psychedelic drugs.

In the second part of the movement to free Tibet, these initially casual contacts between the Dalai Lama and the counterculture turned out to be instrumental in sustaining the Tibetan cause through its darkest years since the 1950 Chinese invasion.

Chapter 9

Wheels Within Wheels

Nonviolent resistance had always appealed to the Dalai Lama as the way to preserve Tibet's independence. In the years since the Chinese invasion, he had received numerous direct appeals to sanction armed resistance, but he never did so. At most, he had tacitly condoned it.

Now, with no immediate prospect of rolling back the Chinese forces occupying Tibet, the Dalai Lama turned his leadership to the twin challenges of survival and reform. The immediate imperative was sheltering and caring for the waves of refugees, more than 80,000, who followed him into exile.

At first, the Dalai Lama settled in Mussoorie, but the small hill town was inadequate for the growing numbers of Tibetans. There was another alternative, Dharamsala, in the Indian state of Himachal Pradesh. Overlooking the Kangra Valley, in its heyday Dharamsala was a summering spot for British colonial administrators fleeing the hot lowlands of the Punjab region.

On the hillside above Dharamsala, a *faux* English village called McLeod Ganj had risen in the mid-nineteenth century. Named for its founder, Lt. Governor of the Punjab David McLeod, it included the Victorian-styled St John's Church in the Wilderness located off a one lane road with a forested hillside thick with pine and deodar cedars. Lord

Elgin, the Viceroy of India, liked Dharamsala so much that he might have made it the summer capital of the British Raj, the seat of government administration, had he lived longer. His death in 1862 foreclosed the possibility, but Elgin staked a permanent claim by having himself buried in the graveyard at St. John's Church. Other headstones, etched with the date 1905, bear witness to the earthquake that devastated McLeod Ganj in the same year. By 1947, the year when India and Pakistan were partitioned after independence from Britain, most of the town's remaining residents were Moslem. Along with millions of other Moslems from India, they joined the exodus to Pakistan, leaving the village empty of people.

When the Tibetans began streaming into India twelve years later, McLeod Ganj was a virtual ghost town. The buildings which managed to withstand the 1905 earthquake were vacant and decaying, their survival in doubt. The town was badly in need of rebuilding, of commerce, and of people. A local Indian merchant who had clung optimistically, even stubbornly, to the hope that somehow the town would recover, petitioned the Indian government to consider McLeod Ganj for the Tibetans.

When word reached the Dalai Lama that Dharamsala and McLeod Ganj might serve as home until a return to Lhasa was possible, he sent a delegation to examine the twin towns. Himachal Pradesh was a region where monkeys and wild peacocks roamed freely in the woods. The peak of Dhauladhar towered some 17,000 feet above McLeod Ganj. In winter, a mantle of snow capped the mountain top and sometimes cascaded below onto the town's narrow streets and occasionally even further down the steep hillsides into Dharamsala, enfolding the land in a blanket of white memories of Tibet. When the delegation reported that "the water of Dharamsala is better than the milk of Mussoorie," the Dalai Lama and his followers moved.

Political reform had long preoccupied Tenzin Gyatso. In a 1961 speech marking the second anniversary of the March 10, 1959, uprising, the Dalai Lama introduced the concept of a Tibetan Charter, a new constitution that would transform the country's traditional institutions into a modern democracy.

The idea made Indian Prime Minister Nehru nervous. It looked too much like the formal establishment of a Tibetan government on Indian soil, one whose legitimacy would rival the puppet Tibetan government installed in Lhasa. Ever fearful of provoking China, Nehru asked the

Dalai Lama not to take steps to implement the charter. In deference to his Indian hosts, the Dalai Lama held off.

CHINA STARTS A BORDER WAR WITH INDIA

Nehru had good reason to be nervous about aggravating China. High in the Himalayas, the two countries shared a disputed border between Kashmir and Tibet and were squabbling over another area further east. Across the ill-defined boundaries, the People's Liberation Army and India's Assam Rifles border forces faced each other uneasily. On October 10, 1962, after almost a month of border skirmishes, the PLA launched a decisive attack against India's North East Frontier border. On November 14, the Indians counterattacked, but were badly beaten.

Fearing an all-out invasion by China, Prime Minister Nehru asked President Kennedy for help. Kennedy sent special envoy Averell Harriman. Riding along on the flight were Desmond FitzGerald and new CIA Tibet Task Force head, Ken Knaus. The United States promised support for India, including aid from the CIA in converting the Tibetan resistance into a force that could serve India.

The CIA proposed to share the Mustang base and let the Indians use it as a staging ground for gathering intelligence on Chinese troop and supply movements and for launching harassment attacks. FitzGerald suggested that the Tibetans being trained at Camp Hale could become the bulwark of a reconstituted force to guard India's Himalayan borders. India seized the offer.

But rather than risk a broadening war in the Himalayas, Mao Zedong withdrew PLA forces from India in December 1962. The border fighting, however, had changed the dynamic between India and China. Nehru's attempts to coexist peacefully with Mao having ended badly, he was now a supporter of an armed Tibetan resistance. Word spread among the Tibetan exiles that India was recruiting troops to fight the Chinese, and a repeat of the situation at Mustang took place. Tibetans flocked to the old British hill town of Dehra Dun in northern India to join the newly created Special Frontier Force. Gyalo Thondup worked with Mullik, India's director of the newly named Central Intelligence Bureau, whom he had first met in Darjeeling. They agreed that the Tibetans would fight for independence, but under Indian command and control. Eventually, the Special Frontier Force grew to a contingent of 12,000 Indian and

Tibetan men. The Indian unit charged with clandestine support for the Tibetans was called Establishment 22. Its purpose included developing contingency plans for the day of Tibet's liberation.

Support from India had come just in time to keep the spark of Tibetan armed resistance flickering. This would not be the last time their fate was determined by the shifting gears of international politics.

THE DALAI LAMA LAUNCHES
DEMOCRATIC REFORMS

When the Dalai Lama brought up the Tibetan Charter again in 1963, not only were there no objections from Nehru, but he was now an enthusiastic supporter of Tibetan political reform. Establishment 22 might have plans for postliberation Tibet, but so did Tenzin Gyatso.

"To build and prepare for the future is one of our primary responsibilities," the Dalai Lama said in his 1963 speech marking the fourth anniversary of the March 10 uprising, "For this purpose, I have prepared a future Constitution for Tibet which is consistent with the teachings of Lord Buddha and with the rich spiritual and temporal heritage of our history and democracy. This Constitution provides for effective participation by the people and also for securing social and economic justice. I have decided that upon Tibet regaining freedom the Constitution shall immediately come into force . . . I invoke the blessings of Divine Providence on all mankind."

The introduction of the Charter marked a turning point in the country's history. For the first time, Tibetans would have fundamental human rights enshrined in a written constitution. Democratic procedures were created to elect representatives. The Dalai Lama had taken the first steps toward creating a Buddhist democracy. While the Charter would govern the operations of the Tibetan government-in-exile, its provisions extended to all Tibetans, including those living in occupied Tibet.

NEW LAND AND NEW LIVES

The number of Tibetans fleeing to India continued to grow. There were now Tibetan refugee camps springing up in Northern India, as well as in Nepal. One of the urgent problems was the lack of a livelihood for many Tibetans, who had left behind virtually everything when fleeing the

Chinese. The problem was especially acute for those who lived pastoral or nomadic lives. Many had come across the Himalayas without livestock and were now landless.

The government of India offered virgin forest land in the south. Tibetans were used to the thin air of high altitude and had rarely experienced sweltering heat. Tropical and humid, this was utterly foreign to them. But the land was arable and, when the Dalai Lama accepted India's offer with gratitude, the refugees marched away in columns to clear the trees and establish settlements, much like pioneers to North America had done 200 years earlier.

For others, the available work was grueling manual labor building and maintaining roads. There were no road graders, tractors, or dump trucks available to ease the work, which had to be done by hand at a tedious pace. Some of this work was done in India and some in Sikkim, but everywhere it was harsh. Daily hazards included rock falls, slides, and cave-ins, sometimes caused by the dynamite used to shatter rock formations and by the instability of excavated hillsides and mountains. The Tibetans on the crews lived along the roads they were building, sheltering under plastic tarpaulins and makeshift tents where children were raised and mothers gave birth to babies before returning to the menial labor of carrying loads of dirt to level roads or fill potholes or widen passageways. It was true that Tibetans had, for generations, done unpaid work on road maintenance as a form of levy, the *courvée*, that could be imposed by local aristocrats. But that had been temporary work, lasting only until the tax was paid off. This was permanent, the refugees' new existence outside Tibet.

There were other pressing problems. The fighting inside Tibet produced many orphans. Parents who wanted their children to grow up free in India smuggled them across the border, but then returned to Tibet to care for their own mothers and fathers or other elderly relatives too feeble to make the trek across the mountain ranges. In addition, illness and death in the refugee camps, on the road crews, and in the struggling settlements of the tropical lowlands to the south created still more orphans. The need for homes and schools was urgent.

THE TIBETAN CHILDREN'S VILLAGE IS BORN

In the hills above McLeod Ganj, the Dalai Lama and his sister Jetsun Pema took long walks, talking over the many challenges facing the

Tibetans. She remembers the first days in the early 1960s as a time when she was able to draw close to her brother, something that would not have been possible if they had remained in Lhasa, where his religious and official duties would have left him little free time. But in the early days of the Tibetan diaspora, the destruction of the old had left a vacuum, and they filled it with plans and hopes for the future. On these treks, the Dalai Lama always took his American built walkie-talkie, so that he could be called back to town when emergencies arose.

Amidst the cedar trees there was a park-like expanse that answered the need for land on which an orphanage and residential school could be built. International humanitarian agencies donated funds, and the Tibetan Children's Village (TCV) gradually grew, one building at a time. They were simple concrete structures at first, housing up to 50 children and two foster parents per residence. Inside, they were brightly painted, with meditation shrines and photos of the Dalai Lama near the entrance. There were separate rooms for the boys and girls, lined with rows of bunk beds, tidily kept and spartan. There were also common rooms for playing games and socializing. Everyone helped in the kitchen and on the patios —even the tiniest of refugees pitched in by shelling beans and preparing meals.

The TCV was more than a place for orphans to shelter with a foster family. It was also a school, founded in 1960 by Tsering Dolma, the Dalai Lama's elder sister, with the motto "Others Before Self." Later, Jetsun Pema took over its administration. Eventually, the TCV became home to some 2000 students. Today, teachers and their families live on the grounds and the student-run bakery is renowned for its bread. There are separate libraries for younger and older students, who respectfully greet the librarian before entering and pause to give thanks as they leave, and a cultural center that features exhibits on Tibet and has showcased all the Dalai Lama's international awards. The school curriculum is rigorous. Eighty percent of the TCV's graduates go on to college or university, primarily in India.

Not all refugees, of course, stayed in India. Some found help relocating through international relief groups. Chögyam Trungpa, after a dangerous but adventurous journey to India, had been appointed by the Dalai Lama as spiritual adviser to the Young Lamas Home School in Dalhousie. He was working there when a friend named John Driver helped him get a Spalding sponsorship through the Tibet Society of the

United Kingdom. The sponsorship paid for passage on the Princess & Orient line of ships, and in 1963 Trungpa sailed from Bombay to England to study comparative religion, philosophy, and fine art at Oxford University.

ALLEN GINSBERG'S INDIAN JOURNEY: EAST MEETS WEST

In October 1961, the Beatnik poet Allen Ginsberg and his artist-lover Peter Orlovsky, with whom he had exchanged vows, that at life's end they would journey to heaven together, set sail on the *S.S. America* for a 28-month long global spiritual quest. Their first stop was Paris, where they hoped to find the writer William S. Burroughs.

Ginsberg and Burroughs had a tangled history. They met in New York, but in the late 1940s Burroughs and his wife, Joan, moved to Texas, where they bought farmland to grow marijuana. The rural idyll was shattered in 1951 when William tried to reenact the Swiss archer William Tell's feat by shooting an apple off Joan's head. Using a gun instead of a bow and arrow, William hit her in the forehead. The fatal shot opened the way for Burroughs and Ginsberg to begin an affair that lasted until Allen broke it off in 1953. A few months later, Burroughs left America for Morocco, where he lived for the next 15 years. Ginsberg and Orlovsky had stayed with Burroughs in Tangiers on an earlier trip, when Burroughs was editing his new novel, *The Naked Lunch*.

For the remainder of spring and early summer, Ginsberg and Orlovsky stayed in Paris at 9 rue git le Coeur, known as "The Beat Hotel," hoping to hook up with Burroughs. When he didn't show by July, they pushed on for Tangiers. They found Burroughs at his Moroccan home. But the older author and Orlovsky clashed, and the artist left for Israel. Ginsberg departed as well soon thereafter and spent the following several months alone in Greece.

Ginsberg read widely during his Grecian solitude that summer and during his onward travels to India in 1962. His choices show that Tibet was on his mind. He read Lama Govinda's 1959 text, *Foundations of Tibetan Mysticism* and Helmut Hoffman's *Religions of Tibet*. He also read political tracts about Tibet's struggles: *Tibetan Interviews* by Anna Louise Strong, *Tibet Fights for Freedom*, published in India in 1960, *The Rape of Tibet* by Nikkil Mantra, and *On the Himalayan Front* by Dr. Satyanarayan.

Many such pro-Tibetan tracts received wide distribution in paperback or pamphlet form, thanks to secret funding provided by the CIA. In a literal sense, CIA officer Howard Bane was subsidizing Allen Ginsberg's reading list.

Orlovsky and Ginsberg reunited in Israel. Three months later they set off for Kenya, where both participated in an anticolonial protest in Nairobi. After just a few weeks in East Africa, they booked passage across the Indian Ocean and up into the Arabian Sea. They disembarked in Bombay on what would turn out to be a 15-month sojourn as Ginsberg searched out every guru and holy man he could find.

GINSBERG MEETS WITH THE DALAI LAMA

During his stay in India, Ginsberg kept a journal. After he visited Kalimpong, Darjeeling, and Dharamsala, Tibetan references and symbols increasingly populated his journal notations and poetry. He referenced Tibetan gongs, Tibetan music, and Tibetan skirts. He wrote about Tibetan skeletons dancing in fire, he had dreams of "Tibetan skull-choppers," and he tuned in to the politics. In a journal entry under the heading *The Fights*, Ginsberg listed conflicts around the globe, including the item "Tibet Lamas vs. Chinese Tibetan secularists."

These references are significant because they document the first involvement of what would turn out to be the most potent social force of the decade, the American counterculture, with Tibetan Buddhism. For Ginsberg personally, it was the start of a fascination with Buddhism that included going on semiannual meditation retreats until the end of his life. The Beatnik poet was the first member of the counterculture to build bridges between Tibet and the West.

His India sojourn was also drug laced. Ginsberg, like other Beat Generation writers and artists, was experimenting with the use of drugs to expand consciousness and gain enlightenment. Marijuana, hashish, LSD, and psychedelic mushrooms feature in his Indian journal and were part of the spiritual quest he and Orlovsky had undertaken. Many of the Tibetan references in the journal appear in the context of drug use, showing how deeply Tibetan influences had taken hold of Ginsberg's mind. This is not generally true of the political references, however, from which it is clear that he devoted a substantial amount of lucid reflection to America's involvement in Cold War conflicts, specifically including Tibet.

Ginsberg was particularly anxious to know whether Tibetan mysticism involved mental experiences similar to LSD-induced visions. His interest was more than socioanthropological. He wanted practical advice on how to handle hallucinations while on acid.

In one encounter with a Tibetan lama, the poet gave a rambling 45-minute introduction of himself, part biography and part confessional, disjointed because he was probably under the influence of LSD during the meeting. Ginsberg asked how to react to things that might appear to him in the psychedelic state.

"If you see anything horrible don't cling to it, if you see anything beautiful don't cling to it," the Nyingmapa Lama told him, "Watch the wheels within wheels of anything you see, but don't get attached."

In Dharamsala, Ginsberg had a 45-minute dialog with the Dalai Lama about Tibetan meditation and enlightenment. In the meeting, the poet expounded on the virtues of LSD. Tenzin Gyatso expressed interest in the proposition that tripping on acid expanded one's perceptual powers, but he wanted to know exactly what it meant. Could Ginsberg, he asked, see what was inside a closed briefcase while on LSD?

In her version of this meeting in *A Blue Hand, The Beats in India*, Pulitzer-nominated biographer Deborah Baker recounts that Ginsberg wanted to know if the states of alternative consciousness induced by drugs corresponded to specific states of mind achieved through meditation. The Dalai Lama offered his view that while the altered consciousness was real, the drugs themselves could divert attention from the real problem of ego. But when Ginsberg offered to have Timothy Leary send psilocybin mushrooms to the Dalai Lama, he did not object.

The anecdote is amusing, but also deeply revelatory. At the time, the Dalai Lama bore the burdens of heading Tibet's government and being top spiritual leader. He was charged with looking after the welfare of Tibet's refugees and handling diplomacy with India and the United States. And still, he made time to meet with Ginsberg and other Westerners like him, people without any official writ, who were spiritually drawn to the Tibetan leader. Ginsberg's meeting with the Dalai Lama took place half a decade before The Beatles popularized gurus and a journey to India became a rite of passage for the young. A pioneer of the shifting consciousness of the decade, Ginsberg was making connections where none yet existed.

Nor was Ginsberg the only sojourner to meet with the Dalai Lama after experimenting with hallucinatory drugs. The year before Ginsberg's arrival in Dharamsala, another American wayfarer had a similar encounter. The screenwriter Bruce Joel Rubin had been working at NBC News in New York in 1960 when a friend asked if he would store some LSD in his refrigerator. At the time, Rubin was reading the *Tibetan Book of the Dead*. After devoting half a year to studying the tome, he decided one day to take a dose of LSD. At the time, noted celebrities such as Cary Grant extolled the virtues of acid as a tool for self-understanding in *LIFE* magazine.

Rubin's trip was transformative. In his visions, he experienced millions of lifetimes. He quit his job at NBC and left for India where he met with the Dalai Lama. During their three hour encounter, Rubin described the life-changing experience and insights he gained from LSD. Tenzin Gyatso encouraged Rubin to become his student and learn Tibetan Buddhism.

Socialite Zina Rachevsky, the daughter of an American heiress and a Russian prince, was another devotee of the early sixties Beat Generation drug culture who was drawn to Tibetan Buddhism. After reading Anagarika Govinda's *The Way of the White Clouds*, one of the first books to popularize Tibetan Buddhism in the West, she went to Darjeeling in search of a guru. Lama Yeshe, who later proudly called himself a Tibetan Hippie, had just fled across the border from Tibet into India in 1959. Although teaching Westerners, especially women, was culturally alien to Lama Yeshe and other Tibetan monks, he agreed to be Rachevsky's guru. The two went on to found an important meditation center in Katmandu.

A generation earlier, the first European woman to visit Tibet began her journey after a revelatory drug experience. Alexandra David-Neel was an eighteen-year old French woman whose curiosity about Asian mysticism drove her to spend hours reading Buddhist and Hindu texts at the library of the Musée Guimet while seated under a statue of Buddha. When her godmother left her a legacy, Alexandra decided to smoke hashish as an aid in deciding how to invest the money. After coming down from the high she booked passage on a ship, arriving in India in 1892. She settled there in 1911, and in 1915 distinguished herself as the first Western woman to enter Tibet to study the customs and religion.

The Tibetans themselves, particularly in the monastic orders, placed a strong emphasis on spiritual training of the mind through disciplined meditation. However, they did not, as a rule, condemn those who chose to use drugs while on their path to spiritual development. In some monastic vows the use of alcohol is prohibited, but other lamas not only enjoyed alcoholic drinks but believed that so long as an awareness or mindfulness of the changed state they induce was maintained, alcohol could be useful.

The 14th century Nyingma master Kunkyen Longchen Rabjam authored hundreds of sacred texts. Only twenty five have survived, including *The Treasury of Wish-Fulfilling Gems*, where his reference to a "*datura* hallucination" in the context of discussing illusion and reality leaves little doubt that Tibetan Buddhists were familiar with mind-altering drugs. *Datura* is a plant that has hallucinogenic properties.

While the use of drugs is certainly not integral to Tibetan Buddhism, the fact that changes in perception fostered by drug use resulted in Westerners as diverse as Alexandra Neel and Allen Ginsberg being drawn to Tibetan Buddhism is incontrovertible.

Ginsberg's mind turned to politics again and again in his travel notes, published in 1970 under the title *Indian Journals*. Writing around midnight on the train to Benares, in a loose journal passage that is half poetry, half Kerouac "Flashes," Ginsberg muses about convening a meeting of the United Nations. In his imaginary UN session, Mao Zedong, Nehru, Kennedy, and Khrushchev participate in a televised debate translated into every language in the world and watched by billions. Ginsberg wrote that the Dalai Lama should be asked to send a "robed" representative, speculates about whether the reports of Tibetan atrocities are real or concocted, and makes a passing reference to "what America needs, 'an alliance with China,'—Democratic communism." And, as if to underscore his visionary claims for LSD, he imagines a system networking millions of miniaturized televisions, one for each person, with a capacity to send and receive. Did Ginsberg intuit the Internet?

THE BEATNIK SPY

On June 6, 1963, readers of the *New York Times* were treated to the improbable headline "Buddhists Find a Beatnik 'Spy.'" The reputed spy was Ginsberg. After his extended stay in India, he had traveled on to Thailand, Cambodia, and Vietnam to immerse himself in Buddhist culture.

In Vietnam, he showed up at a Buddhist monastery and started asking lots of questions. The monks were suspicious. His beard and long hair looked to them like a cheap disguise. They didn't buy Ginsberg's explanation that he was a crazy poet who liked Buddhism. After he left, they decided he was an American spy. The next day, their spokesman denounced Ginsberg at a news conference attended by international correspondents in Saigon. The hot story at the time was the growing conflict between the government of South Vietnam and the Buddhist monasteries. The reporters were curious about the unmasked spy and pressed the Buddhist spokesman for details. They erupted in laughter when they figured out that the alleged CIA agent was actually Allen Ginsberg.

The Vietnamese Buddhist monks who sensed that the probing, questioning, pestering Ginsberg was in truth a spy were only tapping into a deeper reality, for he was a spy, just not a government spy. Ginsberg was the vanguard of the counterculture, a wanderer in search of cultural treasure to carry home, the riches of enlightenment and the path to salvation, an intellectual and spiritual plunderer.

It was the dawn of the 1960s, of alternative states of consciousness, of making love instead of war, of dropping out, tuning in, and turning on, and Jack Kerouac, Alan Watts, Allen Ginsberg, and Timothy Leary were paving the way. The American establishment and its CIA spies might be cooling to the Buddhist cause, at least in the case of the Tibetans, but the antiestablishmentarians were warming to it, the best of them drawn to Buddhism not because of its exoticism, but because the budding counterculture intuited that the cultural diffusion of Buddhism meant the preservation of the West.

The 1962 Cuban missile crisis had shown how real the danger was, how close the world had come to the end of civilization itself. Nuclear war meant Armageddon. The stand off between the United States and USSR radically altered the consciousness of millions, spawning an interest in nuclear disarmament, world peace, and nonviolence.

The final leg of Ginsberg's quest was to Japan, where he wrote *The Change* on the train from Kyoto to Tokyo. It was the culmination of a journey of transformation. Somewhere on his journey, the ethical obligation to Tibet slipped unperceived from the shoulders of spies and diplomats onto the backs of the poet-seer and a new generation of young bohemians just about to come of age.

THE CIA'S ATTENTION SHIFTS TO VIETNAM

The Vietnamese Buddhists Ginsberg had interrogated had secrets to protect. One of the most shocking of them stunned the world a mere five days after his visit to their monastery. On June 11, 1963, a Buddhist monk named Thich Qung Duc appeared before the international press in Saigon. Newsreel cameramen and still photographers were on the scene, primed to record the event as if at any standard news conference. Instead of giving the protest speech the press expected, the monk soaked his robes in gasoline and sat cross-legged on the street. With great deliberation, he lit himself on fire and then calmly remained seated while the conflagration consumed the oxygen around him, charring his flesh and filling his lungs with smoke. Although the pain must have been agonizing, he did not scream or run in panic, but sat silently bearing the flames until he could sit no more and then merely toppled over as if crumbling from within.

This stoical act of self-immolation was the world's first recorded suicide on camera, and it ignited an explosion of criticism over the abuses of the South Vietnamese government led by Premier Ngo Dinh Diem. After North and South Vietnam were partitioned by international accord, Diem became the first president of South Vietnam. He was Catholic, corrupt, and incompetent. By 1963, Diem's shortcomings put him in conflict with his own military, which secretly plotted against him and pitted him against many Buddhist monasteries, which openly protested his repressive rule.

As an act of passive political resistance, self-immolation boggled the mind. Unlike hunger strikes, a time-honored tactic of underdogs, in which the protestor undergoes gradual, almost imperceptible, starvation that results in organ failure and eventual death unless blocked by force feeding, self-immolation was visible, dramatic, and quickly fatal—perfect for the TV age. Seen on television sets and in cinema newsreels across the planet, the burning Buddhist monk became an international symbol of 1960s protest.

In November, Diem was ousted and assassinated by his own military. The CIA knew in advance of the plot, but in Vietnam the Agency was not driving policymaking as it had done in Tibet. The coup had been orchestrated by U.S. Ambassador Henry Cabot Lodge.

The Cuban Bay of Pigs had been a major setback for the CIA. President Kennedy assigned General Maxwell Taylor to review the fiasco. Taylor's probe was welcomed by many who felt the CIA had overstepped its legitimate role of collecting and analyzing intelligence. Among them was Eleanor Roosevelt.

"Over the past few years," she wrote in her column in June, 1961, "The CIA has become an agency not for gathering information and reporting it to those who make policy and take action, but it has itself made policy and taken action. I hope . . . General Maxwell Taylor's committee looking into the CIA will bring about some drastic changes in what has become a situation that never should have been permitted in our CIA."

Taylor reported back that the CIA was ill equipped to conduct large-scale paramilitary operations. Taylor was a military man and his proposed remedy was predictable: the Pentagon, the General said, should be in charge of operations that called for the use of military force. Taylor did not succeed in wresting control of the fledgling secret war in Laos from the CIA, but his assessment put the Pentagon in the driver's seat in the budding Vietnam conflict. Aside from running the secret war in Laos, the Phoenix program in Vietnam, and assorted special operations in Cambodia, the CIA was a supporting player, more or less relegated to an advisory role.

FitzGerald was a regular attendee at the Pentagon strategy sessions on the war, where he struggled to get across his view that reform of South Vietnam's government was crucial to quell the growing Viet Cong insurgency. FitzGerald's years in running guerrilla operations convinced him that unpopular governments fueled insurgencies. Escalating military force, he warned, was not the answer. In one meeting, he clashed openly with Defense Secretary Robert McNamara over the Pentagon's reliance on Viet Cong body counts as a yardstick to measure whether progress was being made in the war. The overly technocratic McNamara bristled at FitzGerald's criticism of his metrics. McNamara threw FitzGerald out of the meeting and told him never to come back to a Pentagon strategy session.

The 5412 Special Group still controlled the Tibetan operation, even though there was waning enthusiasm for its paramilitary aspects. The epicenter of Cold War conflict had shifted East and, with it, many of the players who had been central to ST BARNUM and ST CIRCUS. Ellsworth Bunker moved on to Southeast Asia and would become Ambassador to Vietnam. Air America and Col. Aderholt's Air Commandos dusted off their flight charts for Cambodia, Laos, and North Vietnam, running special operations across the Mekong River from a base at Nakhon Phanom, Thailand. Tony Poe and the Missoula Mafia smoke jumpers and others who had trained the Tibetan resistance fighters and built the aerial supply lifeline were drafted into clandestine operations spanning all of Southeast Asia, especially the secret war in Laos.

Laos was to be Poe's undoing. Isolated in the country's highlands, where he commanded irregular forces made of Hmong and Meo tribesmen, Poe started drinking excessively. Fearing he had gone native after a decade in the bush, the CIA removed him from active duty with paramilitary forces.

Roger McCarthy moved on to a new assignment, turning over the Tibet Task Force to Ken Knaus. Desmond FitzGerald was running Western Hemisphere Operations, where he became deeply involved in various anti-Castro plots, including assassination attempts. With each personnel change at CIA, the human commitment to the Tibet operation weakened.

THE TIBET TASK FORCE CHANGES FOCUS

By 1963, Ken Knaus, now head of the Tibet Task Force, could read the handwriting on the wall. With few or no organized guerrilla groups inside Tibet, both the nature and the center of resistance would have to adapt. The direction in which it needed to evolve was political, and the center of resistance would have to shift from the Tibetan Plateau to world capitals.

Unlike the knuckledraggers and paramilitary officers on the Tibet Task Force, Knaus had always understood the importance of developing a political program to strengthen the Tibetans' sense of purpose and unity. As a trainer at Camp Hale, he had emphasized the political aspects of guerrilla warfare, while teaching the practical skills needed to disseminate information and build popular support for the resistance movement.

As ill equipped as Tibet had been to counter Chinese aggression, it was even less prepared for the challenges of global diplomacy. Tibet's historical isolation meant it had no foreign embassies, no diplomatic corps, and no pool of graduates from foreign universities who understood how the rest of the world worked. The handful of administrators and civil servants who managed to flee Lhasa for India were desperately needed to cope with the urgent tasks of running the Tibetan government-in-exile. Knaus saw the problem and wanted to use Agency resources to build Tibet's capacity to govern and to promote its cause internationally.

In a September 1963 report to the 5412 Special Group, William Colby, the CIA's new Far East Division Director, recommended a substantial shift in Tibet operations. Instead of concentrating resources on armed resistance, Colby advised building support for Tibetan autonomy. The resistance fighters were to be used primarily against high-value targets. The goal was not liberation, but the collection of intelligence.

In early 1964, the 5412 Special Group adopted Colby's proposals. The new policy was to "keep the political concept of an autonomous Tibet alive within Tibet and among foreign nations" and to support the sense of unity among the Tibetans. The sum of $1,735,000—a substantial amount at the time—was earmarked for programs supporting the new policy, including $15,000 monthly for the support of the Dalai Lama and his government-in-exile.

Instead of teaching guerrilla warfare at Camp Hale, the CIA would help create a Tibetan civil service. Knaus put together a plan for a different kind of training calling for Tibetans to undergo a year of academic study at Cornell University in world history, politics, government, and English. The 5412 Special Group funded the program for $45,000 annually. The first group of students arrived at college in the fall of 1964.

Ernest Gross, who advised the Dalai Lama on international diplomacy, suggested that the Tibetans open offices in Geneva, Switzerland, and in New York. Because Tibet was no longer recognized as an independent country, and therefore could not open official diplomatic missions, Gross had the idea of featuring Tibetan crafts and calling them cultural information offices. It worked. The offices provided venues for publicizing the Tibetan cause while serving as informal resources for diplomatic legwork. Building on the success of the New York and Geneva centers, the Tibetans soon opened an additional office in London.

This was a dramatic shift for the Tibetan operation. In less than a decade, it had gone from a full-fledged guerrilla war to a training program for civil servants and diplomats.

Chapter 10

Cultural Revolutions

Inside Tibet, at the same time that the CIA support to the resistance was tapering, China was clamping down harder than ever. In 1965, the Tibetan Autonomous Region (TAR) was created by the Chinese government. The newly drawn boundaries for the region encompassed a mere fraction of the land traditionally inhabited by Tibetans.

Vast portions of Eastern Tibet were annexed into adjoining Chinese provinces, instantly converting Tibetans who lived in Amdo and Kham into minorities in larger Han Chinese provinces. The TAR covered mainly Western Tibet, the old province of U-Tsang. This area was targeted for repopulation by Han Chinese, so that over time the Tibetans would be transformed into a minority within the entirety of their own homeland.

Calling the region "autonomous" was a classic piece of communist propaganda. The TAR was not free or autonomous from China in any sense whatsoever. It was administered by a Communist party official appointed and controlled by Beijing. To dispel any confusion about what "autonomy" meant for Tibet under Chinese rule, Vice Premier Hsieh Fu-chih, Beijing's representative, declared to the first People's Congress of the newborn TAR that "National regional autonomy is a system of people's democratic dictatorship . . . it must be the right of the working people to be masters of society, never a dictatorship of the serf-owning or any other exploiting class."

The TAR was to be the first step in imposing Marxist reforms on Tibetan society. The country, even before the Chinese invasion, had never been Shangri-La. Wealth in Tibet had been unequally distributed, with large tracts of arable land concentrated under the ownership of some 200 powerful Tibetan families. This traditional aristocracy restricted social mobility and monopolized economic opportunity. Landless tenant farmers did resemble European serfs in the age of feudalism. Landlords enriched themselves by taking the bulk of the harvest as rent. But by 1965, most of the aristocracy had fled Tibet for India. Others were dead or imprisoned as a result of the guerrilla fighting. The claim to liberate oppressed peasants from an exploitive ruling class was mere propaganda.

China's interest in Tibet was not reform. It was resources, both land and mineral. To control the country, Beijing needed to break the will of the people to resist, even if it meant destroying Tibet's civilization and rebuilding it in the image of China.

The remapping of Tibet to create the TAR fit the classic "conquer and divide" pattern of colonialism. European powers used similar designs in Africa during the Age of Imperialism, creating geographic units that cut across traditional tribal boundaries. With the people divided from one another politically, any form of cohesion, especially opposition to the colonizing power, was doubly difficult.

Just in time for the TAR's creation, the "famous No. 4 Team" of Tibetan construction workers, as the Chinese called them, laid down their tools. Their work on the Museum of the Tibetan Revolution was complete. Deliberately sited across from the Potala Palace, as if to confront the past, the edifice was a cornerstone in China's plans to transform the ancient Tibetan capital of Lhasa into a showplace of modern socialism.

The Museum's 50,000 square feet of space featured propagandistic exhibits to reinforce China's claim that Tibet was a backward region needing liberation. The country's fabled monasteries and Buddhist theocracy were shown as exploiting not only the Tibetan people, but also young monks and nuns who were themselves taken advantage of by higher ranking lamas. The country's hereditary nobles were depicted as ruthless toward tenant farmers, who were compared to Russia's serfs. Tibetan nomads were portrayed as proof of chronic underdevelopment. The socialist revolution, brought about by Chairman Mao at bayonet point, was featured as welcomed by cheering crowds. Photographs of smiling Tibetans greeting their PLA liberators adorned the walls.

In glass display cases, treasures looted from the Potala and Norbu-lingka Palaces were presented to corroborate China's claim that the Dalai Lama was nothing more than a feudal lord, rich beyond imagination. For good measure, the Museum's curators included an exhibit featuring the dungeon supposedly discovered deep inside the Potala where prisoners were tossed and left to be stung by venomous scorpions. The exhibit had been especially built to buttress the propaganda claims by Anna Louise Strong and the other journalists on her junket.

THE GREAT PROLETARIAN
CULTURAL REVOLUTION

Despite the museum's opening in 1965, Mao's revolution was in trouble. The first of his ambitious development schemes, the Great Leap Forward to introduce Marxist collectives in China, had not gone as planned. Documents captured by the Tibetan resistance and turned over to the CIA showed how bad things were. Attempts to create collective farms had caused famine. Morale in the military was poor. There was grumbling within party ranks, too. Mao was convinced that obstructionists, scattered throughout society and extending even into the upper ranks of the Communist Party, were to blame for the collapse of his plans.

His solution was an even more radical revolution than the one he had completed militarily in 1949. That revolution had overthrown the government and China's economic elite. Mao believed, however, that the Communist party members who had been energetic revolutionaries in 1949 had grown complacent and bureaucratic. The situation called for a new revolution, one in which the masses would have to rise against the Party elite.

In speeches, Mao began calling for a "Great Proletarian Cultural Revolution." It would reach up, down, and across society in an attempt to bring about a complete transformation of China's 5000-year-old civilization. Zhou En-lai, Chairman Mao's hand-picked Premier, described it as a plan to transform not only all of Chinese society but the nature of human consciousness. Zhou called it a "total change in outlook." The new revolution Mao wanted was not against the state or government but against the very essence of the culture itself.

This development was foreshadowed by the last encounter between the Dalai Lama and Mao Zedong a decade earlier. The Dalai Lama accepted an invitation from Mao to come to Beijing for an extended stay in 1954. Although Tenzin Gyatso was only 19 years old at the time, Mao was impressed with his composure and articulateness. The Dalai Lama, in turn, was affected by Mao's friendliness and lack of pretense.

In their first of many meetings during the Dalai Lama's visit, Mao welcomed him with a hearty handshake.

"Your coming to Beijing is like coming back to your own home," Mao said, "If you need anything, you just tell me directly."

Tenzin Gyatso warmed to the chain-smoking revolutionary, dressed in scuffed shoes and a peasant's tunic with slightly frayed cuffs on the sleeves. They discussed the ways the Dalai Lama wanted to reform Tibetan society, and Mao gave him advice on governing. Tenzin Gyatso began to hope that Tibet might be able to coexist peacefully with China. For the remainder of his stay in the Chinese capital, he concentrated on finding middle ground between Chinese claims of sovereignty and Tibet's right to preserve its unique culture and religious identity.

But that all changed after another encounter with Mao in 1955, on the eve of the Dalai Lama's return to Lhasa. Mao summoned him to his house for a final chat. There, the chain-smoking Chairman told Tenzin Gyatso that "religion is poison." The Dalai Lama later wrote in his autobiography that at that moment he realized Mao was truly "the destroyer of the Dharma after all."

In 1955, it was premature for Mao to declare war on Chinese and Tibetan culture. Such a move would have precipitated a dangerous backlash that might have caused the downfall of the Communist regime. Despite numerous reassurances given to the contrary between 1951 and 1959, the Chinese leadership had planned for years to impose socialist reforms on Tibet. In a November 1959 interview in Beijing's Great Hall of the People, Premier Zhou En-lai told journalist Han Suyin "We cannot, in a socialist country, have a region where serfs work for priest-landowners. History does not walk backward. . . Tibet must move forward. It cannot become a museum for an antique social system, or a preserve, like the Red Indians of America."

THE RISE OF THE RED GUARDS

In September 1965, Mao felt confident that the time had come to launch his Cultural Revolution. An historical play penned by the deputy mayor of Beijing, Wu Han, set in the Ming dynasty, featured a minor official challenging the Emperor's authority. Claiming the play was a challenge to his own power, Mao used it as a pretext to set up a five-man commission to investigate not only the play, but any feudal or capitalist tendencies in Chinese literature and theater.

Beijing Mayor Peng Zhen was forced to head the probe of his deputy mayor's play. When his report was presented to the Standing Committee of the Politburo, four of the five commissioners exonerated Zhen's deputy of any intention to undermine Mao. But the crucial commissioner, Kang Sheng, a chain smoker who headed China's security agency, dissented.

Sheng's dissent gave Mao grounds to strike the opening blow of the Cultural Revolution. Targeting the hapless Beijing Mayor and the Minister of Propaganda and Minister of Culture, Mao purged them from office. This was the beginning of Mao's cleansing of the ranks, like a fire to rid the party and the state of impurities.

The men who lost their posts were political allies of Mao's ultimate target, Chinese President Liu Shaoqi. As second in line behind Mao in the Party hierarchy, he was widely believed to be Mao's successor. Mao no longer thought he was ideologically pure, but Liu Shaoqi had already built an independent base of power within the party. He also grasped the threat Mao posed to his ascendancy. In the summer of 1966, Liu Shaoqi decided to preempt Mao by being even more radical than the Chairman. He authorized "work teams" to fan out across China's colleges and universities to root out academics lacking in revolutionary zeal.

The work teams were little more than state-sanctioned terrorists. Yet they managed to command the allegiance of students. If the teams told students that their instructors should be punished, the students obeyed, and in some instances battered the hapless intellectuals to death. The episode came to be known as the "Fifty Days of Terror" because of its duration.

Mao countered by calling a meeting of the Central Committee that August which included a special Group in Charge of the Cultural Revolution. They presented a 16-point manifesto that gave the Cultural Revolution a formal basis in policy. The plan was to carry out a thorough purge of Chinese society, including the Communist Party.

Liu Shaoqi objected. This was ideological heresy. It was impossible, he argued, for the masses to rise against the party without themselves becoming counterrevolutionaries. This nicety of logic was unpersuasive to Mao, who felt that if the Communist party itself had become corrupted by capitalist tendencies the masses had every right to overthrow it.

At the end of the week-long meeting, Mao mustered his masses. On August 18, 1966, 5,000,000 Red Guards, specially recruited youthful radicals, strutted across the pavement of Tiananmen Square. By the end of the year, there had been eight parades of the radical youths, fists pounding the air with copies of *The Quotations of Chairman Mao*, the plastic-jacketed, pocket-sized little Red Book that would become the bible of the Cultural Revolution.

STRIKE DOWN, STRIKE DOWN, STRIKE DOWN

No less than 15,000,000 Red Guards were unleashed across China in a torrent of fury. Everywhere they sought out class traitors, obstructionists, and people Mao called "capitalist-roaders" who opposed communist reforms. The Red Guards were incited by Lin Biao, vice-chairman of the Communist party, a gaunt iconoclast whose speeches, phrased in triplicate for impact, exhorted them to "strike down strike down strike down all the old culture old customs old habits."

Strike down they did, and nothing was exempt. They pillaged houses and offices and hauled suspects before their own revolutionary courts. Ideological purges meant sessions of extended interrogation that went on for days and even weeks. The Red Guards tried to break down the defenses of those they accused by keeping them awake to the point of physical exhaustion. Entire departments of the Chinese government were rendered inoperable as heads of units and bureaus were seized by the Red Guards for these *thamzing* sessions of criticism, questions, and reeducation. Beatings were common and often fatal.

No one was immune. Peng Zhen, the former Beijing Mayor whose deputy's play had given Mao his opening to launch the Cultural Revolution, now found himself on trial by the Red Guards. In the early 1960s, Zhen had reviewed the reasons for the failure of Mao's first Great Leap Forward and concluded it was not due to obstructionists lower down in the party ranks, but resulted from a failure of leadership. The Red Guards used his own findings against him and went after him as one of those very leaders who had let down Chairman Mao.

Zhou En-lai tried to use his influence to spare cultural treasures, such as the Tunhuang grottoes on the Silk Road, as well as individual party members, artists, and scientists. He was cornered in his house, surrounded by a throng of Red Guards who screeched at him for 22 hours until he collapsed from a serious, but not fatal, heart attack. Then the Red Guards went after President Liu Shaoqi. They mustered more than 100,000 students in a round-the-clock, 24/7 "noise war" of shouts and slogans broadcast by loudspeaker that went on for days.

One of their slogans was "Destroy the four olds; erect the four news." It meant to eradicate outmoded ideas, customs, behavior, and attitudes. The Red Guards interpreted it as a mandate to destroy anything old, including books, scripts, cultural treasures, even entire buildings. Fires raged across China as the Red Guards literally attempted to "purify" the culture by burning everything old.

MAO'S CULTURAL REVOLUTION
REACHES TIBET

For Tibet, the Cultural Revolution was catastrophic. While the destructive power of Mao's injunction was felt all across China, its consequences for Tibetans were particularly devastating. Mao's belief that religion is poison combined with the admonition to "destroy the four olds" gave the Red Guards license to wage war against the physical manifestations of Tibetan civilization—the monasteries, the artworks, the libraries—as well as the very ways of the people and their Buddhist beliefs. Because the religion, the culture, and the people's sense of identity were so closely intertwined, it was impossible to strike down any one aspect without literally crushing the people themselves.

The Cultural Revolution started in Tibet on August 25, 1966. The Red Guards invaded the Jokhang, the city's main temple, and desecrated hundreds of sacred wall paintings and priceless statues. For days, smoke billowed from fires in its courtyards while the Red Guards burnt scriptural texts and other Buddhist treasures that had been archived there for safekeeping from monasteries throughout the country. A few days later, this assault on the old was followed by the pillaging of the Norbulingka, the summer home the Dalai Lama left behind.

The Red Guards confronted the old guard of the Chinese Communist Party's Central Committee in the Tibetan Autonomous Region, subjecting them to the same harassment, harangues, and violence as had been done in China. This intra-Chinese struggle was about ideology. As the Cultural Revolution progressed, the infighting became more intense. Factions of Red Guards fought one another using weapons seized from PLA arsenals, each claiming to represent the true revolution. The intensity of the infighting became so fierce that China was virtually engulfed in civil war.

When it came to the Tibetans, however, there was an added element of cultural chauvinism, even racism. China's dominant ethnic group is the Han, and they composed the majority of the Red Guards. Their fanatical zeal was especially harsh in dealing with the Tibetan minority, whom the Han looked down on as "barbarians." The very ideas, customs, behavior, and attitudes of the Tibetans were tantamount to the "four olds."

The Red Guards banned the practice of the Buddhist religion and ceremonies, folk dancing, the celebration of Tibetan holidays, and even the burning of incense. Buddhist prayer flags were torn down, and Tibetans were ordered to surrender "forbidden" religious items, such as small devotional household shrines. *Thamzings* were already commonplace in Chinese-occupied Tibet, but now loudspeakers blared a steady stream of Maoist propaganda.

The monasteries, or *gompas* as they are known throughout the Himalayas, were next in the line of fire. Before the Chinese invasion, there were 6254 monasteries perched along the hilltops and hillsides throughout Tibet. Some of the most ancient monasteries, built in a simple style on flat ground, were more than a thousand years old. They predated the Mongol invasions of the 14th century that gave rise to the Gelug sect and the enthronement of the Dalai Lama as Tibet's temporal and spiritual leader. Later monasteries, built after the Mongol invasions, were strategically located on hilltops and hillsides and dated from the late middle ages. Many had been in continuous use for centuries. The *mandala*, symbol of the universe, was the model for the layout of a classic Tibetan monastery. In the center was the temple, the inner sanctum, surrounded by rooms and cordoned off from the outside world and its preoccupations by an outer wall. At the four cardinal points of the compass stood an equal number of guardian deities. Tibet's first monastery, built at Samye in 779, followed this plan.

The monasteries were not isolated retreats; rather, they were central to the society. Much more than spiritual centers or places of worship like a Western church, they are the hub of Tibetan civilization. The monasteries are centers for education and learning and evolved over the centuries into great universities where subjects as diverse as civil engineering, medicine, and psychology were taught along with philosophy, language, and astronomy.

In addition to functioning as Tibet's school system, the monasteries were also artistic centers. Traditional Tibetan arts such as *thangka* painting, featuring meditation deities painted on elaborate scrolls according to precise artistic proportions, were taught master to pupil and practiced in an uninterrupted tradition dating back centuries.

Monasteries also functioned as banks, lending money to merchants and farmers at a rate of one-fifth of the amount borrowed annually, keeping the wheels of the economy greased. Sited along trade routes, monasteries sheltered merchants and travelers from the dangers of bandits and evolved into commercial centers for trading goods, including salt, barley, and wool. At times, the monasteries served as tax collectors for the Tibetan government, for in the Tibetan theocracy the line between religion and state was always thin.

But their prime function remained spiritual. Tibetans turned to the monks and lamas to bless animals, crops, land, children, and to perform spiritual services connected with life milestones such as birth and death ceremonies. Tibetans gave offerings to the monks, in the form of barley, money, even beer, to earn merit and improve their karma.

At the start of the Cultural Revolution, thousands of monasteries scattered throughout the country remained in pristine condition. Despite some instances of substantial damage in the fighting of 1956 to 1959, such as the destruction at Litang, the majority of the country's monasteries and shrines survived the initial Chinese incursion relatively unscathed. A few were completely deserted when the monks and nuns who had inhabited them followed the Dalai Lama into exile in India. In 1959, China had created a Cultural Articles Preservation Commission that was formally charged with inventorying the contents of the monasteries but was, in fact, working to identify the most valuable artwork and artifacts with the aim of transferring them to Beijing. There was so much intact that by 1966 only the biggest of the monasteries around Lhasa, Gyantse, and Shigatse and the larger monasteries in Kham and Amdo had undergone thorough review.

Chinese Premier Zhou En-lai had made lists of national treasures and religious shrines in Tibet, Yunan, and Sichuan. They were to be respected by the Red Guards and preserved from destruction. In Tibet, however, provincial officials simply ignored Zhou's orders. In the fall of 1967, the systematic ransacking of the monasteries began. Red Guard brigades fanned out across the land, armed with notebooks to tally the contents of the monasteries. Anything of value, especially objects of precious metals like gold, silver, or bronze, was stripped from the monasteries. So were significant artworks, provided they were moveable like *thang-ka* paintings of buddhas or deities and *mandalas*, elaborate designs of sacred circles representing the cosmos, with their outer rings of fire symbolizing a barrier to the mysterious world within and at the center a sacred city with Buddha, the primal force, surrounded by lotus flowers.

What was not sent to China was dismantled and destroyed, sometimes down to the sun-dried bricks with which the monasteries had been so laboriously built over the centuries. The Red Guards forced Tibetan work gangs, conscripted from the local people whose generosity and voluntary donations had created the monasteries, to carry out their destruction.

The spire-like *stupas* that adorned the tops of monastery temples were pulled down, their metal recovered and smelted. Statues that could not be removed were smashed or defaced. Wall paintings of bodhisattvas and deities were desecrated. In scenes reminiscent of Nazi book burnings in the 1930s, Red Guards tossed precious copies of the sutras of Lord Buddha and commentaries into bonfires. Stones bearing incised prayers, called *mani* stones, were carted off for use in paving roads and lining public toilets.

While the work was carried out, red banners emblazoned with Maoist slogans were hoisted by the Red Guards, fluttering in the wind in place of the traditional Buddhist prayer flags. When there was nothing left to sack, the buildings were dynamited or, less frequently, used by the PLA for artillery practice. The massive Ganden monastery, sacred to the Dalai Lama's Gelug sect and a major university that was home to 10,000 monks, was blasted until only shattered remnants were left.

The Red Guards' obliteration of the monasteries was an all-out assault on Tibetan civilization. For three years, they rampaged throughout China and Tibet. By the time they were done, Tibet's monasteries had been reduced from more than 6,000 to a few hundred. No more than eight of the Tibetan monasteries were left truly intact.

Nor were the people spared the Red Guards' fanaticism. In Tibet, where the culture itself was the target, virtually anyone qualified as a "class enemy," "reactionary," or "counter-revolutionary." Buddhist priests, especially higher ranking lamas, and Tibet's noble families were of course suspect, as were merchants, administrators, and even Tibetans who were members of the Communist party. But not even the so-called serfs and nomads were immune from persecution.

A group of 400 families gathered for woodcutting at Po Tramo were singled out by the Red Guards. Young girls were separated from their families, stripped of clothing, and forced to undergo *thamzing*. As a final humiliation, the Red Guards gang raped them. It was not an isolated incident. There were more gang rapes in Shigatse, Tibet's second-largest town, as bands of Han Chinese marauded in what amounted to open season on Tibetans.

In China proper, Red Guards also committed atrocities during the revolution—murder, gang rapes, severe beatings—but during the worst periods of lawlessness in China the authorities would intervene. Those who committed the crimes in China were generally executed. When absolutely necessary, Mao didn't hesitate to order the PLA to step in and impose order, although under very strict rules of engagement that prevented the military from using weapons against the people. The Red Guards, radical youth licensed by Mao to root out his enemies, were little threat to the PLA even when the Guards had guns. They were undisciplined and no match for trained combat troops.

But, in Tibet, appeals to the authorities to restore order were worthless. Mao's restrictions against the use of force by the military against the people didn't apply to Tibetans. The PLA not only would not protect Tibetans against rampaging Red Guards, the military joined in the violence. Reports from refugees fleeing to India indicated that the repression was as bad as it had been in 1959, immediately following the Tibetan National Uprising.

China also imposed communal policies on the Tibetans. Nomads were ordered to live and work in group arrangements, their individual livestock confiscated and redistributed for the benefit of the commune. Traditional crops like barley were supplanted by wheat, which the Chinese preferred, and then exported to compensate for the tremendous agricultural production losses inside China as a result of the disruption caused by the Red Guards. The result was a severe shortage of food in Tibet. The famine took at least as many lives as were claimed by the violence unleashed by the Red Guards. The combined death toll in these years is estimated by the government-in-exile to be as high as 1,000,000 Tibetan lives. In China, Mao's turmoil and purges killed between 40 and 60 million people in the years from 1950 to 1972. Most of the deaths occurred after the 1965 start of the Cultural Revolution, making Mao the world's greatest mass murderer ever. Not even Adolf Hitler came close to Mao's death mania; the Chairman personified the evil Desmond FitzGerald feared and that he had expressed in the gloomy letter to his daughter, Frances.

By summer's end in 1967, even Mao realized that events were spiraling beyond control. He ordered Zhou En-lai to bring the Cultural Revolution to a close. The PLA was authorized to use all force necessary to establish order. The Red Guards were prohibited from looting weapons from PLA arsenals. When a contingent of Red Guards in Guangxi refused to relinquish their control of arms depots near the Vietnamese border—critical for the supply of North Vietnam—PLA general Wei Guoqing responded by shelling the radical youth with mortars, followed by a direct military assault. Those who surrendered were sent to forced labor camps.

CULTURAL REVOLUTION'S CHAOS
HARDER TO CONTROL IN TIBET

It took longer to reestablish control in Tibet, where the Red Guards' war against the people had provoked another uprising. Tibetans took literally Chairman Mao's call to rise up against the entrenched party bureaucracy and, by 1968 there were revolts, major and minor, in 20 of the 51 administrative districts composing the Tibetan Autonomous Region. In restive Kham and Amdo, largely excluded from the TAR by China's gerrymandering of boundaries, there was also rebellion.

It was hard to keep track of all the factions involved in the chaos and violence inside Tibet. The Red Guards splintered into three competing groups that often fought one another. PLA troops inside Tibet also took sides and they too were splintered.

Tibetans fought back, sometimes siding with one or another faction, or, as in the Nyemo Rebellion of 1969, simply to assert their independence. At daybreak on June 13, 1969, a local uprising took place against Chinese troops at the Barkhor district headquarters. Dozens were slaughtered by Tibetans using any weapons at their disposal, from knives to stones. When the rising was quelled, the Chinese put the Tibetans they considered responsible on public parade. The men's arms were bound with wire, their heads bowed, bearing signs with their names dangling from their necks reading "Execute Dorje" and "Execute Rindron." As the crowds watched, they were summarily executed.

Another uprising took place in Pala that same year as word spread among nomads that the Chinese intended to force them to give up their lifestyle and move to collective farms. The nomads adopted the name of a Red Guard faction, Gyenlo, and then promptly followed Mao's dictate to purge the party bureaucracy by dispatching several local Communist officials to their graves. Others were imprisoned, and the nomads asserted local control over their own affairs. It was an ingenious, if ultimately ill-fated, interpretation of Mao's injunction to root out corrupt party officials. For a brief three months, the Gyenlo Uprising succeeded and the nomads enjoyed self-rule.

Because of the factional infighting, the PLA in Tibet had become impervious to Beijing's commands. To end the infighting and reestablish Beijing's control, PLA troops from the Xinjiang Military District in Northwest China were mobilized to enter Tibet. While the Cultural Revolution was basically over in China by 1970, it took almost another five years before the repression and cultural destruction instigated by the Red Guards finally subsided in Tibet.

Tibet's cultural devastation was immeasurable, but not complete. Two factors prevented the utter disappearance of Tibet's civilization. The first was the relatively short duration of the Cultural Revolution, which had lasted from 1966 until 1975. A culture cannot be eradicated in a decade, especially one as resilient as the people and civilization of Tibet.

The second factor was the Dalai Lama's prescience. His awareness in 1955 that Mao was to be the destroyer of the Dharma allowed him to make cultural preservation a priority almost immediately after reaching India in 1959. Many Tibetan sacred scriptures had been smuggled to India, and secular texts in Tibetan medicine and astrology and other sciences had also been preserved by the exiles. Still, there was no escaping the fact that Tibet had undergone immense destruction, worse than anything to date.

THE WEST HAS A COUNTERCULTURE REVOLUTION

China, of course, was not the only country undergoing a youth-led revolution in the 1960s. A world away in America, something new was tentatively groping its way into being. It was the first glimmerings of a counterculture movement that would sustain the cause of freedom in Tibet, morally, politically, and financially, when America's foreign policy establishment began withdrawing its support from the Dalai Lama. In the vanguard were Allen Ginsberg and a Harvard professor named Timothy Leary.

Tibet was at the forefront from the very start of the counterculture revolution. In 1964, Leary published *The Psychedelic Experience: A Manual Based on the Tibetan Book of the Dead.* The book was no analytical study. It was a user's guide to "psychedelic sessions" that included not only meditations but also instructions and dosages for the use of hallucinogenic substances such as psilocybin, mescaline, and LSD. Based on Leary's own readings in Tibetan Buddhism and his professional training in psychology, the book was an explicit call for a revolution in consciousness. Leary believed that without this revolution, the Cold War trajectory of nuclear stand off between the superpowers would result in the destruction of civilization. Heedful perhaps of Ginsberg's meeting with the Dalai Lama and his admonition that the central problem was ego, Leary devoted a substantial portion of his manual to the explicit discussion of how to overcome it.

Ginsberg's interest in LSD predated Leary. He first experimented with the psychoactive substance in a controlled setting at Stanford University's Mental Research Institute in the spring of 1959, as a volunteer test subject. Ginsberg met Leary the following year at a psychiatry conference and, under Leary's guidance, tried psilocybin mushrooms. These were scientific research sessions. Leary was not yet advocating the general use of hallucinogens.

Leary's fascination with Tibet included the legendary powers of the country's adepts to levitate and perform other magical feats. When he learned about the group of Tibetans Ken Knaus had brought to Cornell University, he made a trip to the campus in Ithaca, New York, to meet them. Leary commandeered an auditorium and performed what he thought were Tibetan rituals, accompanied by drumming. According to Knaus, Leary's audience was mystified. They hadn't seen anything like it in Tibet. Leary asked whether any of them witnessed an adept vanish from one spot and materialize in another. None had.

The publication of *The Psychedelic Experience* transformed Leary from an academic to a political activist. In writing the book, Leary relied heavily on his interpretation of Lama Govinda's commentaries on the *Tibetan Book of the Dead*, published by Oxford University Press in 1959, combined with insights from the European schools of psychoanalysis He believed his psychedelic manual could—combined with the use of what he termed "visionary chemicals"—speed the process of spiritual enlightenment. To Leary, LSD and magic mushrooms promised liberation at a time which he warned was a critical moment in human history.

THE PSYCHEDELIC MOVEMENT

This was the start of the psychedelic movement. It began as a search for the liberation of consciousness and personal enlightenment, goals also shared by Tibetan Buddhism. Before the sixties were over it would metamorphose into a mass movement with profound social and political ramifications that also applied to Tibet.

The psychedelic movement was about to run head on into the baby boomers, the largest demographic cohort of young Americans ever in history. While most baby boomers never truly became hippies and only a tiny fraction actually sought enlightenment through LSD, mind-expanding, counterculture values would prove infectious to the entire generation. The baby boomers' embrace of the counterculture ethos made the fringe psychedelic movement go global and, with it, however imperfectly understood, a glimmering of awareness of Tibetan Buddhism. As the social and economic impact of the baby boomers increasingly permeated popular culture, the late 1960s and 1970s introduced Buddhism to the West on a mass basis.

GINSBERG BECOMES A POLITICAL ACTIVIST

In 1965, Allen Ginsberg set out on a jaunt to Cuba. In Havana, he found himself in trouble when it was reported that he thought Fidel Castro was "cute" and speculated that his brother Raul was gay. The Cubans decided that Ginsberg lacked the proper respect due to revolutionary authority and packed him on a plane to Prague, where he went to work dictating poetry. Using a tape recorder he bought with $600 that Bob Dylan fronted him for the trip, Ginsberg narrated a poem, *Wichita Vortex Sutra*, calling for an end to the Vietnam War.

From Prague, Ginsberg made a brief trip to Russia, where he met poet Yevgeny Yevtuchenko. He arrived back in Prague just before the May Day celebrations and was crowned the "King of May" when Czech poet Joseph Skyvorecky became ill and asked him to stand in at the popular street festival. A crowd of more than 100,000 young Czechs lauded the Beatnik poet. Czech authorities weren't so benign. After checking into the suspicious foreigner, they used the pretext of his journal entries to expel him from the country as an unwanted cultural subversive.

Next Ginsberg landed in London, where Bob Dylan was about to perform at the Royal Albert Hall. Together, they collaborated on producing a short film that is arguably the world's first music video. After the 1965 Albert Hall performance, Ginsberg and Dylan partied with the Beatles, who had not yet reached the heights of their musical careers.

A month after Dylan's gig at the Albert Hall, Ginsberg organized a read-in of poets at the same venue. Before an audience of 7000, the leading lights of the Beat Generation, including Lawrence Ferlinghetti and William Burroughs, read aloud. A few weeks after this literary feat, Ginsberg returned to the United States, where, he discovered, the FBI had taken a sudden interest in him.

That fall, Ginsberg began organizing peace protests. During a protest in October, members of the Hells Angels motorcycle gang began disrupting a march against the Vietnam War. The police stood by and refused to interfere. Using a microphone, Ginsberg began chanting "Om" to the Hells Angels and their mood changed. Instead of harassing the marchers, they joined the peace protest. Instead of composing poems, Ginsberg put together a detailed pamphlet on how to organize successful, nonviolent peace protests that avoided confrontations with the police.

At the start of 1967, poetry and rock music fused in New York at the "Human Be-In." It was a combined event featuring musical artists like The Jefferson Airplane and The Grateful Dead with poetry readings by Ginsberg, Ferlinghetti, and Gary Snyder. Timothy Leary spoke about expanding the frontiers of consciousness, and activist Jerry Rubin talked of political and social transformation.

The youth revolution was going global.

In London in 1967, British stalwarts of the Socialist Workers Party hawked copies of Mao's little Red Book while 100,000 people marched in the streets calling for a ban on the submarine-launched Polaris missile, the latest technological innovation in the U.S. nuclear arsenal. In France the following year, a massive student uprising in the streets of Paris nearly toppled the government of President Charles De Gaulle.

To the West, in America, 1967 was the Summer of Love. From Big Sur to San Francisco, the California coastline drew waves of hippies and youthful wanderers from across the country and around the world. The physical epicenter of the youth revolution was the corner of Haight and Ashbury Streets in San Francisco, but its metaphysical epicenter was the Beatnik movement and its evolution into the psychedelic revolution. Allen Ginsberg and Jack Kerouac had been foremost among the Beatniks in seeking to infuse Buddhism into the growing exploration of alternative consciousness, their efforts carried forward by others like the novelist Ken Kesey and his Merry Pranksters and Timothy Leary. Happenings, acid tests, love-ins, teach-ins, and rock music festivals that lasted for days and attracted crowds of thousands combined with transcendental meditation, psychedelic drugs, marijuana, and Buddhist teachings to create the catechism of the counterculture.

THE TIBETAN CAUSE LOSES FITZGERALD

In July, 1967, as the crowds gathered at Haight Ashbury, across the continent in rural Virginia, Desmond FitzGerald stepped onto a tennis court for a set of doubles with British Ambassador Patrick Dean and his wife. FitzGerald's 200-year-old country home was in the quaint town of The Plains, in the heart of Virginia's horse country, set among rock walls and miles of white fences bounding green hills and grassy pastures. Here FitzGerald savored rare personal time with his family, although he wasn't beyond bringing work with him. Admittedly, the work might include exotic new weapons to test, such as combined rifles and grenade launchers.

Ambassador Dean felt right at home in this horse-and-hounds setting, spotted with historic inns and handsome stone houses predating the American Revolution, except for the weather. It was nearly 100 degrees when FitzGerald and his wife Barbara squared off with Sir Patrick and his spouse. FitzGerald was swinging his racquet when he felt as if someone kicked him squarely in the chest. It was a heart attack. The architect of the CIA's support for the Tibetan National Uprising and the resistance fell onto the hot court, dying.

TIME magazine ran his obituary in its August 4th issue.

FitzGerald's star had still been on the rise inside the CIA. He might have moved on to Director of Central Intelligence. Howard Bane counted his death a personal setback. He had lost a valuable mentor, a man with whom he shared the adventure of a lifetime in the Tibetan operation. President Lyndon Baines Johnson awarded FitzGerald the National Service Medal. Bobby Kennedy, whose candidacy in the upcoming 1968 presidential campaign would help push Johnson into taking himself out of the running for reelection, attended the posthumous ceremony for his longtime friend.

For the Tibetans, FitzGerald's sudden death was a gloomy omen that foreshadowed the end of an era. They had lost one of their staunchest allies in the struggle against the Chinese, an individual who was as deeply repulsed by everything that Chairman Mao's China represented as if he himself was a victim of Chinese repression.

The ground in Washington was shifting. President Kennedy had decided early in his short tenure in office that the People's Republic of China was a fact to be lived with and that hopes for the revolutionary regime's collapse were fantasies. The Johnson Administration inherited this policy framework after Kennedy's assassination in 1963.

By the time of FitzGerald's death, Johnson's presidency had become consumed by the Vietnam War. President Johnson was fighting a war he knew could not be won but from which he had no idea how to disentangle himself. His policy options exhausted, Johnson withdrew from a bid for a second term in office, leaving it to the next president to find a way out of the Vietnam quagmire. Meanwhile, the death toll soared in the mountains and rice paddies of Vietnam.

The Vietnam War politicized the psychedelic movement, creating a generation of political activists who would later become the main source of Tibet's support. Without the movement, the struggle to free Tibet would have ended a few years after Desmond FitzGerald's death. The Tibetan government-in-exile was about to face its worst existential crisis since the 1950 Chinese invasion.

Chapter 11

Nixon Embraces China

1968 was a pivotal year for the movement to free Tibet, and the reason was the American presidential campaign. Eight years earlier, then-President Eisenhower had confidently told CIA Director Dulles and Desmond FitzGerald that Nixon would be certain to keep up the Tibetan operation if he won the presidency in 1960. But Nixon lost to Kennedy and, by the time he ran for president in 1968 as the Republican nominee, Vietnam had changed his outlook.

In the United States, antiwar protestors marched in the streets by the thousands, chanting refrains like "all we are saying is give peace a chance." They defied authorities by staging rallies to burn draft cards, which were mandatory for all males over the age of eighteen. To mutilate or destroy a draft card or to fail to register for the draft was a criminal offense. In October 1967, the largest war protest to date took place when tens of thousands of marchers converged on the Pentagon. The centerpiece of the protest was a "Pentagon Exorcism," written by Allen Ginsberg, and read to the assemblage by Tuli Kupferbug and Ed Sanders of The Fugs, a popular rock band.

Ginsberg was not in attendance. He had journeyed to Wales from London in the summer of 1967, where he dropped acid and wrote the poem *Wales Visitation* before traveling on to Italy for a long-anticipated meeting with the poet Ezra Pound. Shortly after Ginsberg's return to the

United States, a few months after the Pentagon Exorcism, he was arrested along with Dr. Benjamin Spock and several hundred others at an antiwar rally in New York. It was Ginsberg's first arrest for protesting the Vietnam War.

In 1968, political activist Abbie Hoffman decided to organize a "Festival of Life" to coincide with the Democratic National Convention in Chicago, under the banner of the Youth International Party. The Yippies, as they quickly became known, shared many of the tenets of the counterculture. Ginsberg was invited to the event and, although he had reservations about the prospects for avoiding confrontation, decided to attend along with his friend Jerry Rubin.

In late August, demonstrators gathered in Chicago by the thousands, including luminaries like author Norman Mailer, only to discover that Democratic Mayor Richard Daley refused to grant a permit for the Festival of Life. Daley was determined not to let the Yippies disrupt the Democratic Party convention. Young voters had been energized by Robert Kennedy's primary campaign, but his candidacy was cut short by assassin Sirhan Sirhan in early summer. Democratic Senator Eugene McCarthy was a favorite of the antiwar protestors, but incumbent President Lyndon Johnson wanted the nomination to go to his Vice-President Hubert Humphrey. Daley was loyal to Johnson and believed it was his partisan duty to keep the antiwar protestors under control.

The Mayor's decision to withhold a permit for the Yippie festival didn't stop it from happening. But, without permission, the event was an illegal gathering and gave the Chicago police a pretext for breaking up any protest rallies taking place during the week-long Democratic Convention. What happened next was later deemed by an investigative commission to have been a "police riot." In an orgy of violence, the Chicago cops viciously attacked the peaceful demonstrators. No one was immune. Journalists were beaten, as were Hippies and Yippies and students and, frequently, innocent bystanders whose only offense was to witness the brutality. On the morning after the worst of the police brutality, Ginsberg once again chanted "Om" over a loudspeaker for seven hours to calm the shaken protestors.

The Chicago bloodshed backfired. Instead of the smooth convention Daley wanted, televised images of the violence in Chicago only further undermined the Johnson Administration and Democratic Party. No event had so radicalized American youth and the counterculture as the police riot. Mayor Daley's determination to block protests alienated the youth vote from Democratic nominee Humphrey and Republican challenger Richard Nixon narrowly won the presidency in the fall of 1968.

In his victory speech, Nixon told a heartwarming story about seeing a little girl in Deshler, Ohio, toward the end of the campaign, with a sign that said, "Bring Us Together Again." The *New York Times* reported that the girl originally bore a more prosaic placard that said, "LBJ convinced us—vote Republican." But, the *Times* said, she lost it and then found the unifying slogan—"Bring us together again"—lying on the ground. It's a cute tale, but the truth is that the sign was given to her by Steve Bull, one of Nixon's campaign advance men, so that the photo could be staged for the press.

Nixon inherited the Vietnam War from the Johnson Administration. The war had destroyed Johnson's presidency, limiting LBJ to one term in office that ended in political disgrace. Nixon was determined not to let Vietnam destroy his presidential legacy.

From the start of his presidency in January 1969, Nixon knew he had to find a way to end the Vietnam War. In his book, *The Real War*, written after he had left the White House, Nixon revealed that he thought it had been a mistake to give the Pentagon control over the Vietnam War in the first place. In his view, written with the benefit of hindsight, Nixon said the CIA had a much better feel for the nuances of fighting a guerrilla war than the military. But it was far too late, by 1969, to salvage the failed military strategy.

Instead, Nixon pursued a diplomatic solution. The key, he believed, was to induce the Soviet Union into wanting the war to end. In February of 1969, as a first order of business, Nixon asked National Security Advisor Henry Kissinger to circulate the rumor among the USSR's Eastern European satellite states that America was exploring a way to engage China. Nixon believed that the fear of a U.S.-Sino rapprochement would prompt the Soviets to curb aid for the war before the United States could establish diplomatic relations with its archrival.

Nixon had given a hint of his intent to engage China in a 1967 article in *Foreign Affairs*. He wrote that "we simply cannot afford to leave China forever outside the family of nations, there to nurture its fantasies, cherish its hates, and threaten its neighbors. There is no place on this small planet for a billion of its potentially most able people to live in angry isolation."

The article drew little attention. Published in the run-up to the 1968 Republican presidential primaries, it was a clear indication of Nixon's plans. However, for a Republican candidate to embrace Maoist China would have opened up Nixon to charges of being soft on communism. Had he been more explicit about his goal of establishing relations with China, he would have risked a primary campaign controversy that could have cost him the Republican nomination.

Even as president, it was risky for Nixon to declare his intentions openly. He had no way of knowing in advance whether the Chinese leadership would welcome or rebuff his overtures. American policy was to back the claim of the Nationalists on the island of Taiwan as the legitimate government of China. They had supporters in the Senate and the House who would try to stifle any initiative to engage the PRC. For an opening to China to stand any chance of success, Nixon had to explore its potential in absolute secrecy. The only man he fully trusted for this delicate undertaking was Henry Kissinger, the Special Assistant to the President for National Security Affairs. By keeping the initiative inside the White House, Nixon minimized the chance that damaging leaks from the State Department or CIA would generate political opposition.

KISSINGER ORDERS A REVIEW
OF CHINA POLICY

Kissinger seized on Nixon's directive to reassess U.S. policy toward China across the board. America's support for the Nationalist Chinese government on Taiwan was one obstacle, but there were other factors to be considered, such as regional relations with India, and, by extension, with its adversary, Pakistan. One of the most longstanding obstacles, however, was the fundamental question of whether the Soviet Union and China were truly antagonistic.

Nixon's belief that the USSR would cooperate in ending the Vietnam War if the United States engaged China depended on whether the two countries were enemies. Reports of the Sino-Soviet rift had been reviewed by Western intelligence agencies since the late 1950s. Inside the CIA, the question of whether the rift was real or an elaborate deception had been unresolved for years.

James Jesus Angleton was one of the principal advocates of the theory that the Sino-Soviet rift was nothing more than a deception operation—disinformation—designed to lure the West off base. Angleton's theory was that International Communism was monolithic and tightly controlled by Moscow. False schisms were created and fobbed off on Western intelligence agencies by double agents to diminish the true threat posed by a unified Communism.

Within the CIA, Angleton had legendary status as a counterintelligence officer. His pedigree in spying was familial; Angleton's father had been a Lieutenant Colonel in the wartime OSS, the CIA's precursor agency. After a childhood spent in Italy, Angleton was educated at Harvard and Yale, where he edited an avant-garde poetry magazine with Ezra Pound and e.e. cummings. A tall man of refined habits who favored bourbon, branch water, and fine cuisine, Angleton chain smoked on the job. His main outdoor hobby was fly-fishing, where he limbered up what otherwise appeared to be perpetually stooped shoulders, rounded perhaps from bearing decades of secrets and intrigue.

Angleton's determination to prove that the Sino-Soviet fissure was an illusion was dogged. Anatoliy Golitsyn, an important but controversial Soviet defector, had persuaded him of the truth of the theory. Armed with information Golitsyn provided after debriefings in 1962, Angleton marched straight to the Eisenhower Executive Office Building in the White House compound. There he briefed a panel called the President's Foreign Intelligence Advisory Board (PFIAB) on the phony nature of the Russian-Chinese split. The PFIAB members were alternately spellbound and mystified to learn that what they believed to be one of the most significant developments concerning International Communism was a hoax. Several called CIA Director McCone to ask why they hadn't been briefed earlier about this vital intelligence assessment, only to be told that it was just one of Angleton's pet theories.

Ironically, the Tibetan resistance had captured secret Chinese documents that helped prove the veracity of the Sino-Soviet rift. The reports from the Chinese commander's bloody satchel showed the limited extent of cooperation between Moscow and Beijing. Still, Angleton clung to his theory. Then, in March 1969 the USSR and the PRC clashed. Combat was isolated to the border between the two countries, but it was significant enough to put China on a state of high alert.

The previous fall, Chinese Defense Minister Lin Biao had warned of the danger of nuclear war. Alarmed by the Soviet invasion of Czechoslovakia in the summer of 1968, China's leaders feared conflict between the USSR and China would be next. Directive Number One, issued in October 1968, put China on a war footing. It required a massive civil defense effort, including building underground tunnels and air raid shelters in every city able to withstand nuclear attack. If this was a deception, it was very elaborate. To all but Angleton, the question of whether the rift was real was put to rest by the border fighting.

KISSINGER REMOVES OBSTACLES
TO U.S.-CHINA RAPPROCHEMENT

Using files from the 5412 Special Group and evaluations on the program from the CIA, Kissinger reviewed the effectiveness of the Tibet operation. The Dalai Lama's government-in-exile was getting a stipend of $15,000 a month and the 5412 Special Group had earmarked another $1.5 million for the Tibetan resistance fighters. The 1800 rebels at Mustang, divided and quibbling, were of dubious value either for guerrilla warfare or intelligence collection. Without a clear purpose, instead of being an intelligence asset they had become a liability. To Kissinger, the Tibetan operation had the potential to derail any diplomatic initiative with China, just as the shooting down of Francis Gary Powers' U-2 over Russia had derailed Eisenhower's plans for a comprehensive nuclear test ban.

Kissinger was a believer in "great power" diplomacy and the fate of Tibet held little interest for him compared to the advantages to be gained by playing Russia against China. Moreover, Nixon had given him his marching orders to engage China as a way of ending the Vietnam War. Both Kissinger and Nixon believed that ending the war was critical to the success of Nixon's presidency. Whether or not they stayed in power depended on finding a way out of the Vietnam quagmire.

KISSINGER CUTS OFF
THE TIBETAN RESISTANCE

Soon after Kissinger's review got underway in early 1969, Gyalo Thondup was told that the CIA was winding down its support for the resistance fighters. There would be a three-year transition period to settle the fighters outside Mustang and reintegrate them into civilian life. After that, funds for Mustang would be cut off entirely.

Gyalo felt betrayed. He had been personally involved in recruiting Tibetan fighters starting with the first group trained on Saipan. He had visited trainees at The Ranch and The Farm to monitor the progress of the young recruits. He became the public face of the struggle in New York and London and Geneva, making appearances before diplomats, journalists, and dignitaries, such as Eleanor Roosevelt.

Gyalo liked and trusted the CIA officers he worked with. For more than a decade, at personal peril, he had put his services and those of his friend, Lhamo Tsering, at the disposal of the Agency. He and Desmond FitzGerald bonded closely. In the face of opposition from Ambassador Galbraith, Howard Bane and Gyalo became joint allies in the struggle to keep the resistance alive. But with FitzGerald dead, and Bane on a new assignment, the resistance no longer had strong champions within the Agency. No one at the CIA fought hard to keep the rebel base at Mustang.

Without Gyalo's assurance that the United States was a reliable ally, the Tibetans might have chosen a different course than armed resistance. Now he felt as if the rug had been pulled out from under him. The sudden reversal of policy had the inevitable effect of raising doubts among the community of Tibetan exiles about the soundness of Gyalo's judgment. His personal effectiveness compromised, he turned over the delicate matter of winding down the Mustang base to Lhamo Tsering and withdrew from Tibetan political causes, at least temporarily.

Mustang was not an isolated case. Other Far East Division operations and intelligence activities were also put on ice. One CIA officer operating under non-official cover in Japan at the time recalls widespread mystification among his colleagues over the sudden halt to activities targeting the Chinese. No explanation was given for the suspension of intelligence activities. Kissinger was minimizing risks of any embarrassing incident that might upset the delicate path toward normalizing relations with Beijing, even a CIA attempt to recruit a Chinese spy.

The CIA officers involved in the day-to-day Tibet operations had no idea that Henry Kissinger was laying the foundation for the restoration of diplomatic relations between the United States and China. In fact, no one—not even at the very highest echelons of the Agency—was aware that Nixon and Kissinger were planning a U.S.-Sino rapprochement. The two were notoriously secretive, and Nixon himself had a paranoid streak. He obsessed over leaks and enemies and did not trust anyone outside of a tight circle of White House loyalists.

Counterintelligence chief James Angleton guessed that something was up. To Angleton, Kissinger's activities raised suspicion. He thought Kissinger might be a Soviet mole. Angleton asked his prized Soviet defector whether Kissinger fit the profile of a KGB spy. Golitsyn reinforced his fears that Kissinger could indeed be a Soviet deep-cover agent. Angleton instructed the CIA's Counterintelligence staff to open an investigation of the Special Assistant to the President for National Security Affairs.

SECRET COMMUNIQUES WITH CHINA

Kissinger was justified in fearing that if the CIA found out about Nixon's intentions toward China opponents like Angleton might try to strangle the fledgling diplomatic initiative. In the utmost secrecy, Kissinger began putting out feelers and leaving diplomatic hints among governments with good access to Chairman Mao and Zhou En-lai that the United States was ready to talk with China.

Pakistan's president, Yahya Khan, was one such leader who relayed word to China. Pakistan had developed close ties with China to offset its regional rival, India, and Khan was a willing conduit for the United States. Another go-between who forwarded the back-channel diplomatic messages from President Nixon to Beijing was Nicolae Ceausescu, the quixotic dictator who ruled Romania under his personal brand of Marxism.

Zhou En-lai was the first among China's leadership to grasp the seriousness of these diplomatic feints. Despite the continuing friction created by China's support for North Vietnam in the ongoing Vietnam War (or perhaps because by 1970 the cost to China of supporting the war effort had reached an all-time high), China was receptive. Both sides agreed to hold preliminary talks in Warsaw, Poland.

But Kissinger's fears of a disruptive incident came true. In 1970, a coup attempt was made against Prince Norodom Sihanouk in Cambodia. Sihanouk was closely allied with China, and the failed putsch strained the atmosphere. The talks, which were scheduled for May, were postponed because of China's view that they were "inappropriate at this time."

In November, Zhou sent a message to Kissinger via the U.S. Ambassador to Pakistan. Zhou, Kissinger was told orally, welcomed "an emissary from Washington" to talk about Taiwan. Zhou En-lai received in return a typed reply on plain paper bearing no official designation or watermark to identify it, saying a discussion should be broader than Taiwan's future and ought to extend to the general improvement of relations and an easing of tensions between the United States and China.

This was a tectonic policy shift. Kissinger followed it by stating that as tensions lessened, the United States anticipated reducing its military forces in Asia. This was an unmistakable signal to China of linkage between the reestablishment of relations and an end to the Vietnam War. Kissinger undertook this initiative without the involvement of the U.S. foreign policy bureaucracy or Congress. The document delivered to the Chinese bore no traces of official U.S. origins, precisely so that Nixon and Kissinger could deny its existence if needed.

This was the ultimate covert operation, conducted so secretly that not even the CIA and the FBI were aware of it. Angleton had at his disposal the CIA's Counterintelligence staff to scrutinize Kissinger's movements, but the crafty National Security Advisor eluded him as well.

Flush with anticipation over the impending diplomatic breakthrough, Nixon and Kissinger spoke by telephone about who would make a suitable presidential envoy to lead the U.S. delegation. The first contender they discussed was George H.W. Bush. The call, secretly recorded by Nixon, was declassified in 2001:

Nixon: "How about Bush?"

Kissinger: "Absolutely not, he is too soft and not sophisticated enough."

Nixon: "I thought of that myself."

Kissinger: "I thought about (Elliott) Richardson, but he wouldn't be the right thing."

Nixon: ". . . Nelson (Rockefeller)—the Chinese would consider him important and he would be—could do a lot for us in terms of the domestic situation. No, Nelson is a wild hair running around."

Kissinger: "I think for one operation I could keep him under control. To them a Rockefeller is a tremendous thing."

Nixon: "Sure. Well, keep it in the back of your head."

Kissinger: "Bush would be too weak."

Nixon: "I thought so too but I was trying to think of somebody with a title."

Later in the call Kissinger and Nixon make it plain that the driving factor in establishing relations with China was to end the Vietnam War:

Nixon: "Put Nelson in the back of your head. What did (Alexander) Haig think about this?"

Kissinger: "He thinks it is a great diplomatic move and if we play it coolly and toughly as we have until now, we can settle everything."

Nixon: "He said that."

Kissinger: "Mr. President, I have not said this before but I think if we get this thing working, we will end Vietnam this year."

Nixon and Kissinger relished in their planned coup's impact on domestic political opponents:

Kissinger: "We are beginning to hold the cards."

Nixon: "That's true but we are going to hold it. The demonstrators may overplay their hand."

Kissinger: "John Chancellor, whom I had lunch with today, thinks the tide has turned."

Nixon: "What turned it?"

Kissinger: "He thinks what happened this week has ruined them."

Nixon had claimed to have a secret plan to end the war in Vietnam, and the news anchorman apparently believed the contacts with China had not only vindicated Nixon's claim but also left the antiwar movement with little to protest.

Nixon: "John Chancellor . . ."

Kissinger: "Absolutely. He doesn't know exactly what you have up your sleeve but. . . ."

Nixon: "I am not saying anything about China except that the proposals are at a very sensitive stage and I don't intend to comment on the future and next question, gentlemen."

Kissinger: "Right."

Nixon: "I don't want to get into the proposal of a two-China policy, UN membership, Taiwan *and so forth. [Italics added]* I am going to finesse all questions by saying developments here are significant, and I don't think the interests of the nation will be served by commenting on it further."

Kissinger: "I think that would be the best position to take, Mr. President."

If Tibet was a factor at all in Nixon's thinking, it was relegated to that category of "and so forth." Next, Kissinger and Nixon exulted in the fact that not even the Cambodian coup against Sihanouk had derailed their initiative.

Kissinger: "If anyone had predicted that two months ago, we would have thought it was inconceivable."

Nixon: "Yeah, yeah. After Laos. . ."

Kissinger: "After Cambodia, the same thing. . ."

Nixon: "Yeah. But look at after Laos, the people over two-to-one thought it had failed and yet here comes the Chinese move, the Ping Pong team and something more significant that pales that into nothing."

And there were self-congratulations.

Nixon: "Henry, it wouldn't have happened if you hadn't stuck to your guns. We played a game, and we got a little break. It was done skillfully and now we will wait a couple of weeks."

Kissinger: "We have done it now. . ."

And so, on July 9, 1971, Kissinger and a crew of American diplomats boarded an aircraft at a base in Pakistan and flew to Beijing for a secret meeting with Zhou En-lai and his circle of advisers.

The Chinese were initially put off by what they perceived as Kissinger's arrogance. The former Harvard professor had begun his dialog with a learned presentation that struck the Chinese as a philosophy lecture. Zhou En-lai is credited with turning the conversation to practical matters. By the end of the visit both sides had agreed to issue a communiqué on July 15 summarizing the objective of the talks.

On the appointed date, Nixon parted the veils of secrecy and stunned the nation with his announcement of talks with China, but what followed truly strained credulity. Nixon said he planned to pursue the dialog by visiting China in the coming year. The presidential trip was scheduled for February 1972.

NIXON COURTS CHAIRMAN MAO

To make arrangements for an official visit, the White House Office of Presidential Advance sends out staffers skilled at planning presidential events and schedules. The teams are composed of White House staff and press advance, Secret Service advance, and representatives of the White House Communications Agency, who are drawn from the various branches of the armed services. Collectively called the advance team, this group must develop the detailed, minute-by-minute plans for the President's activities and movements in coordination with the foreign host government.

Nixon's advance men worked tirelessly, but one troubling problem persisted. After spending time in Beijing, a number of the team felt as if

Chinese hospitality was chafing their backsides, literally. Several had developed an irritating rash on their hindquarters after using Chinese toilets. The seats were lacquer-coated wood, and the team concluded that something in the lacquer was irritating their skin.

While this was inconvenient for the advance team, it wouldn't do at all to let the President's posterior become aggravated. The problem was how to politely convey this delicate matter to the Chinese government. After deliberating, they decided the most diplomatic way to raise the problem with their Chinese counterparts was to rely on the eavesdropping bugs they knew the Chinese had planted in their hotel conference room.

At exaggerated length, the advance men discussed their dilemma and ways to avoid irritating Nixon's bottom. The next day, when they returned to their hotel rooms after the maid service, each toilet had a lace doily covering the seat. The Chinese had gotten the message. The way was now clear to a smooth presidential visit.

Nixon was elated by the 1972 trip. Although he found Mao Zedong "enfeebled by age and ill health," in Nixon's view he was "sharp and there was no question that he was in command."

The breakthrough was viewed as a bold act of statesmanship. After isolating "Red China" for two decades, Nixon was praised for courageously overcoming political resistance from the right wing of the Republican Party to bring about the historic rapprochement with Beijing.

Nixon saw no essential differences between the United States and China. "The hostilities between China and the United States in the 1949–1972 period," he wrote later, "were the result of politics, not personality; they stemmed from a clash of national interests, not national cultures. Therefore, as policies changed and interests shifted, hostility could more readily be replaced by respect, cordiality, even friendship."

Best of all, from Nixon's vantage, was that this budding friendship between Washington and Beijing came in 1972 during his presidential reelection campaign.

"It was an election year," Nixon wrote in 1980, "and I wanted the political credit for what I believed were genuine advances toward a stable peace."

But despite his diplomatic and political coups, Nixon couldn't bury the paranoia. That same year CREEP—the Committee to Reelect the President—sent a team of former spies and political operatives to bug the

Democratic National Committee headquarters at the Watergate Hotel. An alert night watchman noticed tape covering the locking mechanism to a door that the Watergate burglars had picked and called the police. Nixon hadn't yet won the reelection campaign, but the seeds that would destroy his presidency had been sown.

THE TIBETAN RESISTANCE
GOES OUT FIGHTING

In 1968, a young man with a bright future, Lhasang Tsering, read a stirring article in *Reader's Digest*. The piece, "Raid Into Tibet," told of the exploits of the Tibetan resistance in Mustang and a cross-border foray against the Chinese.

Born in Tibet, Lhasang grew to maturity as an exile in India. He was an able student and his teachers nurtured his education. In the late 1960s, a handful of international organizations made funding for scholarships available. The Tibetans selected their best and brightest to pursue higher education in Indian universities and, for the lucky few, to study abroad.

Lhasang was offered a coveted scholarship to study medicine in the United States. The Tibetan exiles badly needed skilled people, and the scholarship was his ticket to a highly respected and financially secure position within his community. More importantly, from his Buddhist perspective, he knew it was a way that he could be of valuable service to his people. He was poised to take up his studies when he stumbled across the article in *Reader's Digest*.

At that moment, he realized that his course of study wasn't right for him. His *karma* was to join the fight for Tibet's independence. He passed on the scholarship and set out for Mustang to join the Tibetan resistance and fight for the liberation of his country, unaware that international currents swirling around him would short circuit his ambitions and put the cause of Tibetan freedom in its greatest peril since the Chinese invasion.

Lhasang Tsering had barely arrived in Mustang when Gyalo got word from the CIA that the resistance was to be demobilized. Neither Tsering, nor anyone else at Mustang, had been informed of the CIA decision to cut their funding. Baba Yeshe, the monk from Eastern Tibet, still refused to give up command. Other Tibetans compared him to a warlord. He was accused of misappropriating money intended for the base, especially after he began building up a collection of rare artworks and antiques from Tibetan refugees fleeing the Chinese. Some said he fleeced the refugees, others that he was an extortionist who took their valuables and religious heirlooms in exchange for safe passage.

Wangdu, one of the original CIA trainees from 1957, was sent to Mustang to wrest command from Baba Yeshe as gracefully as possible. Called Walt by the Americans, Wandgu was a nephew of Gompo Tashi Andrugstang, the now-deceased founder of the original *Chushi Gangdruk* resistance. Wangdu had combat experience inside Tibet. He was dedicated and loyal. If anyone could turn things around at Mustang, it was Wandgu.

To help ease the transition, Baba Yeshe was ordered to Dharamsala for a meeting with the *Kashag*, the Cabinet of the Tibetan government-in-exile. He was thanked for his service and asked to retire and accept the rank of deputy *Kashag* minister. This diplomatic solution might have worked except that Baba Yeshe found an excuse to slip back to Mustang, where he resumed his command and old tricks. With no missions to undertake, but with plenty of weapons, the men divided into separate factions under Baba Yeshe and Wandgu.

In 1971, the CIA convened a meeting of the resistance leadership in New Delhi. It was at this meeting that Wangdu first learned that his force was to be disbanded and that CIA support for the resistance was ending. Gyalo Thondup and Lhamo Tsering were in attendance to help cushion the blow, but just as Gyalo had taken it as a betrayal when he learned funding was being cut off, so did Wangdu now. He pleaded for more time to demonstrate the merit of the Mustang force, but to no effect. Gyalo maintains that the CIA officers at the New Delhi meeting explained the reasons for the cut off in funding as the price Nixon agreed to pay in exchange for reestablishing relations with China. By 1971, of course, with Nixon and Kissinger's secret diplomacy out of the bag, anyone could see the cause-and-effect relationship. It may have made it easier for CIA officers to explain their government's actions by depicting it as a precondition imposed by the Chinese, but the opposite is true.

The Nixon Administration chose to abandon the Tibetans in order to build ties with China. The Chinese leadership didn't have to insist on anything with regard to Mustang and the Dalai Lama. The decision to cut off aid to the Tibetans was taken unilaterally by President Nixon and Dr. Kissinger.

The Sino-Soviet rift had undercut the logic of Eisenhower's National Security Directive 5412/2. Signed by the president 16 years earlier, the premise of the document was that monolithic communism— "International Communism" was the phrase used in 5412/2—was a global danger that had to be opposed by the United States using covert means. But, if the USSR and China were not working together and, in fact, had become adversaries, then 5412/2 reflected an outdated world view. By 1971, reality contradicted the directive and it was time for a new foreign policy. So thought Nixon and Kissinger, and they acted on their views.

Lhamo Tsering had the unenviable task of overseeing the demobilization of the fighters. The initial plan envisioned moving 500 fighters annually out of Mustang and into other occupations. After three years, that would leave a token force of 300 men, under Indian control, as a kind of rapid response force in the event of new hostilities between China and India in the Himalayas. The plan fell apart when the faction of resistance fighters loyal to Baba Yeshe refused to cooperate.

The majority of the Mustang fighters sided with Wangdu. At a Tibetan New Year's Day celebration, a fighter loyal to Baba Yeshe threatened Wangdu and was arrested. When Baba Yeshe's men tried to rescue their comrade there was a fight and several were killed. Next, a trio of couriers carrying CIA cash to Wangdu were ambushed by Baba Yeshe's fighters. One was killed, but Baba Yeshe failed to get his hands on the money.

In Dharamsala, news of the fighting at Mustang created a fierce controversy within the Tibetan government-in-exile. What had begun as a force to be used against the Chinese had degenerated into Tibetan killing Tibetan for no clear cause. The *Kashag* decided to adjudicate the matter, but each time a date was set for hearings before the cabinet, Baba Yeshe simply refused to appear.

In 1972, King Mahendra of Nepal died. His policy toward the Tibetan fighters in the neighboring kingdom of Mustang had been one of benign neglect, at least so long as the CIA station in Katmandu kept him on the payroll. Even when the Tibetan fighters created trouble for their neighbors by pillaging or looting livestock, Mahendra downplayed the incidents.

His successor, Prince Birendra, took note of Nixon's trip to China. If the United States was cozying up to Mao, it made sense for Nepal to follow suit. In 1973, King Birendra demanded the demobilization of the

Mustang fighters and threatened to use the Nepalese army to accomplish the task if the resistance would not disarm and decamp willingly.

The Mustang force could not defeat the Nepalese army. Moreover, thousands of Tibetan refugees had settled in Nepal. If they tried to fight, they might jeopardize the asylum that Nepal had given Tibetans, thereby creating a humanitarian crisis.

To try to defuse the growing crisis before the Nepalese acted unilaterally to clear out Mustang, the Dalai Lama made a tape recording. It was taken to Mustang and played for the resistance fighters. Tenzin Gyatso urged the men to put down their weapons, accept his thanks for their valiant defense of Tibet, and begin new lives. Many of the men wept openly upon hearing the Dalai Lama tell them to cease their resistance.

Some, it is said, committed suicide rather than lay down their arms. CIA officer Howard Bane had been away from the Tibetan operation for years by the time the end came, but he said afterward that he had never heard or seen any CIA reports of suicides at Mustang. However, in his excellent book, *Buddha's Warriors*, author Mikel Dunham recounts an interview with a Tibetan resistance fighter with first-hand knowledge of cases of self-destruction. He reported that some men plummeted to their deaths by jumping off ledges, others used knives. For Buddhists who believed in living their *karma* and who prize human life as the highest form of incarnation short of enlightenment, suicide was rare. But many of the resistance had, in a sense, accepted suicidal odds, while others literally accepted CIA-provided cyanide pills.

Most of the Tibetan fighters heeded the Dalai Lama's call to disband. But some remained and the Nepalese army made good on its threat. Baba Yeshe, perhaps seeing an opportunity to crush his rival Wangdu, guided the Nepalese troops to the Mustang base. At the same time, acting in apparent coordination with the Nepalese, the Chinese moved extra troops to the border between Tibet and Mustang to seal off any escape.

Wangdu tried to break out of the trap. He collected the records for the base and other equipment that might have compromised the CIA's operational methods, taking them and a small band of trusted men with him. They moved south and west across the rugged terrain seeking refuge in India, playing cat and mouse with the Nepalese army as they wound their way by horse down from the Himalayan heights. By August of 1974, only the Tinker-La mountain pass separated Wangdu and his group from safety in India. About a mile from the summit, they took a saddle break.

Wangdu and a few men went over a small crest looking for water for the horses. They rode straight into an ambush. Within minutes, Nepalese sharpshooters had gunned them all down. Some of those who remained on the other side of the crest managed to escape the slaughter and eventually reached India. They reported that Wandgu had charged on horseback into the fusillade of bullets, a warrior to the end. He had been one of the first CIA trainees on Saipan. Now he was one of the last of the CIA trainees to die in combat.

In that same month of August 1974, Richard Nixon, facing an impeachment crisis stemming from the Watergate break in and a clumsy presidential cover up, resigned the presidency in disgrace.

The Agency airlifts dropped a total of 49 trainees from Saipan and Camp Hale into Tibet. Only 12 survived the fighting. Ten managed to evade the Chinese and escape to India after disastrous battles or completing their missions. One man surrendered, and one was captured. The other 37 were killed or died in battles, including some who swallowed cyanide when the odds against them became insurmountable.

The CIA conducted a study on the effectiveness of the Tibetan operation. It was published by the CIA's Center for Intelligence in a classified 1976 edition of its in-house journal, *Studies in Intelligence.* Insiders who have read the document say the Agency concluded that an inadequately supported guerrilla war cannot succeed, but that the operation was not a total loss. The report found that the intelligence collected by the Tibetan resistance fighters, some from wiretaps placed on phone and telegraph lines and some from seized documents, was extremely valuable in helping the United States shape its new policy toward China.

The study is still classified.

For the next 20 years, the Kingdom of Mustang was closed to Westerners to avoid any chance of it being used as a springboard for intelligence activities in Tibet. For a generation it was known as the Forbidden Kingdom of Mustang, a mysterious land that beckoned travelers but remained beyond reach. It took until the 1990s before Westerners could reenter Mustang. When the ban on foreigners was finally lifted, tour operators at the 1997 Adventure Travel Show in Chicago billed Mustang as the closest thing still available to old Tibet, a kingdom of

walled cities where the gates were shut at night against intruders and fero-
cious mastiffs were best kept at bay with a stout staff.

SEVERED LIFELINES, NEW LIFELINES

After the debacle at Mustang, Kissinger dropped another bombshell
on the Tibetans. He had already cut funding for the resistance fighters,
but now he wiped out the annual stipend of approximately $180,000 a
year that supported the Dalai Lama and the Tibetan government-in-exile.
No formal U.S. government decision was taken on this matter; the funding was cut at the verbal directive of Henry Kissinger.

Next on Kissinger's list was the Tibet Office in New York, which
Ernest Gross helped the Tibetans establish. Through sales of Tibetan arts
and crafts, it had the potential to become self-supporting. Kissinger saw it
as an impediment to reaching an agreement with China to open liaison
offices between the two countries. He directed the CIA to instruct Gyalo
Thondup to shutter the office.

Gross was asked to break the news. He and Gyalo met at a Chinese
restaurant on Lexington Avenue. Gyalo heatedly refused to go along.
Bluntly, he told Gross that the United States could put the head of the
Tibet office, Phuntso Thonden, in jail if they wanted, but it would not be
closed down. When Gross relayed the word, Kissinger backed down.

The government of the United States had used the Tibetans for its
own purposes when it believed that Russia and China were allied against
it. Now that the United States was playing China against Russia, it no
longer needed the Tibetans. Unceremoniously, the political establishment washed its hands of the superfluous Tibetans.

Desperately poor India could not be expected to replace the U.S. government's financial assistance to the Tibetan government-in-exile. The
exiles themselves were impoverished and barely able to sustain their existence. If the cause of freedom for Tibet was to survive, support would
have to come from the wealthy countries of the West, where Buddhist
Dharma centers were just taking root thanks to the bohemians, spiritual
seekers, and counterculture personalities who had embraced Tibetan
Buddhism. For Buddhist monks, accustomed by centuries of tradition to
getting their daily sustenance by taking a begging bowl into the streets
and appealing to the people, the way forward was clear.

Chapter 12

Counterculture to the Rescue

Geshe Wangyal introduced America to Tibetan Buddhism. He may literally be considered the father of Tibetan Buddhism in the United States. Wangyal's accomplishment began humbly with the Lamaist Buddhist Monastery of America, the center he established in the old garage at Howell, New Jersey, for the Kalmyk refugees who settled there after World War II. When it later moved to a farm outside Howell, it was renamed the Tibetan Buddhist Learning Center. It was the first Tibetan Buddhist dharma center in the United States.

In many ways, Wangyal was the living link between the often contradictory forces that collected around Tibet's struggle. He was vital to the CIA's role in Tibet, from introducing CIA officers to the Dalai Lama's family to flying to Saipan to train Tibetan resistance fighters. His translation work was crucial to the CIA's ability to communicate with its agents deep inside Tibet. And, from his safe house in Georgetown, he translated the radio broadcasts that kept President Eisenhower informed of the Dalai Lama's daily progress on the trek to India.

Yet he was also an early inspiration to the Beat Buddhists and, later, to the baby boomers. On a personal level, his life was a crossroads between the phase of militant resistance to Chinese domination and the Dalai Lama's path of nonviolence, between the CIA and the counterculture, and between Tibetan Buddhism's historic isolation and its emergence as a global phenomenon. Dharma centers like Wangyal's became the means of introducing Westerners to Tibet's rich culture, sources of fundraising, and bases from which to host travel by Tibetan lamas, including the Dalai Lama. These centers spawned the next generation of leaders in the movement to free Tibet.

FROM DHARMA BUMS TO DHARMA SCHOLARS

The stories of three different Americans—Robert Thurman, Sarah Harding, and David Gardiner—show the way in which Tibetan Buddhism began its diffusion into the West. Their paths were separate, but each became involved in the Tibetan cause after making personal journeys of discovery typical of the counterculture ethos of the 1960s and 1970s.

The First American Tibetan Monk

Twenty-one-year-old Robert Thurman had an existential crisis after being blinded in the left eye while trying to change a tire in the early 1960s. He left behind a young ex-wife, Texas oil heiress Christophe de Menil, and their child and began wandering the world in search of himself. Like Ginsberg, Thurman's knowledge quest took him to India, but his father's death would call him home to New York. Around the time of the funeral, he met Geshe Wangyal.

Thurman was immediately drawn to the Mongolian monk. During his globe trekking, Thurman had searched for a spiritual teacher. Now he was surprised to find the man he thought would fill that role living in New Jersey, literally "just down the road" as Thurman put it, from New York City. In his book *Inner Revolution,* Thurman recounts an overwhelming power and intensity in Wangyal's Buddhist temple on its one-acre plot next to a Russian Orthodox Church, but far more so in the man himself, as if it emanated from within him.

To Thurman's disappointment, Wangyal refused to become his guru. He didn't feel he was the right teacher for the young American. Instead, he told Thurman to start reading Tibetan texts. This was a problem. Thurman couldn't read Tibetan. They made a bargain. In exchange for Thurman teaching some of Wangyal's resident monks English, Thurman could eat at the monastery and Wangyal would teach him to read Tibetan.

Thurman sold his return ticket to India and stayed in New Jersey reading about Tibetan Buddhism.

Gaining knowledge through texts only made Thurman persistent about learning more. Wangyal decided to take him to India to find the right teacher. In 1964, they traveled to Dharamsala, where Wangyal introduced him to the Dalai Lama as a "crazy American boy" with a good heart. Although intrigued by Westerners wanting to learn their religion, the Tibetans also sometimes thought them slightly strange.

Wangyal succeeded in finding a guru for Thurman. He was Khen Losang Dondrub, abbot of Namgyal College, the Dalai Lama's personal monastery. Thurman spent the next year in Dharamsala, studying Buddhist philosophy, Tibetan astrology, medicine, and astronomy. In 1965, he was personally ordained by the Dalai Lama as a Buddhist monk. He was the first American to become a Tibetan monk. He was only 24 years old.

After his return to the United States, Thurman realized the monastic tradition was not his calling. At a party in New York, he met a former magazine model named Nena Birgitte von Schlebrügge. She had been married to Timothy Leary, who had put behind him forever his life as a Harvard professor. Instead, he pursued what he called "the politics of ecstasy" with Ginsberg, advocating the use of LSD by writers and poets and artists so that the experiences and insights of creative minds on psychedelic trips could be infused into the culture as a whole. In their quest for cosmic awareness, Leary and the Beat Buddhists linked Tibetan Buddhism and LSD, although the Tibetans themselves did not use psychedelic drugs in their meditation or religious practices. As they did for Leary and Ginsberg, drugs opened the gateway to Buddhism for many Americans. A 1996 reader survey by *Tricycle*, a respected Buddhist magazine, shows 40% of respondents said LSD or mescaline sparked their interest in Buddhism, while 83% of the practicing Buddhists in the poll said they had used psychedelic drugs.

Thurman fell in love with Nena. They married, and his attention shifted to earning a college degree and then attending graduate school while helping to raise their young family. The couple had two children, the older a boy named Ganden, and the younger a girl, Uma. Wangyal had suggested the boy be named for the future Buddhha, Maitreya. Uma was named for the Indian Mother-Goddess. She would grow up to become an internationally known actress.

When Thurman returned to Dharamsala in 1970 on a graduate research grant, he and von Schlebrügge took the children with them. Thurman was tense about seeing Tenzin Gyatso again after the five-year absence. He felt he had let the Dalai Lama down by becoming an academic instead of a monk. But when three-year-old Ganden clambered unbidden onto his lap and knocked his glasses askew, the Dalai Lama laughed. Thurman knew then their relationship would endure. He explained his ambition to work from American society's equivalent to the monastery, the Ivory Tower of the university, and the Dalai Lama not only gave his blessing to the young couple but offered Thurman advice on his doctoral dissertation.

His research in India finished, Thurman returned to the States to complete his doctorate and begin teaching. His odyssey was part of a broader pattern taking place in lives on both sides of the world, in distant Dharamsala, Southern India, and the Himalayan kingdom of Nepal, as well as in the United States and Europe.

From College Dropout to America's First Woman Lama

Sarah Harding's journey as the first American woman to become a Tibetan Lama began in the ferment of the 1960s. When she was still in high school, Harding became intrigued by Buddhism after reading *The Life of Milarepa*. Then she dated a Tibetan while attending college in Arizona. They talked about her interest in Buddhism, but he never tried to convert her. In fact, he urged her not to change her religion.

At the age of 19 she dropped out of college to travel. With a friend, she headed for Europe, and they journeyed together for a few years. In Italy, her friend was asked to be the lead singer in a rock band. Staying in Italy wasn't Harding's idea of an adventure, so the two friends parted ways.

Harding bought a Volkswagen van and traveled to Turkey, eventually making her way to Nepal. Foreigners were flocking to Katmandu to meet lamas and gurus, and Sarah joined in the scene. She got a job teaching English to the wife of North Korea's ambassador. It covered her living expenses, including the rent on a little hut, and left her time to learn about Buddhism.

She met two teachers, Lama Yeshe and Lama Zopa, who were introducing Tibetan Buddhism to Westerners and went on her first meditation retreat. It lasted a month. Afterward she saw a picture of Kalu Rinpoche. She knew nothing about him, not even where to find him, but felt drawn, as if compelled, to meet him. Kalu Rinpoche was in fact a great meditation master who would later be credited with playing a major role in awakening people the world over to Tibetan Buddhism.

What happened next is almost magical. Sarah left Nepal and set off for Darjeeling, India, by train. When she got off at the station, she ran into a Westerner who off-handedly asked Sarah if she wanted to meet Kalu Rinpoche. She said yes, and the stranger took her to his house.

Sarah knew immediately that Kalu would become her teacher. She realized it was odd, but she felt completely familiar with him even though they had only just met. Kalu Rinpoche assigned a monk to teach her to read and speak Tibetan. The very next day, he had her start practicing language lessons. Every other day, she and six other Westerners crowded into the Master's small bedroom, where he held teachings. For several months, Harding's studies continued this way.

One problem nagged at her, however. Her documents weren't in order. In her passage from Nepal, she neglected to get the proper Indian visa. She was also a woman traveling alone, a risky proposition that drew unwelcome attention. Before long, she found herself under the scrutiny of the Indian security services. Sarah's access to the North Korean ambassador's wife in Nepal, her apparently aimless wandering, and her sudden arrival in Darjeeling, which at the time was a restricted area, invited suspicion. Indian intelligence officers surmised that she worked undercover for the CIA. When she attended teachings in Kalu Rinpoche's room, he kept space under the bed cleared so that she could hide there if Indian officials came looking for her. Eventually, the authorities caught up with her and expelled her from India.

Sarah went next to Burma (modern Myanmar), where she continued her Buddhist studies. But she kept in touch with Kalu Rinpoche. In Tibet, he had run long-term Buddhist retreats for monks. He now was running meditation retreats not only in India, but also in the United States. He asked Harding to join him on one of his U.S. trips.

During the stay, he told her he wanted to establish the first three-year retreat for Westerners. Unlike other long-term retreats, which can be completed in phases, Kalu Rinpoche wanted this to be in the traditional Tibetan style. It would last for three consecutive years, requiring a real depth of commitment from the participants. He proposed adapting it to

Westerners by including both men and women. And, because many of those who wanted to attend were French, he proposed locating it in France near Dijon.

Sarah knew immediately that she wanted to take part in it. However, she was only 22 years old and Kalu Rinpoche was reluctant to include her. She persuaded some of the other participants to plead her case and he finally relented. In 1976, Sarah and 13 other Westerners began the three-year retreat. Of the seven men and seven women who had been accepted by Kalu Rinpoche, Sarah was the youngest. Her goal was to learn more about Buddhism and experience what it was like to withdraw from the world for 36 months.

The first learning experience consisted of manual labor. The retreat participants had to build the houses they would live in for the next three years. There was grumbling from those who didn't understand the relationship between practical duties and the purpose of the retreat. But once the spiritual studies and meditation began in earnest, the disgruntlement vanished.

Changing his methods to adapt to the West wasn't always easy for the retreat Master. In Tibet, the only women in long-term retreats were nuns. Among his group of seven, only one was a Buddhist nun. To Kalu, it seemed that any woman who would commit herself to completing the three-years of study and meditation would naturally want to be a nun. For the duration of the entire three years he tried unsuccessfully to convince the other six women, all of whom were single, to become nuns.

On top of her earlier studies, the retreat qualified Sarah to become a Tibetan Lama. She was no longer just a student of Buddhism, but a high teacher. She had found her life's calling. Lama Sarah Harding would become one of the pioneering Buddhists spreading the Dharma in America.

From Road Warrior to Buddhist Professor

Unlike Sarah Harding, whose interest in Buddhism was kindled while she was still in high school, David Gardiner had no early interest in Tibetan Buddhism. He grew up in a CIA family in northern Virginia. His mother and father met in Vienna, Austria, where both worked for the Agency.

After high school, Gardiner entered Amherst College. During his freshman year he mainly studied psychology and political science. Other students, however, raved about a popular instructor named Robert Thurman who taught an introductory course on Asian religions. To see if Thurman's class lived up to its reputation, Gardiner enrolled in his sophomore year, although he had little interest in religion.

Within weeks, Gardiner became hooked. Thurman's lectures on Daoism, Confucianism, Shinto, and Hinduism were riveting, and his knowledge of the cultures of India, China, and Japan held Gardiner's attention. Thurman taught that the key to understanding the "heart" of these countries was Buddhism.

Gardiner had never been drawn so strongly to a topic before. He decided that he wanted to study Buddhism, but he wasn't particularly interested in majoring in religion. Instead of enrolling as a junior the next fall, he decided to take the year off. Before leaving he asked Thurman for recommendations of what to read.

At the top of Thurman's list were books by Lama Govinda, the charismatic Tibetan Buddhist teacher in the West, including *Way of the White Clouds, Psychological Attitude of Early Buddhist Philosophy,* and *Creative Meditation and Multidimensional Consciousness.*

Armed with the books, Gardiner set off on a voyage of self-discovery by going on an extended road trip in the best traditions of Jack Kerouac. Using his thumb as his principal means of propulsion, Gardiner took to the highway, criss-crossing America six times, one lift at a time.

Creative Meditation and Multidimensional Consciousness became his bible. By the time Gardiner returned to Amherst, he had settled on Asian studies as his major. He enrolled in more classes with Thurman on Buddhism, Buddhist scriptures, and a survey course in Asian religions.

In his senior year, Gardiner met Lama Lobsong Jampsal, a geshe, and Thupten Kelsang Rinpoche. Thurman had invited the monks to stay in his house while he took his family on a sabbatical to India. In his absence, Gardiner studied with Lama Jampsal and Kelsang Rinpoche, not so much in an academic sense as in the traditional Buddhist method of guru and student.

Six months after graduating from Amherst, Gardiner went to India. For a few months he traveled around the country, much as Ginsberg and Thurman had done a decade earlier. In Dharamsala, he took classes at the Library of Tibetan Works, renting a room at its dormitory. There he found an eclectic mix of monks and nuns, dharma bums, scholars, and hippies, all drawn to the Dalai Lama. He studied texts in the library and attended lectures on Buddhism.

After a few months, he left for central India, where Tibetan monks had built a new Drepung monastery to carry on the traditions of the ancient Drepung in Tibet. The new monastery was only about ten years old when Gardiner arrived. To him it looked like a small college campus in the middle of dry, barren fields. There were less than half a dozen buildings and a small community of monks and nuns numbering in the low hundreds. The Drepung in Tibet, in contrast, had been home to more than 10,000 monks.

Armed with a letter of introduction from Thurman, Gardiner presented himself. By chance he had arrived the day after the monks completed a new building intended specifically to house visitors. He was welcomed to stay in one of its two apartments, without charge, although he was told if he wished to make a donation it would be accepted. He paid $50 a month for his lodgings and began studying Tibetan, meditated for up to six hours daily, and hung out in the cafeteria talking with the monks and nuns.

One of the lamas, Khensur Yeshe Thupten Rinpoche, offered teachings from *Entrance to the Bodhisattva Path*, one of the most influential texts in Tibetan Buddhism. Twice a week, Gardiner and other students gathered in Lama Thupten's room at the foot of his bed. The Lama sat cross-legged in bed, reading a verse from the text, explaining what commentators had said through the centuries about its meaning, and then asking his students for questions. It was the traditional Tibetan teacher-student way of passing knowledge from one generation to the next.

During these six months in India and two in Nepal, including a month at Drepung, Gardiner considered becoming a monk. But he realized his true calling was in academia. He returned to the United States and applied for graduate school at the University of Virginia (UVA.)

Gardiner was unaware when he applied that the UVA program was one of the most prestigious—and competitive—programs on Tibetan Buddhism in the entire country. Another of Geshe Wangyal's acolytes, Jeffrey Hopkins, had founded the program. Gardiner was accepted and began studying for his Masters in Asian Religions.

One day, he noticed a poster featuring an upcoming speaker. It was Lama Thupten from Drepung. They hadn't seen one another for five years and master and pupil reunited gleefully. Americans no longer had to travel to India or Nepal to find Buddhist teachers. Growing academic interest in Tibetan Buddhism made colleges and universities important centers for exchanges between the Tibetans and Americans. Campuses were associated with the counterculture because of Vietnam War protests and known as havens for advocates of social and political change. Derided by some as hotbeds of radicalism, the universities were to become spawning grounds for the new generation of pro-Tibet activists.

BEATS GO WEST: ALLEN GINSBERG AND CHÖGYAM TRUNGPA

As the 1970s progressed, colleges weren't the only places where Americans could encounter Tibetan Buddhism. Meditation centers began springing up, slowly at first, pioneered by monks and lamas like Geshe Wangyal. One of the most successful at establishing new Tibetan Buddhist institutions in America was Chögyam Trungpa Rinpoche.

Trungpa had followed the Dalai Lama into exile and become head of the Young Lama School in India before receiving a scholarship to study in England. After studying comparative religion at Oxford University, Trungpa went to Scotland in 1967 and founded Samye Ling. It was among the first Tibetan Buddhist meditation centers in the West.

Then he met Diana Judith, a fair-haired teenager, and they fell in love. Trungpa gave up his monastic vows and married her at the registrar's office in Edinburgh. They posed for their wedding pictures in a photo booth and got a strip of four shots in muddy black and white. Diana took Trungpa's family name, Mukpo, and the couple settled at Samye Ling. She was 16 years of age.

Even though Trungpa was just in his early twenties, his marriage to a teenager was not well received at Samye Ling. One member of the community, Christopher Woodman, took it upon himself to persuade the London Buddhist Society that Trungpa was, to use Trungpa's words, "a neurotic criminal."

Trungpa and Diana left Samye Ling. They moved first to Canada and then the United States, where Trungpa was invited to start a meditation center in northern Vermont. The site was a 430-acre farm, purchased by former students, nestled against tree-lined mountains. His students dubbed it Tail of the Tiger. Today it is known as Karmê Chöling.

In 1970, Ginsberg and Chögyam Trungpa met when trying to hail the same taxi. In an encounter made short by the necessity of getting Ginsberg's elderly father to the hospital, Trungpa asked Allen to come to Tail of the Tiger, where fellow Beat poet Anne Waldman was already spending time on meditation retreats. Intrigued, Ginsberg promised to stay in touch, and the two exchanged addresses.

COLORADO AGAIN BECOMES BASE CAMP

It was also 1970 when Trungpa was invited by a group at the University of Colorado at Boulder to teach. When he and Diana moved to the States, his eight-year-old Tibetan son, Osel Rangtrol, was supposed to stay at Samye Ling until the couple was settled. Christopher Woodman, however, went to court to prevent the boy from joining his family when Diana returned for him. The lad was sent to live in a children's home in Sussex until the court case was resolved.

Trungpa flew to Sussex to see his son, and then traveled directly from England to Colorado. With its high altitude and backdrop of the Rockies, Trungpa felt the same sensation of homecoming in Boulder that the Tibetan trainees had experienced at Camp Hale.

From a modest house on Alpine Street that he named Anitya Bhavan —House of Impermanence—Trungpa introduced a small gathering of students to Tibetan Buddhism. Diana joined him in Colorado, and in 1971 she gave birth to their first son, Tendzin Lhawang Tagtrug. A second son, Gesar Arthur, was born two years later.

America in the early 1970s proved to be a culture ready for transformation, and Trungpa found Boulder a community that was open minded and tolerant. He set up a meditation center called Karma Dzong, Fortress of Action, and then set up the 360-acre Rocky Mountain Dharma Center near Fort Collins. Its first inhabitants were a group of young hippies who called themselves "The Pygmies."

It was in the 1970s that Trungpa evolved a method of practicing Tibetan Buddhism suited to the cultural expectations of Western students. It was called Shambhala Training and involved contemplative practice and studies, but also mingled elements of Zen with the arts, psychology, and Tibetan Buddhism. Like other religions, Buddhism took on different "clothing" as it was introduced to different parts of the world. There is no monolithic Tibetan Buddhism. There are many schools, many teachers, many different views and approaches. But even with the new forms, the essence and the core teachings do not change. As long as people studying Tibetan Buddhism actually practice meditation and study the original teachings of the Buddha and the many commentaries that followed, nothing is lost or diluted.

By the mid-1970s, Trungpa was ready to take his vision for Tibetan Buddhism in the United States to the next level. He wanted to establish a university for contemplative studies, and Boulder seemed right. He called it the Naropa Institute.

In 1974, Trungpa invited Allen Ginsberg, John Cage, Diane di Prima, and Anne Waldman to create a school for the study of poetry at Naropa. Ginsberg and Waldman came up with the Jack Kerouac School of Disembodied Poetics, named after their late colleague who had died five years earlier in 1969. "Disembodied," Waldman explained, because "so many of our faculty would be peripatetic, and also our inspiration was from many writers long gone."

A quote attributed to Trungpa came during his first trip to the United States: "Where are the poets? Take me to your poets!"

Ginsberg later recalled the intent: "It would be a way of teaching meditators about the golden mouth and educating poets about the golden mind."

Trungpa admired Kerouac's poetry, which he called "a perfect manifestation of mind." Trungpa thought that for Buddhist teachers to be able to successfully teach liberation in America, they would have to be poets. Ginsberg likened this to Kerouac's insights about poetry as "spontaneous divinity" and "spontaneous mind" where the first thought is the best thought, and lines like "hydrogen jukebox" flow. Addressing a small group at Naropa, wearing his glasses, looking more like a professor than a lama in his light grey suit and tie, speaking softly, Trungpa explained the connection:

"Poetry is the expression of one's phenomenal world in the written form," he said, "It could be either prose or poetry, it's not so much from a Buddhist point of view is what you write good poetry, particularly, but how your thought patterns become elegant, that you see the phenomenal world as a process."

Naropa flourished and over time it became an accredited institution, making it the first Buddhist University in America. Ginsberg later described it as "one of the single community commune meditation-oriented projects of the ethos of the sixties that survived. . . ."

Ginsberg and Waldman began teaching regularly at Naropa. Ginsberg found the Buddhist tradition more open to bohemia, and Trungpa's methods of holding classes and teaching poetry based on meditation particularly effective. Unlike other communal experiments of the era which failed, like the many hippie communes, Naropa flourished, in part, Ginsberg believed, because Buddhism had thousands of years of experience organizing similar communities. Ginsberg also thought that Buddhists were better at solving practical problems like fundraising to sustain their communities than were the hippies.

As meditation centers proliferated across the United States, Trungpa saw the need for a national organization. The result was Vajradhatu, national offices for the chain of meditation centers he dubbed Dharmadhatu, or "space of dharma." Vajradhatu became the umbrella organization for approximately 100 meditation centers and retreat centers around the country.

Colorado was once again central to the support of Tibetan Buddhism. The growing network of Buddhist organizations not only spread Tibet's religion and culture, but also became sources of financial support for the Dalai Lama and the Tibetans in exile. Vajradhatu eventually took on the name Shambhala and spread internationally.

TRUNGPA ADAPTS TIBETAN
BUDDHISM TO AMERICA

Peter Volz had studied Zen Buddhism half-heartedly while attending college at Berkeley in the early 1970s. In 1973 a speech Chögyam Trungpa gave at the Unitarian church in San Francisco intrigued him.

"He was adapting to our culture," Volz explains, "He wasn't making us adapt to his culture. He demystified himself by taking off his Tibetan robes, donning American clothes, and understanding who we (Americans) are."

Core American values, Trungpa believed, would influence how Tibetan Buddhism needed to be taught and practiced by his new audience. He quickly recognized as cornerstones of American culture such values as efficiency, the belief that hard work lead to success, self-reliance, the pursuit of happiness, and individual freedom. This was true even for hippies and counterculture acolytes and the bohemian poets Trungpa found when he arrived in America in the early 1970s. They may have denied it, but these values were rooted deep down even then, as they are today. Trungpa also knew he was encountering a culture firmly ground-ed in the Judeo-Christian tradition and that the theism inherent in that tradition was also ingrained.

"One of the first things Rinpoche had people do," Volz explains, "was to sit and do nothing. Literally. He did not even give them any particular meditation technique to follow, let alone any fancy visualizations or prayers. He told people to just sit and be present."

He was trying to teach that there was no goal, per se. One of his first books, *Journey Without Goal*, was a teaching to undercut the ambition to become a "higher" spiritual being. He considered this goal very naïve and childish and a major obstacle to the genuine practice of Buddhism.

"If people actually possess Buddha-nature or wisdom," says Volz, "There is no need to try to acquire something foreign or new. Rinpoche pushed people to question their own theism, and he undercut their devo-tion to him when it became theistic or worshipful. He taught that effi-ciency wasn't the point, nor was climbing the ladder. The whole thrust to achieve something, to accomplish one's purpose on the spiritual path was brought into question."

The Myth of Freedom, another early book by Trungpa, counters the assumption that we can find freedom, independence, or happiness by manipulating our circumstances and the outside environment. His teach-ing emphasizes the idea that true freedom is freedom from the tyranny of ego and grasping, or clinging to hope and fear.

Trungpa and other Tibetan teachers believed materialism was the biggest issue that needed to be confronted when teaching Tibetan Buddhism in America. While materialism is hardly unique to America or Western cultures, he found it had a particularly strong hold on students in the United States often unknowingly. His book, *Cutting through Spiritual Materialism* explored the theme that our materialistic outlook has physical, psychological, and spiritual components.

When trying to prove his point that materialism was an empty pur-suit, Trungpa could be dramatic. He once drove a Mercedes into the ocean to demonstrate the meaninglessness of status symbols.

Some of Trungpa's efforts to provide insights to his students back-fired. The most notorious happened in 1976 on Halloween. Trungpa held a retreat near Snowmass, Colorado, that was attended by many writers, including the poet W.S. Merwin and his companion Dana Naone. Trungpa wanted the students to attend the Halloween festivities in the nude instead of costumed.

Merwin and Naone refused to join in and blocked themselves in their room. Trungpa had other students force their way into the room, strip the couple, and bring them to the Halloween party. They left the next day. The contretemps remained private until three years later when Ginsberg was interviewed by Tom Clark of the *Boulder Monthly* about what came to be known as "The Merwin Incident." Trungpa defended the couple's treatment as part of his teaching, but the explanation failed to deflect criticism. As the participants explained and rationalized their involvement, the continuing controversy came to be called "The Poetry Wars" because of the high-caliber of the writing.

Trungpa's unorthodox techniques were premised on his belief that the teacher can't tell a student the truth. All the guru can do is give hints; the students have to intuit truth for themselves.

"It is too personal and nuanced and subtle to simply say, 'Here's the story,'" Peter Volz explains, "It requires intensive training in meditation. And in that training all kinds of things come up—repressed feelings and thoughts and things you just haven't dealt with that your teacher will help you to work through."

Trungpa was consumed with finding the language that Americans could hear and understand. Volz explains it with a baking analogy:

"Tibetan Buddhist tradition is passed down, much like a recipe for baking fresh bread is passed down from grandmother to mother to daughter. You don't just sit around studying the recipe, though, you make the bread and you eat it and enjoy it. And the way you make the bread is to hear about how to make it, you see how to make it, you make it—it is passed down human-to-human. The Tibetans call this an 'ear whispered lineage.'"

Complex and sometimes misunderstood, Trungpa deserves enormous credit for the successful transplantation of Tibetan Buddhism to the United States. His methods drew criticism, but their result was the creation of a new lifeline of support.

CHANGING OF THE GUARD

Subtly, imperceptibly, the mantle of the Tibetan cause was being rewoven and passed to a different set of actors. Desmond FitzGerald and the CIA were out of the picture, but new leaders like Thurman, Trungpa, and Wangyal were emerging. They would take on the Tibetan cause just as energetically as the Cold Warriors, but with more conviction because their support stemmed from shared spiritual values instead of political expediency. Their concept of liberation, both political and personal, was expansive far beyond the imaginings of the most creative of the spies; transcendental, universal, eternal, personal, cultural, social, perhaps impossibly optimistic. But of the two, the counterculture's support would be more enduring.

This shift in leadership happened because of what may seem, superficially, to be chance intersections, the thread of one life crossing another. One person meets another after a funeral. A poet and a lama encounter each other on the street while both try to hail a taxi cab, as happened in 1970 when Ginsberg bumped into Trungpa in New York.

And so what appeared as a double-cross by the American government—cold-hearted reneging on solemn promises to support the Dalai Lama during his exile—was in reality a criss-cross, a moment in time when the surging counterculture took over from an establishment that had discarded the goal of Tibetan liberation.

Part Three: Hope

Germinating in his mind during the first decades of exile was a concept the Dalai Lama almost dared not raise with the independence-minded Tibetans. Tenzin Gyatso had been developing his autonomy proposal, The Middle-Way Approach, as a solution that China and the Tibetans could accept. Autonomy within the People's Republic of China was controversial for Tibetans, because it meant backing away from Tibet's right to be independent. Yet it offered hope that a negotiated resolution of the longstanding conflict could be achieved, especially if the growing power of the free Tibet movement was harnessed to push China into talks.

Hope for a breakthrough with China suffered a serious setback after the death of reformer Hu Yaobang and the crackdown on democracy activists in Tiananmen Square. Despite this, the 1990s was a strong decade of growth for human rights across the world. Democracy spread across Eastern Europe and Russia, and South Africa's apartheid regime fell. The movement to free Tibet grew as a new generation was introduced to the cause by a combination of campus activism, fresh interest from Hollywood, high-profile rock concerts, and the Dalai Lama's growing international stature. At the end of the 1990s, the Seventeenth Karmapa, one of the three major spiritual leaders of Tibetan Buddhism, escaped to join the Dalai Lama in India.

As the 21st century dawned, China became a member of the World Trade Organization and was given the privilege of hosting the 2008 Summer Olympic Games. Beijing's commitment to improve human rights raised hopes that the Games would be a turning point in resolving Tibet's future. Hu Jintao's repression of the 2008 National Uprising dashed expectations, but China's growing integration into the world economy created the conditions for a new kind of pressure to be effective in finally accomplishing the goal of a Free Tibet.

Chapter 13

The Dalai Lama Finds
a Middle Way

Bitterness would have been a natural response to the dilemma in
which the Dalai Lama found himself in the 1970s. Refugees from
Tibet reported that the country was still being ravaged by the
Cultural Revolution, yet the U.S. government had abandoned both the
resistance and the Tibetan government-in-exile and was cultivating relations with Chairman Mao. But, as a March 1972 encounter with ethnic
Chinese writer Victor Chan shows, bitterness was alien to Tenzin Gyatso.

After finishing college in 1971, Chan bought a Volkswagen van and
began touring Europe. He made his way from Holland to Turkey and
then through Iran to Afghanistan. Along the way, he joined up with two
girls, an American named Cheryl Crosby and a German named Rita. In
Kabul, the trio were kidnapped and held briefly until their captors
crashed the vehicle they were moving them in and Chan and the girls
managed to escape.

When Cheryl, a practicing Buddhist from New York, suggested they
go to Dharamsala, Chan agreed. She had a letter of introduction to the
Dalai Lama and wanted to ask him about meditation. The audience took
place at the Dalai Lama's gated residence, lightly guarded by Indian
troops. After discussing her questions, Tenzin Gyatso turned to Chan.

Thinking that his Chinese heritage must kindle resentments, Chan
asked the Dalai Lama whether he hated the Chinese. In his book, *The*

Wisdom of Forgiveness, Chan recounts the disarming reply. Tenzin Gyatso looked directly into his eyes and said not only that he didn't hate the Chinese, but that he had truly forgiven them.

By the early 1970s, the Dalai Lama had started to see the relationship between Tibet and China as interdependent. Applying Buddhist precepts about the interrelatedness of everything in the world, the long chain of cause and effect whereby something that happens in one place or time extends its reach at a distance, he began to envision a joint future for China and Tibet. His thoughts were not yet concrete, and it was premature to introduce them to the Tibetan exile community, which was still wedded to regaining independence from China.

But the preliminary idea of forging a new relationship with Beijing had taken hold. It was rooted in the ability to forgive the evildoing of the Chinese communists who, acting under the influence of Maoist propaganda, were still ignorantly destroying Tibet's culture and people. The Dalai Lama started a dialog with the leadership of the Assembly of Tibetan People's Deputies, the Kashag ministers, and Tibetan thinkers and scholars. The substance of the talks was to find a middle ground between the Chinese position that Tibet was subservient and Tibet's right to political, cultural, and religious independence.

THE NECHUNG ORACLE PROPHESIES CHANGE IN CHINA

During a consultation at the beginning of the 1970s, the Nechung oracle foretold a period of Chinese decline followed by the collapse of all that Mao's rule had created. When a catastrophic earthquake in Tangshen followed, killing hundreds of thousands of Chinese, the oracle's prediction of a change of fortune seemed at hand.

Then, on January 8, 1976, Zhou En-lai died. The leadership vacuum was filled by Hua Guofeng, a Mao loyalist who had been Minister of Public Security. When Mao Zedong died on September 9, 1976, Hua Guofeng became Premier and Chairman of the Chinese Communist party. During Mao's extended illness, his wife Jiang Qing was at the apex of a quartet of party radicals known as the "Gang of Four." Moderates saw the Gang of Four as the principal impediment to economic reforms that would help modernize China. With Mao dead, security forces arrested the Gang of Four.

This appeared to be the change in the Chinese regime prophesied by the Nechung oracle. And indeed, in 1977, an official said China "would welcome the Dalai Lama and his followers who fled to India . . ."

It was the beginning of a thaw. With Mao and Zhou both dead, the Gang of Four's grip on power manacled, and the United States and China entering into a rapprochement, it is possible that Chairman Hua Guofeng sensed an opportunity to resolve the Tibet problem. Whatever the motivation, the immediate result was an easing of religious restrictions for Tibetans.

In Lhasa, residents and pilgrims were allowed to freely circumambulate the Barkhor and the Lingkho during the Buddhist Saka Dawa celebrations commemorating the anniversary of Buddha's birth, enlightenment, and death. Chinese officials called for a restoration of Tibetan culture and urged Tibetans inside the country to invite their exiled relatives to return to their homeland because of the "good conditions."

CHINA MAKES AN OVERTURE

Deng Xiaoping, who was rising through party ranks, sent an unofficial envoy to Gyalo Thondup with an offer to set up direct communication between the Dalai Lama and the new Chinese leadership. After two-and-a-half years of delicate diplomatic maneuvering, the contacts resulted in the Chinese agreeing to the Dalai Lama's proposal to allow a high-level, fact-finding delegation to examine conditions inside Tibet. It was a prelude to his possible return from exile. The agreement called for the Dalai Lama's representatives to inspect each region of the country and report back to him. If China's governance in Tibet had indeed been beneficial, discussions about the terms of the Dalai Lama's return would commence.

In the summer of 1979, the first delegation went to China and then into Tibet. When ordinary Tibetans learned that emissaries from the Dalai Lama were visiting, their cars were besieged. People wanted to make contact so badly that windows were broken and crowds climbed on the vehicles, hands outstretched just to get a glancing touch of one of the Dalai Lama's representatives. The mob scenes unsettled the Chinese hosts, who feared the pandemonium that might ensue if the Dalai Lama himself were to return.

The delegation returned to Dharamsala in late December 1979, where they submitted their report to the Dalai Lama in confidence. Their findings chronicled the depth of destruction and repression. Circumstances in Tibet were far worse than the exile government had known.

A second delegation was dispatched in 1980 with the specific goal of examining education conditions in the homeland. Jetsun Pema, one of the Dalai Lama's younger sisters, was part of the team. She was appalled by what she saw, as well as the stories she heard about torture, death, hunger, and destruction from her fellow Tibetans.

"In every region we went through, we heard the same stories of atrocities. . ." Pema recounts in her book, *Tibet, My Story.* "As I listened to these accounts, looking at the emaciated faces and fleshless bodies, I could not prevent myself from shedding tears. The delegation I led lived in a state of permanent shock. We often cried with the people who had come to meet us. We could see how moved they were at being able to talk to us for the first time in 30 years. Sometimes, after talking amongst ourselves about the day's experiences, exhaustion and discouragement overcame us and we sobbed silently."

There was friction between Pema and her Chinese handlers when large crowds blocked their progress in order to see the Dalai Lama's sister. Instead of letting her pause and make an appearance, the Chinese literally locked Pema in her vehicle.

The final straw came during the delegation's visit to Ganden Monastery on the 571st anniversary of its founding. The ruined buildings were being laboriously restored by faithful Tibetans, using whatever scraps of lumber they could find and laying stone after stone by hand on their one day off from work each week. On the day Jetsun Pema's group arrived, some 5000 people were at the monastery, crowded around some 80 trucks laden with materials for its restoration. The gathering turned into an impromptu demonstration, with thousands of Tibetans shouting for a free Tibet.

By the end of her 130-day mission, Jetsun Pema and her delegation had traveled 8500 miles inside Tibet, often on roads that were barely passable. Despite the risk of Chinese reprisals, Tibetans greeted the delegation in every town, city, and village along the route. Pema came away from her trip desolated by the abysmal conditions facing most Tibetans. Her countrymen and women had lost family members as well as their identities, religion, monasteries, homes, and livelihoods. But, even in the face of these atrocious circumstances, the Tibetans were steadfast in their religion and belief in the Dalai Lama as their spiritual leader.

HU YAOBANG CALLS FOR
ENLIGHTENED REFORMS

When word of the negative reactions of the the the Dalai Lama's delegates reached Beijing, Chinese Communist Party (CCP) Secretary Hu Yaobang and Vice Premier Wan Li went to inspect conditions for themselves. They were the highest ranking Chinese officials to visit Tibet during China's 30 years of occupation.

Appalled at what he found, Hu Yaobang set up a new liberal Tibet policy called the Six-Point reform program. Among Yaobang's six points, the fifth point speaks clearly of preserving Tibet's culture, education, and religion:

"So long as the socialist orientation is upheld, vigorous efforts must be made to revive and develop Tibetan culture, education and science. The Tibetan people have a long history and a rich culture. The world-renowned ancient Tibetan culture included Buddhism, graceful music and dance as well as medicine and opera, all of which are worthy of serious study and development. All ideas that ignore and weaken Tibetan culture are wrong. It is necessary to do a good job in inheriting and developing Tibetan culture. . . Education has not progressed well in Tibet. . . efforts should be made to set up universities and middle and primary schools in the region. Some cultural relics and Buddhist scriptures in temples have been damaged, and conscientious effort should be made to protect, sort and study them. Cadres of Han nationality working in Tibet should learn the spoken and written Tibetan language. It should be a required subject; otherwise they will be divorced from the masses. Cherishing the people of minority nationalities is not empty talk. The Tibetan people's habits, customs, history and culture must be respected."

Although not universally supported by communist party officials, Yaobang's reform program brought temporary relief for Tibet. Some monasteries were reopened. The Tibetan language was allowed in business and on commercial signs for shops and offices. Chinese administrators were replaced by Tibetans, and travel restrictions were eased for those wanting to visit family outside Tibet.

Hu Yaobang's reforms were an effort to undo some of the damage caused by the Cultural Revolution in Tibet. But they failed to yield further progress in the dialog between Beijing and Dharamsala. Chinese officials, perhaps opponents of Hu Yaobang's efforts at reconciliation, gave the press the misinformation that the Dalai Lama had agreed to unification with China without any guarantee of independence for Tibet. The Tibetan government-in-exile formally repudiated the misinformation. The fourth delegation never completed its fact-finding tour and the diplomatic overture stalled.

DALAI LAMA ARRIVES AT THE MIDDLE WAY

Before the Chinese overture, the Dalai Lama had opened the door to a new approach to China. By 1979, a consensus had been achieved. The Dalai Lama changed paths. He moved away from seeking independence for Tibet and began openly advocating a Middle-Way Approach. But in keeping with the democratic process of the Tibetan government-in-exile, the new approach was not imposed on the Tibetan people. Instead, it was subject to a series of democratic procedures before formal adoption took place.

The roots of democracy in Tibetan Buddhism can be traced to the Vinaya Teaching, in which the rules and regulations that govern monks are not simply imposed by the abbot of a monastery, but subject to discussion in a monastic assembly. The object of such an examination was to arrive at a valid ethical decision to govern the rules of the monastery. It's not unlike New England town hall democracy.

The concept of a valid ethical basis for rules is what distinguishes a democracy from the arbitrary use of state power in the hands of a governing elite. The divine right of kings to rule is no longer accepted in the West as an ethical basis for government. Nor is Marxism, the dictatorship of the proletariat, accepted in the West. The essence of democracy is the belief that the people are sovereign, with inviolable fundamental rights, and that there can be no legitimate government without their assent.

SLOW PATH TO DEMOCRACY

The Tibetans' pathway toward democratization was slow and sometimes tedious. Although both state and religious leadership were vested in the Dalai Lama, his approach toward democracy building was consensual. Rather than impose reforms on the people, he wanted democracy to take root and flourish. This required a gradualist approach based on winning acceptance of reforms rather than imposing them by decree.

Democratic reforms began for the Tibetans-in-exile on September 2, 1960, when for the first time ever Tibetans voted formally to elect representatives. With the Tibetan exile community scattered in settlements across the vast breadth of India and others in refugee camps in Nepal, voting for an assembly helped create a sense of unity and identity as Tibetans. The election of representatives provided a bridge between the seat of the government-in-exile and far-flung communities and fostered a spirit of cohesion among the exiles.

Initially, many Tibetans found the idea of voting alien. Some wanted to know who the Dalai Lama wanted them to select. There was also cultural resistance to the idea of putting oneself forward and asking for votes, as well as ingrained habits of deference to traditional authority figures from historical Tibet—the hereditary aristocracy, tribal leaders, monastic hierarchies, and large landowners. But once the strangeness of choosing their own representatives wore off, Tibetans took to it enthusiastically.

In March 1963, on the fourth anniversary of the Tibetan National Uprising, the Dalai Lama proposed a draft document outlining Tibetan self-rule. The timing coincided with the end of major guerrilla fighting inside Tibet. The Dalai Lama's plan was ambitious in that it extended beyond the scattered exile communities to encompass all of Tibet. This plan was the precursor to the Tibetan Charter, equivalent to Tibet's constitution.

To win popular support, public education programs were mounted. They involved sending teams from Dharamsala to Tibetan exile communities across India to explain the reform agenda. Patience was the other factor crucial to winning broad acceptance of his reforms; the Dalai Lama had the political foresight to give his people time to see for themselves how the principles of self-rule would play out in practice.

The result was a gap of 27 years between the introduction of the democratic reform agenda and its final implementation. On June 15, 1988, the Dalai Lama appeared before the European Parliament and presented what has come to be known as his Strasbourg Proposal. The initiative was intended as a basis for productive talks with the Chinese, now under the leadership of Deng Xiaoping, and had a direct bearing on Tibet's prospects for democracy.

THE ELEMENTS OF THE MIDDLE-WAY APPROACH

The Strasbourg Proposal envisioned Tibet accepting China's sovereignty under conditions that permitted a wide range of autonomy. The Dalai Lama proposed that the three provinces of Tibet—U-Tsang, Kham, and Amdo—would be reunited as one entity with self-rule in domestic and religious affairs. While nominally part of China, the state of autonomy would guarantee local political freedom. Foreign policy and national defense, however, would remain the exclusive domain of Beijing. Adoption of the Strasbourg Proposal would set the stage for the Dalai Lama and other exiled Tibetans to return to their homeland.

Autonomy was a familiar concept to the European parliamentarians in the Dalai Lama's audience. After the death of Spanish dictator Generalissimo Francisco Franco in 1975, Spain had returned to democracy. The country had two ethnic minorities, the Basques and the Catalans, each with their own language and regional traditions. Before the Franco dictatorship, the Basques briefly had their own independent republic, and the Catalans had a long tradition of independence from Madrid. Franco had tried unsuccessfully to repress Basque nationalism and Catalan separatism. As Spain returned to democracy, statutes of autonomy gave each region its own legislature, local administration, and police force, within the political framework of the Spanish state. Visitors to Barcelona or Bilbao might never be aware of the fact that they are in politically autonomous regions of the kind the Dalai Lama now proposed for Tibet.

The main components of the Middle-Way Approach, as outlined by the Central Tibetan Administration, are as follows:

1. Without seeking independence for Tibet, the Central Tibetan Administration strives for the creation of a political entity comprising the three traditional provinces of Tibet;
2. Such an entity should enjoy a status of genuine national regional autonomy;
3. This autonomy should be governed by the popularly elected legislature and executive through a democratic process and should have an independent judicial system;
4. As soon as the above status is agreed upon by the Chinese government, Tibet would not seek separation from, and remain within, the People's Republic of China.

5. Until the time Tibet is transformed into a zone of peace and nonviolence, the Chinese government can keep a limited number of armed forces in Tibet for its protection;

6. The Central Government of the People's Republic of China has the responsibility for the political aspects of Tibet's international relations and defence, whereas the Tibetan people should manage all other affairs pertaining to Tibet, such as religion and culture, education, economy, health, ecological and environmental protection;

7. The Chinese government should stop its policy of human rights violations in Tibet and the transfer of Chinese population into Tibetan areas;

8. To resolve the issue of Tibet, His Holiness the Dalai Lama shall take the main responsibility of sincerely pursuing negotiations and reconciliation with the Chinese government.

It helps to understand the Buddhist basis for the Middle-Way Approach in order to appreciate the Dalai Lama's concept of autonomy. Even though he had thought about this approach for quite some time before 1988, the changing world was making an ever stronger case, in the Dalai Lama's mind, to seek a change in policy that offered mutual benefits to China and Tibet. Tenzin Gyatso was inspired by the central Buddhist concept of "interdependence"—all existent things are a *whole* composed of *parts* that are dependent on each other to maintain the *whole*.

About the Middle-Way, he explained that the whole globe was heavily interdependent. Tibet's economy and environment were heavily dependent on China. China's prosperity would benefit Tibetans, provided that Tibet remained "in China."

"If we separate, in long run, Tibetans may face more difficulty," he said, "My Middle-Way Approach, not separate from China—economically bound to the PRC. Meanwhile, full autonomy, self-government, culture, education, environment, spirituality—these things we Tibetans can manage better. I'm quite sure that our Tibetan traditions, Tibetan spirituality, can help millions of Chinese. Already some Chinese artists, some Chinese thinkers are showing interest in Tibet, in Tibetan Buddhism. So China and Tibet not separate. Help each other, interdependent."

Not all Tibetans embraced the Middle-Way Approach. Lodi Gyari, the Dalai Lama's special envoy, had been chairman of Tibet's parliament and was a high-ranking official in the government at the time of the debate. He was descended from the Khampa warriors whose resistance to the Chinese had persuaded Desmond FitzGerald that there was a guerrilla movement worthy of support inside Tibet. In addition to Gyari's mother, Dorjee, his aunt had also taken up arms in 1956. When she learned that he had been in possession of the draft document laying out the Strasbourg Proposal, she told Gyari that if she had known she would have "torn it to shreds."

Approximately one-third of Tibetans shared her view, but another two-thirds supported the Dalai Lama's change of policy. The Dalai Lama hoped that the Middle-Way Approach would become a basis for serious negotiations about Tibet's future. Deng Xiaoping had said unequivocally that with the exception of the issue of independence, any other matters could be negotiated.

MARTIAL LAW IN LHASA

In 1988, Hu Yaobang's efforts to soften Chinese rule in Tibet suffered a setback. It was the same year that the Tenth Panchen Lama, Tibet's second highest lama, died shortly after publicly denouncing the Chinese for causing more harm than good during their occupation of Tibet. Two months later, on the 30th anniversary of the Tibetan National Uprising, Tibetans marched in protest. There were three days of demonstrations, fueled by popular suspicion that Chinese authorities had assassinated the Panchen Lama in order to silence him.

A somewhat obscure forty-six-year-old party bureaucrat named Hu Jintao was China's top administrator in Lhasa. His father had died when Hu was five, leaving the boy to be raised by his aunt, Liu Bingxia. He lived with her in the city of Taizhou in Jiangsu Province until he left to attend Tsinghua University. After graduation he was sent by the Communist party to work in its propaganda department in Gansu, a far-flung, barren province on the edge of the Gobi Desert.

It was hardly a promising beginning for an ambitious bureaucrat, yet some who have known Hu for decades insist that he was indeed ambitious, so much so that he believed he was predestined to be part of China's top leadership. His biographer, Ma Ling, says that from the time he was a teenager Hu guarded his words carefully to avoid political missteps or giving unintended offense with career-derailing potential.

Hu spent 14 years in Gansu before being appointed to head the Communist Youth League. At the age of 39, he became the youngest cadre to ever be appointed to the powerful Central Committee. This honor was followed by becoming the youngest ever provincial Party Secretary when Hu was appointed top administrator in Guizhou in the mid 1980s.

This rapid ascent was possible because of Hu's patronage. Deng Xiaoping had taken a personal interest in his career after a party leader named Song Ping advised him that Hu Jintao had potential. Another one of his patrons was Hu Yaobang, the Communist Party Secretary whose zeal for reform sparked China's nascent democracy movement.

Hu's next move up the career ladder was Tibet, where his patron, Hu Yaobang, had introduced reforms intended to reverse the damage caused by Chairman Mao's Great Proletarian Cultural Revolution. Hu Jintao's career had become firmly aligned with the liberal clique of the Communist Party by the late 1980s. His political prospects depended in large measure on the fate of his patrons, Deng Xiaoping and Hu Yaobang, and the success of their reforms.

There were riots in Lhasa in the fall of 1987, prompting a severe response from Hu. In the aftermath, hundreds of monks were imprisoned. Stern measures earned Hu praise in Beijing, especially from political quarters outside his main networks.

It had been an embarrassment to Hu Jintao when the Panchen Lama, while on a trip to Shigatse in Tibet, used the occasion to criticize Chinese rule. But his death turned into a political crisis. The demonstrations in Lhasa on the 30th anniversary of the Tibetan National uprising were a direct challenge to Hu's career prospects. The unrest continued for three days. To contain the damage, Hu Jintao declared martial law.

TIANANMEN SQUARE
CRUSHES HOPES FOR TIBET

A few months after the Lhasa protests and Hu Jintao's imposition of martial law, his patron Hu Yaobang died. The demise of the popular reformer catalyzed the 1989 protests at Tiananmen Square. Fearing that events were spiraling out of control, Chinese authorities mobilized the People's Liberation Army and ordered the violent dispersal of the protestors. Hundreds were killed and thousands more injured when the military used tanks and armored vehicles to mow down the hapless protestors.

The Dalai Lama was in Dharamsala when he learned about the PLA's repression of the protestors, mostly young people and university students. He sent a car and driver to bring Lodi Gyari, who was serving as foreign minister, to his residence.

Gyari found him uncharacteristically pacing, agitated. The Dalai Lama told him he wanted to immediately issue a statement condemning the harsh treatment of the youthful protestors. In true diplomatic fashion, Gyari cautioned that condemning China's action would probably destroy any prospects for further negotiations. Tenzin Gyatso understood, but he also knew that if he didn't speak out in support of freedom and democracy for the Chinese now, he would lose all moral authority to ever make such an appeal. Resignedly, Lodi Gyari listened to the main points the Dalai Lama wished to convey and issued a statement criticizing the Chinese leadership's action.

Deng Xiaoping took the criticism as a personal affront and broke off further discussions with the Tibetans. In any case, with the death of Hu Yaobang, China's political pendulum had swung away from the reformers and toward the authoritarians. Fortunately for Hu Jintao, his tough measures in Tibet and imposition of martial law had realigned his political future with the hardliners. When he left Lhasa to return to Beijing to take up a post on the Standing Committee of the Politburo, one of China's most powerful party institutions, Hu handpicked the party officials he wanted to rule over Tibet. They were, according to Tibet scholar Robbie Barnett, "very aggressive, very hard line." Hu's crackdown had elevated him to the inner circle in Beijing, and he didn't want to jeopardize his legacy by appointing weak successors in Lhasa. The state of martial law remained in effect for a full year before it was finally lifted in April of 1990.

Chapter 14

The 1990s: The Tibetan Movement Goes Global

Four months after the tragic events at Tiananmen Square, the Nobel Institute announced that the Dalai Lama had won the 1989 Nobel Peace Prize. The 54-year-old Buddhist monk beat out former Soviet premier Mikhail Gorbachev and Czech writer and political activist Vaclav Havel for the prestigious award.

Calling it a Western plot to split the country and restore feudalism in Tibet, Chinese authorities denounced the decision as "preposterous" interference in China's domestic affairs. In truth, the five-member Nobel selection committee was deeply influenced by the crackdown on democracy in China. Jakob Sverdrup, director of the Nobel Institute and secretary to the Nobel selection committee, said that although the Dalai Lama had been a favorite from the start, China's brutality gave him an edge. When the Nobel committee settled on the Dalai Lama, the members fully intended to have an impact on Beijing.

THE DALAI LAMA ARRIVES
ON THE WORLD STAGE

For the Dalai Lama, the Nobel Peace Prize was vindication that he had been correct to speak out against the bloodshed in Tiananmen Square.

The award would put him in the global spotlight, amplifying his moral authority worldwide.

The first steps toward Tenzin Gyatso's arrival on the world stage began shortly after the loss of U.S. government support in the mid-1970s. Whatever sense of betrayal he may have initially felt over Nixon and Kissinger's courtship of Chairman Mao, the Dalai Lama didn't waste time dwelling on it. Instead, he turned his energy to developing new sources of support, moral as well as financial, for the Tibetan cause.

Until 1973, he had rarely traveled outside Tibet and India. That September, the Dalai Lama made a four-nation tour that included Italy, Switzerland, the Netherlands, and England. In Rome, he had an audience with Pope Paul V at the Vatican. In Geneva, the Dalai Lama visited Prince Sadruddin Aga Khan, an international figure who was part playboy, part philanthropist, and part international man of intrigue with periodic CIA entanglements. In Amsterdam, he was received by His Royal Highness Prince Bernard. On his final stop in England, he met with the Archbishop of Canterbury, head of the Anglican Church.

The trip marked the beginning of the Dalai Lama's emergence as an international spiritual teacher and champion for human rights, a role that elevated the simple Buddhist monk from an obscure and isolated region of northern India into a global celebrity.

Robert Thurman had foreseen the transformation. The night before the Dalai Lama's arrival in New York, on his first-ever visit to the United States in September 1979, Thurman had a dream. The Dalai Lama, from the top of New York's Waldorf-Astoria Hotel, was manifesting the Kalachakra Buddha's mandala palace and all the corporate titans and denizens and political leaders and celebrities were caught up "in the dance of 722 deities of the three buildings of the diamond palace like pin-striped bees swarming on a giant honeycomb."

There were no trappings of celebrity status during the first U.S. visit. In upstate New York, the Dalai Lama stayed at a small private home instead of a five-star hotel. For three days, he and the monks who accompanied him were guests of Christi Cox, whose friends volunteered to help with the cooking, cleaning, washing of robes, and transporting the Dalai Lama to and from speaking engagements. His security detail consisted of one state trooper. In this manner, using volunteers and speaking and teaching at events organized by local Buddhist centers, the Dalai Lama slowly built a global following.

Ten years later, on December 11, 1989, the Dalai Lama took the podium in Oslow to deliver his Nobel Lecture. The audience of dignitaries included Norway's King Olav V.

"The awarding of the Nobel Prize to me, a simple monk from faraway Tibet, here in Norway, also fills us Tibetans with hope," the Dalai Lama said, "It means, despite the fact that we have not drawn attention to our plight by means of violence, we have not been forgotten."

The Dalai Lama turned to the theme of interpendence and what he termed a rising sense of universal responsibility. Citing developments in modern communications and new awareness of environmental conditions, he made the case that events once confined to faraway places have an impact on all of us in the modern world, from famine in Africa to the loss of the rain forests. The ultimate example of interdependence, he said, is the necessity of preventing nuclear war.

To promote peace, he proposed making Tibet a "peace sanctuary" called Ahimsa, which means "nonviolence." Under his plan, Tibet would be demilitarized. The country, which is approximately the size of the European Union, would become "the world's largest natural park or biosphere." Development would be strictly sustainable, and individuals and organizations working to promote peace would be welcome to set up shop. But it all depended on China agreeing to stop its exploitive and aggressive development, cease testing nuclear weapons in Eastern Tibet, stop its policy of transferring Han Chinese settlers into the region, and accepting Tibet's right to self-determination. The Dalai Lama said the proposal to establish Ahimsa on the Tibetan Plateau was essential to peace and stability for all of Asia.

"With the Cold War era apparently drawing to a close, people everywhere live with renewed hope," Tenzin Gyatso said, ". . . in the struggle between forces of war, violence and oppression on the one hand, and peace, reason and freedom on the other, the latter are gaining the upper hand."

After a generation in which the Tibetan cause had largely faded from the general public, the Nobel Peace Prize helped spark popular interest. Working to rekindle the movement were a combination of familiar faces, like Robert Thurman, along with fresh converts drawn from the ranks of celebrities, musicians, and students.

RICHARD GERE JOINS THE CAUSE

Among the celebrities drawn to the Tibetan cause were actors Richard Gere, Keanu Reeves, and Goldie Hawn. In the 1960s and 1970s, celebrities had taken an interest in India and Tibetan Buddhism, but there was no sustained link between Hollywood and the Tibetans similar to the one that existed between the Beat Generation and the Buddhists. Then, in the 1980s, Richard Gere started making annual pilgrimages to Dharamsala for Buddhist study and meditation. After meeting the Dalai Lama, Gere's initial interest in Buddhism expanded to include Tibet. At the Dalai Lama's urging, Gere, Robert Thurman, and composer Philip Glass cofounded Tibet House in Manhattan. It serves as a cultural embassy and a center for Buddhist religion, art, and philosophy.

Keeping Tibet's unique civilization alive had begun to preoccupy the Dalai Lama, especially after he heard the reports of destruction from the delegations the Chinese had allowed to visit in the 1980s. He realized that exile could last decades. If Beijing continued to repress Tibet's traditional culture while supplanting its people with Chinese immigrants, the civilization could become extinct. Musicians, artists, and poets cannot exist without patrons, galleries to sell their work, or venues to perform. With conditions dire in Tibet, cultural and artistic survival hinged on foreign patronage. Tibet House would play a vital role by promoting the country's culture, not as historical artifacts, but through the ongoing work of performers and creative people.

Working with the Ministry of Religion and Culture in Dharamsala, in 1991 Tibet House inaugurated The International Year of Tibet. The idea of celebrating Tibet's culture caught on quickly. Dozens of countries joined in the movement, spawning more than 7000 events across the world. Philip Glass launched an annual concert to benefit Tibet House, timed to coincide with the Tibetan New Year celebrations. Building on the idea of artists supporting other artists, Christie's auction house in New York held a special sale every other year to which world-famous artists donate works, with the proceeds going to Tibet House.

Also in 1991, an art exhibit, *Wisdom and Compassion: The Sacred Art of Tibet*, was organized by the Asian Art Museum in San Francisco at the prompting of Marylin Rhie, Robert Thurman, and Richard Gere. Curators brought together almost 200 paintings, sculptures, tapestries, and other Tibetan works of art from museum collections, as well as from private collections throughout North America, Europe, and Russia. In 1998, Tibet House opened its own gallery to exhibit works of Tibetan art, both contemporary and traditional.

Not all of Richard Gere's contributions have been as elevated in nature but they are important to the well-being of all Tibetans. Because of the shortage of public restrooms in Dharamsala, Gere funded the construction of toilets on the street corner adjacent to the Dalai Lama's grounds, filling a dire public need. Additionally, to aid Tibetan refugees who cross into India or Nepal often penniless, frostbitten, and without the training for employment in their new world, he established the Gere Foundation. Beyond acts of charity and philanthropy, Gere began using the platform his celebrity provides to promote the movement through media interviews and by speaking at pro-Tibet rallies.

CHINA RESPONDS WITH MORE REPRESSION

Optimism was widespread after the award of the Nobel Peace prize that at last China might be persuaded to open a serious dialog about Tibet. In 1990, the Dalai Lama traveled to Washington, DC, where he met with President George H.W. Bush and was accorded the rare honor of addressing a joint session of Congress.

Much of the legwork for this trip was done by the International Campaign for Tibet (ICT), a Washington, DC-based not-for-profit organization. John Ackerly, head of ICT, had been on a mountaineering trip to Tibet in 1987 when Hu Jintao imposed martial law. Appalled by the brutal treatment he witnessed, he decided to create ICT after meeting with the Dalai Lama in India.

While in Washington, DC, the Dalai Lama also had an extensive interview schedule, including an appearance on John McLaughlin's nationally-broadcast *One on One* television program. At the time of the interview, martial law had just been lifted in Tibet. During the taping, McLaughlin pressed the Dalai Lama in his trademark fashion to criticize China, but he refused to do so. Instead, he emphasized his plan for reconciliation by demilitarizing Tibet and his proposal for autonomy. The TV host was impressed by the Dalai Lama's composure and diplomatic tact. Technicians in the studio that day said they sensed a preternatural calm, not the usual charged and tense atmosphere.

Unfortunately, China did not reciprocate the Dalai Lama's concilia-
tory spirit. By the mid-1990s, it was becoming clear that the Communist
government had no intention of responding to the Dalai Lama's overtures
in his Strasbourg proposal and Five-Point-Peace Plan. In his 1994 annual remarks commemorating the March 10 National Uprising, Tenzin
Gyatso acknowledged that abandoning the goal of independence had not
induced the Chinese to resume their dialog or improved Beijing's behavior. In 1995, Richard Gere took over the chairmanship of the
International Campaign for Tibet. To promote the Dalai Lama's proposals, Gere addressed the United Nations Human Rights Commission, the
U.S. Congress, and the European Parliament.

China's obstinance seemed to harden in direct proportion to the
Dalai Lama's growing fame. Not only did Beijing ignore his initiatives,
but conditions inside Tibet worsened. It was in 1996 when Chinese
authorities made simple possession of a photograph of the Dalai Lama a
criminal offense punishable by up to seven years in jail.

STUDENT MOVEMENT
SWELLS THE RANKS

In 1994, the free Tibet movement spread to colleges and universities,
thanks to a joint undertaking of the International Campaign for Tibet
and the U.S. Tibet Committee to form Students for a Free Tibet. In its
first year alone, the movement sprouted at a rate of six chapters monthly,
reaching a total of 75 college and university campuses. College students
underwent training in political activism emphasizing Gandhian nonviolent protest, and in turn fanned out to high schools and other colleges to
spread their knowledge of political protest tactics.

As student activists began organizing, among their first targets were
businesses operating in China. An economic Action Committee was created to monitor the corporations involved with the U.S. China Business
Council. When the hotel chain Holiday Inn was targeted with a boycott
for collaborating with the Chinese government's plans to increase
tourism, the company eventually closed its facilities in Tibet.

One of the most successful efforts to raise awareness about Tibet
among the young people of Generation X and the Millenial Generation
was the collaboration between musician Adam Yauch of the Beastie Boys
and a 21-year-old woman named Erin Potts. Together, Yauch and Potts

organized the Tibetan Freedom Concerts, a combination of mass movement and large-scale fundraising.

It began in 1994. Two tracks on the Beastie Boys' newly released album, *Ill Communication*, featured Tibetan monks. The band wanted to make sure the monks received royalties. Potts and Yauch cofounded a not-for-profit organization called The Milarepa Fund to distribute the money, named after a revered Tibetan Buddhist, Milarepa, who used music in his teachings. While performing as headliners for the 1994 Lollapalooza Tour, Yauch and Potts hit on the idea of doing a concert series to benefit Tibet.

The first of the Tibetan Freedom Concerts was held in San Francisco on June 15 and 16, 1996, before a crowd of 100,000. Popular bands, such as Rage Against the Machine and Smashing Pumpkins, performed. Robert Thurman and Chinese and Tibetan prodemocracy activists addressed the crowd. The concert netted $800,000, which went into The Milarepa Fund, whose expanded purpose now included broad support for the Tibetan movement.

Concertgoers loved the San Francisco event, but it failed to attract attention from the national press. To elevate the media profile, Potts and Yauch chose New York for the next venue. In 1997, artists ranging from Alanis Morisette and U2 to Björk and KRS-ONE performed over June 7 and 8 at Downing Stadium, Randall's Island, in New York City. Some 30 groups and soloists made appearances, including Nawang Khechog, a former Buddhist monk and Grammy nominee.

Nawang was born in Eastern Tibet to a family of nomads. In the mid-1950s, when Nawang was three years old, his father decided to leave Tibet. He packed his family's belongings onto their livestock, and the family set out by yak for India. The journey covered more than 1000 miles and took three years. In India, Nawang studied Buddhist philosophy and meditation and became a monk. He spent several years as a hermit, deep in meditation in the foothills of the Himalayas. He taught himself music, playing his trademark flute and traditional Tibetan instruments like the long horn. Nawang has performed at Carnegie Hall, toured on several continents, produced five albums, coproduced two more, and composed the music for the New York play *Road Home* by Academy Award winning writer James Lecesne.

He also collaborated with Allen Ginsberg. The two men formed a strong bond and took semiannual meditation retreats together in Colorado during the last decade of Ginsberg's life. Ginsberg had always understood the power of the concert to elevate consciousness. In the summer of 1981, just before he moved to Boulder, Colorado, Allen Ginsberg went on tour with The Clash. He had toured before with Bob Dylan in the mid-1970s, but his performances with The Clash took his revolutionary rhetoric to the new Generation X audience whose members were just coming of age.

In 1997, Allen Ginsberg died in his East Village loft in New York City. That same year, *TIME* magazine named Robert Thurman one of its 25 most influential people in America. Ginsberg's life odyssey had taken him from outcast to counterculture hero to icon of American literature. Thurman's path had evolved from wanderer to Buddhist monk to professor to activist.

Washington, DC, was the site for the third Tibetan Freedom Concert. Nawang appeared again, as did R.E.M., the Dave Matthews Band, Pearl Jam, Blues Traveler, and 17 other bands. The concert took place over June 13 and 14 at RFK Stadium. Despite a tragic lightning strike during an afternoon thunderstorm that injured 12 people, four of them critically, the concert was a success in terms of fundraising and media coverage. The performances netted $1.2 million for The Milarepa fund.

The year 1998 was also when the CIA declassified new information relating to its Tibetan operations. The fact that the United States had given $1.7 million a year to the Tibetan government-in-exile and resistance before Kissinger cut the funding was disclosed for the first time. Adam Yauch and Erin Potts' concert series raised $2.5 million.

The rock concerts reached youthful audiences whose social consciousness was just expanding to embrace causes like freeing Tibet. They boosted the efforts of Students for a Free Tibet to recruit supporters on college campuses. The synthesis of poetry, popular music, and the campuses was crucial in passing the torch to a new generation of activists.

HOLLYWOOD INTRODUCES
A NEW GENERATION TO TIBET

Hollywood's interest in Tibet developed into box-office success in the mid-1990s, when Heinrich Harrer's memoir of life in Lhasa, *Seven Years in Tibet*, was made into a movie. In 1961, during his summer interlude on Greece, Ginsberg had included the book on his reading list. The 1996 movie starred Brad Pitt in the role of Harrer, and the film became a hit. Pitt's popularity and celebrity appeal introduced a new generation of admirers, especially his female fans, to the story of Tibet and the Dalai Lama. Nawang Khechog's music was used in the film's soundtrack. Because of the story's time frame, the movie did not delve into Harrer's subsequent contacts with U.S. diplomats and involvement in efforts to get the Dalai Lama to go into exile nor did the movie touch on the CIA's operations in Tibet.

Martin Scorsese was another Hollywood titan to tackle the story of the Dalai Lama. His film, *Kundun,* is an accurate yet mystical portrayal of the Dalai Lama's early life and the initial period of Chinese repression. It too omits the CIA's involvement. In fairness, at the time Scorsese's film was made only skeletal details of the Agency's Tibetan operations were known.

Through these movies, millions of people who would otherwise have known little about historical Tibet were introduced to the Dalai Lama and his people. More importantly, many of these moviegoers were of a new generation. Without the interest and commitment of celebrities and directors and writers in Hollywood, this new awareness of Tibet in the 1990s would not have been possible.

TIBETANS PRESERVING THEIR OWN ART AND CULTURE

While interest in Tibet was going global in the 1990s, the Tibetans themselves were working to preserve their cultural traditions and civilization. Ten miles below McLeod Ganj, down in the valley on the outskirts of the Indian town of Sidhpur, the Norbulingka Institute for Tibetan Culture was opened in 1995. The compound, built to replicate the Dalai Lama's summer palace in Lhasa, is a school for artists and artisans. There, in an idyllic setting of gardens and overhanging trees and pools of trickling water, apprentices learn the visual and decorative arts master to pupil, as they have been practiced for generations.

The land for the Norbulingka Institute was purchased with a donation from Japan. The Dalai Lama himself undertook the fundraising to erect the buildings, and construction began in 1988. The Institute has approximately 430 professional staff, workers, and students.

Each year, approximately two dozen students are admitted to study *thangka* painting, creating intricate depictions of meditating deities on delicate scrolls, as well as decorative and textile arts. Prospective students must be 18 years of age and submit a written letter of application to be considered for admission. Many are newly arrived from Tibet and learn these traditional arts both as a means of sustaining their culture and themselves by earning a livelihood.

The *thangka* studio, accessible by a narrow stone staircase, is spacious and well lit. The studio accommodates up to 25 artists and pupils, a mixture of monks, a few nuns, and ordinary Tibetans. Artists sit either cross-legged on cushions, or perched on small stools, their backs to the tall narrow windows so the sunlight illuminates their easels. The creation of a *thangka* begins with cloth, the color of unbleached cotton, stretched taut over wooden frames. In good weather, this work might be done outdoors on the rooftop patio just outside the studio door. Before the painting begins, a background color, sometimes red, is applied using paints made from crushed minerals. There are 13 rules and regulations governing proportion, color, and the depiction of deities that the artists must learn. Within them, there is room for creativity. It takes the pupils three years to become certified as *thangka* artists, and the individual *thangkas* they create require two-to-three months for completion of an average work and up to six months for a large-scale piece.

Another studio is devoted to furniture and the applied arts. Here ten artists work at decorating mirrors, chests, and boxes, with carvings and stencils and tempera paint mixed with glue and applied by a syringe to make detailed designs. The resulting pieces are quality furniture art, instantly collectible.

A third studio is dedicated to the Appliqué Section. Rich swatches of cloth, stenciled silk, and sewing tools are everywhere. The studio accommodates nine students and 20 artists. It takes the students three years to master the full course in textile work. They work collaboratively. Textile artists specialize in piecework, which is then sewn together in a team effort, as it was originally done in Tibet. The end result can be decorated pieces up to 14-feet long featuring the work of many different artists.

Collectors from around the world commission the artists and artisans of the Norbulingka to create special pieces. Many *thangkas* are sold before they are painted, destined for meditation centers, household shrines, and individual collections. The fine artwork from the Norbulingka Institute proliferates worldwide.

Many visitors, Tibetans and tourists, come to the Institute just to stroll in the gardens, spin the bronze prayer wheels, watch the artists work, and visit the Doll Museum. It contains miniature displays of scenes and traditional clothing from the different regions of Tibet. Nomads of Eastern Tibet are shown outside their tents, livestock nearby, while a scene from Lhasa shows the Potala Palace and the distinctive garb of the city's administrative classes. There are miniature monasteries, depictions of the courts of past Tibetan rulers, including the ninth-century King Tri Relbachen, who convened the first international medical conference in the Himalayas. The Doll Museum dioramas, painstakingly crafted by monks and nuns in Southern India to show Tibet before the Chinese invasion, particularly fascinate Tibetan children.

A HANDFUL OF MONASTERIES RISE ANEW

Inside Tibet, a handful of monastery restorations began in the 1990s. Many are the work of Tibetans themselves. Others were started by outside groups like the China Exploration and Research Society (CERS), a group of Sinophiles and prominent Chinese-Americans like organizer Wong How Man. They have helped repair and conserve some of Tibet's greatest treasures, monasteries, that were damaged or destroyed during the Cultural Revolution.

In 1994 CERS took on the job of repairing the finest surviving set of Buddhist murals in Western Sichuan at Pewar Monastery in Derge. Pewar is a small monastery in comparison to others. Its original temple, no longer standing, was built nearly 700 years ago. The main temple was built around 1735 by King Denba Tsering. Pewar was the last of his many building projects and, as such, the monastery received the large remainder of his construction budget.

It was not the building that interested CERS, but the murals it contained. While the temple's 100 gold statues, including a 1.5 meter-high gold statue of Sakyamuni were all destroyed or looted during the Cultural Revolution (along with the only Litang edition of the Kangyur—commentaries on Sakyamuni's commandments—left on the entire Tibetan plateau), the one thing the Chinese were not able to take and did not completely destroy were Pewar's murals. The temple's first level contains 28 panels covering some 300 square meters depicting sacred deities, decorations, and images highlighted in gold. Upstairs in the temple's lantern room are some 43 square meters of additional painting.

While all restoration efforts are welcome, the widespread destruction of monasteries means it will take decades, perhaps centuries, to repair the damage. Even with the best of conservation and restoration efforts, inevitably some cultural heritage is irretrievably lost.

TIBETAN LIFEWAYS HANGING ON

Tibetan Buddhism is not simply made up of prayers, chants, prostrations, and turnings of prayer wheels. Tibetan songs, dances, and festivals are all rooted within Tibetan Buddhism, one not able to exist without the other. Previous to the Chinese invasion Tibetans came together to sing, dance, race horses, and celebrate for days on end.

Many of these beautiful Tibetan festivals are allowed to continue inside Tibet, albeit in somewhat edited versions. But, they are celebrated in Dharamsala and throughout different parts of the world in their original ways. These festivals keep the spark of Tibet's cultural and religious freedom from being extinguished and include the following.

Losar, is the celebration of the Tibetan New Year. The exact date varies from year to year according to Tibet's lunar calendar, but it falls on the 1st to 3rd days of the 1st Lunar month.

The **Great Prayer Festival,** or Monlam Chenmo, is Tibet's greatest religious festival and was celebrated inside Tibet since 1409. It is now faithfully celebrated in Dharamsala, India and takes place between the 4th and 11th days of the first Tibetan lunar month.

The **Tibetan Shoton Festival,** sometimes today called the yogurt festival, is an annual celebration of Tibetan Opera rooted in the founding of Drepung Monastery in Lhasa, Tibet.

Tibetan Uprising Day is celebrated every year on March 10th to commemorate the Tibetan people's uprising against the Chinese on that date in 1959. It has become traditional for His Holiness the Dalai Lama to mark the occasion with a special statement.

The **Saka Dawa Festival** is held on the 15th day of the 4th lunar month to celebrate Shakyamuni's Buddhahood and the death of his mortal body.

In Eastern Tibet, the **Litang Horse Festival,** traditionally a part of the Harvest Festival, takes place in August. Horsemen, and observers, gather from surrounding towns to exhibit their dexterity and ability as riders.

In the documentary film, *Tibet, Cry of the Snow Lion,* Robert Thurman explains the Buddhist celebrations: "Religion for Tibetans is a source of fun. They do not feel God created the world to punish and torture them. They don't feel God created the world—or that he has any control over them. The only thing that brings them happiness or can cause them any trouble is their own behavior."

TIBETAN WRITERS ORGANIZE

Lhasang Tsering, who had joined the resistance fighters in Mustang just before their funding was cut off, was one of the organizers of The First National Conference of Tibetan Writers. Held in March 1995, at the Bhagsu Hotel in McLeod Ganj, the conference brought together exiled Tibetan writers from throughout Nepal, the United Kingdom, the United States, Switzerland, and various parts of India to perpetuate the Tibetan language, Tibetan literature, and Tibetan history. It was sponsored by the Amnye Machen Institute (AMI), which was cofounded by Lhasang Tsering and was named for a mountain range in Eastern Tibet. The Dalai Lama inaugurated the writer's conference by stressing the need to keep the Tibetan language alive through literature.

Scholarly writers, such as Dhongthog Rinpoche from Seattle and Rakra Rinpoche from Switzerland, were in attendance, as was Lhagon Kyap, a 21-year-old exile writer recently arrived from Tibet. AMI's purpose is to study the past to help Tibetans understand the present and prepare for the future. The Institute's concerns extend beyond preservation. It is dedicated to informing and raising cultural and intellectual awareness of the Tibetan people, both inside Tibet and in exile. AMI's goal is to make available and accessible to the Tibetan people their rich heritage of literature, culture, and scientific knowledge.

CHINA SLAMS THE DOOR SHUT

False hopes and disappointments were to characterize the 1990s in terms of making concrete progress with China. Although direct contacts between the Tibetan government-in-exile and Beijing ended after Tiananmen Square, both sides periodically used indirect channels to put out feelers and communicate. Several times throughout the decade, China indicated that talks might resume, provided the Dalai Lama agreed to accept preconditions.

The 1998 Beijing summit between President Bill Clinton and President Jiang Zemin is an example of how China kept raising the hurdle to talks by making fresh demands. Just before he left for the summit, Students for a Free Tibet had bombarded the White House with 1.2 million postcards urging Clinton to press Jiang Zemin to negotiate with the Dalai Lama. At their joint news conference, Clinton took the unprecedented step of publicly urging Jiang Zemin to negotiate with the Dalai Lama. The Chinese president responded that "the door to dialog and negotiation is open," provided the Dalai Lama accepted a new precondition. He had already agreed to give up Tibet's claim to independence. Now Jiang Zemin wanted the Dalai Lama to acknowledge that Tibet and Taiwan were integral parts of China before talks could start.

Tenzin Gyatso replied that he could not speak for Taiwan. Reaffirming his commitment to the Middle-Way, he expressed hope that the two sides would be able to start talks in earnest. These messages were relayed through the media and intermediaries. But by December 1999, the Chinese shut off even the informal channels of communication.

Despite the lack of progress with China, it was not a lost decade for the free Tibet movement. It had taken root with a new generation, spreading beyond the counterculture to become a popular global cause. From its culture and arts to its political and religious freedom, Tibet had never had so many supporters around the world. As the number of people backing the Dalai Lama grew, their political leaders became more willing to speak out on Tibet's behalf. Change was growing from the grassroots upwards.

Chapter 15

The Tibetan National Uprising of 2008

Gyalo Thondup received an unusual invitation in July 2000. He was asked to come to Beijing to meet privately with officials from the United Front Department of the Chinese Communist Party. Hoping that this might be the long-awaited response to the Dalai Lama's proposals, Gyalo went to China. There, three senior officials told him bluntly that Tenzin Gyatso should return to China unconditionally. They had no intention of discussing autonomy or any of the Tibetans' other concerns. Despite this fresh disappointment, in September the Dalai Lama sent a letter to the Chinese officials suggesting that he send a delegation to begin a dialog with Beijing.

OLYMPIC PROMISES RAISE HOPES

In the summer of 2000, China's leadership had good reason to encourage the Dalai Lama to bring his two decades of exile to an end. Britain had just ceded its territorial control over Hong Kong to Beijing, removing one of the last vestiges of foreign colonialism. The celebrations to turn over Hong Kong were attended by many world leaders and featured extravagant fireworks and pageantry. Now there were two more initiatives China hoped to successfully complete to boost its international prestige at the start of the new millennium.

The first initiative involved China's long-sought goal of joining the World Trade Organization (WTO). The country's leaders saw WTO membership as crucial to their plans to build their economy by using their competitive advantage of cheap labor, lax environmental standards, and low manufacturing costs to become one of the world's largest exporters.

The second initiative was a bid to host the 2008 summer Olympic Games. The Chinese hoped to use the Olympic Games as their "coming out party," a global public relations blitz to showcase their nation as a modernized country that had made huge gains over the past 30 years.

From the vantage point of China's leaders, winning the competition to host the Olympics and gaining WTO membership would symbolize the country's growing international power. By inviting Gyalo to Beijing in 2000 to tell him his brother should return to the fold, the Chinese hoped to clear away any difficulties the unresolved question of Tibet might pose to either WTO membership or winning the 2008 Olympics.

China knew that the main impediment standing between it and the Games was human rights. In 1993, the U.S. House of Representatives passed a resolution strongly opposing allowing Beijing to host the 2000 Olympic Games. Representative Tom Lantos sponsored the resolution.

"Given the abominable human rights record of Communist China," Lantos said in 1993, "It would be unthinkable and unconscionable to agree to holding the Olympics in China in 2000."

Lantos urged the International Olympic Committee (IOC) to find an alternative venue. It may not have been entirely due to Lantos' resolution, but the 2000 Olympic Games were held in Sydney, Australia. Determined not to lose the Games a second time, China promised the IOC that it would improve on its abysmal record regarding human rights if chosen to host the 2008 Olympics.

The Olympic Charter is explicit about the connection between human rights and the Olympic movement. Contrary to the widespread misimpression that the Games are only about athletic competition, the second principle of the Charter's "Fundamental Principles of Olympism" states:

"The goal of Olympism is to place sport at the service of the harmonious development of man, with a view to promoting a peaceful society concerned with the preservation of human dignity."

Principle # 5 is also indisputable:

"Any form of discrimination with regard to a country or a person on grounds of race, religion, politics, gender or otherwise is incompatible with belonging to the Olympic Movement."

The Tibetans were naturally justified in hoping that China's commitment to improve human rights would be in accordance with the Olympic Charter. If applied to Tibet, the Charter's principles of nondiscrimination based on religion, politics, and preservation of human dignity could have no other meaning than giving the Tibetans the freedoms they had enjoyed before the Chinese invasion. Anything less would mean that the Olympic Charter's principles were a sham.

Jacques Rogge, the Belgian yachtsman who was president of the IOC, repeatedly assured the world that China had made commitments to allow freedom of expression if it won the right to host the Olympic Games. In 2001, China was awarded the 2008 Olympic Games and gained admission to the WTO. Rogge's assurances regarding human rights and the Olympics raised expectations among Chinese democracy activists and Tibetans. The IOC president unwittingly set the stage for the riots that would explode across Tibet seven years later, when those hopes were brutally crushed by China.

CHINA AGREES TO TALK
WITH TIBETAN DELEGATIONS

Soon after it won the competition to host the summer Olympics, Chinese officials accepted the Dalai Lama's offer to send delegations to open a dialog. Between 2002 and 2008, representatives from the Tibetan government-in-exile held talks with the Chinese government on six occasions. According to one delegate, the talks were more like exchanges than a real dialog. Instead of discussing issues, the Chinese highlighted the value of their economic development in Tibet and in China proper and encouraged the Tibetans to accept the status quo. For their part, the Tibetan delegates try to impress on the Chinese that their desire for genuine autonomy is not a ruse or stepping stone to achieve complete independence.

Chinese officials pointed to some $13.8 billion in spending in the Tibetan Autonomous Region (TAR) since its creation in 1965. But the

Tibetan delegates are all too aware that the improvements taking place inside TAR rarely reach the masses of Tibetans. Eighty-five percent of Tibetans live in rural areas outside the major towns of Lhasa and Shigatse, earning little more than a dollar a day. The average annual income of rural Tibetans was $398 in 2007. In contrast, the income of urban dwellers in Tibet, most of whom are now Han Chinese, is $1,588 a year, almost 400 percent higher than in the countryside. The modernization the Chinese officials viewed with pride was seen by the Tibetan delegates as one-sided development intended to benefit China, not Tibet.

As delegation after delegation returned bearing no news of progress, the result was a growing and visible sense of frustration among Tibetan exiles that the Chinese were not negotiating in good faith. Some suspected that China was merely keeping up the appearance of a dialog to avoid criticism in advance of the Olympic Games.

RAILWAY SPEEDS CHINA'S PLAN
TO MAKE TIBETANS A MINORITY

In 2006, China opened a high-speed railway between Qinghai and Tibet. The train made it possible for millions of Chinese citizens and tourists to easily traverse the 1140-km stretch between Golmud in China and Lhasa, Tibet's capital. The government claimed a principal reason for building the $2.3 billion railway was to accommodate the rising numbers of tourists traveling to Tibet, but others suspect the real reason is to transport Chinese immigrants. In its 2007 annual report, the Tibetan Centre for Human Rights & Democracy said that in the first ten months of the year the railway transported 3.72 million passengers, a 50% increase in people traveling to Tibet over the previous year.

China has a policy of encouraging Han Chinese, the majority among the country's 56 separate ethnic groups, to move permanently to Tibet. Through supplemental salary increases, bonuses, and housing allowances, the Han Chinese are rewarded for immigrating to Tibet.

In July, 2007, there were floods in the lower plains of mainland China. Rather than rebuild water-damaged homes and villages, many of the people dislocated by the floods were resettled in Lhasa. Beijing residents uprooted from entire neighborhoods demolished to make room for the construction of new facilities for the 2008 Olympics also immigrated to Tibet. By 2008, it was estimated that between 6 million and 8 million Han Chinese were living inside Tibet's borders. If these numbers are accurate, the Tibetans have already become a minority in their own homeland. In the capital of Lhasa, two out of every three people are non-Tibetans.

One of the major Chinese boasts is that modern development has brought Tibet dramatic improvements in the standard of living. But the benefits are often one sided. Measured by employment and economic opportunity, Tibet has two vastly different economies. The economy of the urban towns is dominated by immigrant Han Chinese, while the much poorer, less developed countryside and rural villages are left to the Tibetans.

In the cities, Tibetans are up against a number of obstacles. The tourist industry is an example of how economic development favors ethnic Chinese. Tourism is one of Tibet's growth industries, but most tour guides are Han Chinese. In 2006, some 70 guides were relocated from China to Tibet under its "Guides from Inland to Aid Tibet" program. The reason for pushing out the Tibetan tour guides and replacing them with Han Chinese is to make it easier for the government to propagate the officially approved version of Tibet's history. In this manner, foreign and Chinese tourists in Tibet are subjected to Chinese indoctrination by their tour guides, whether they realize it or not.

Before a guide can get a license, he or she has to be proficient in Chinese and English. Tibetans who had already learned English in India had their tourist guide licenses cancelled by the Chinese authorities, who require the guides to learn Chinese first and then English in a government-approved facility. The requirement to learn Chinese is a stiff barrier for Tibetans wanting to become guides. Because of deficiencies in the state-run education system for Tibetans, few are able to become fluent in Chinese. This makes it virtually impossible to qualify not only for guide jobs, but most white collar employment because contracts, bank documents, permits, papers, and regulations are all written in Chinese.

Tourism-related industries, such as hotels, restaurants, and even the sale of Tibetan handicrafts and tourist trinkets, pose similar barriers. Many of the souvenir shops in Lhasa proffering Tibetan handicrafts are in fact owned by Han Chinese and their wares are fakes and copies produced by Chinese artisans.

The sheer scale of the recent influx of Han Chinese made matters worse by causing rising unemployment and a spike in food costs. The result was a growing numbers of beggars, both Chinese and Tibetan. To keep Lhasa appealing to tourists, Chinese officials began regular street sweeps to "clean up" the city center by rounding up indigents. Ethnic Tibetans were given strict orders to go back to their rural villages and not return to Lhasa. Chinese beggars, however, were not sent back to their hometowns in China.

THE CASE OF WOESER

Woeser, who uses only one name in the tradition of Tibet, was fired from her job as an editor with the Lhasa-based Chinese language journal, *Tibetan Literature*, for writing about the Dalai Lama. In her 2003 book, *Tibet Notes*, a compilation of 38 of her short stories published by Huacheng Publishing House in Guangzhou, Woeser had a favorable reference to the Dalai Lama. To Shi Jifeng, Deputy Director of China's General Bureau of Journalism and Publication, this was a firing offense.

The official charges against her were praising the Fourteenth Dalai Lama and the Seventeenth Karmapa, Ogyen Trinley Dorje, encouraging reverence and belief in religion, and encouraging nostalgia for the old Tibet. She was barred from her editing work and ordered to leave Tibet.

Woeser didn't fit the usual profile for a Tibetan activist. Her parents were Communist party members, and she herself believed the party line about liberating Tibet's serfs. She learned Chinese, earned a degree in Chinese literature, and began writing poetry. She didn't awaken politically until China interfered in the selection of Tibet's second-most important religious leader after the Dalai Lama, the Panchen Lama.

After being forced out of Tibet, Woeser began writing a blog from the apartment in Beijing, where she lives under house arrest. Her husband, Wang Lixiong, supports her now that she has lost her job. She has written a history of the Great Proletarian Cultural Revolution as experienced by some 70 Tibetans she interviewed, but it is not yet translated into English. In China, the book, along with her other works, was banned by the authorities. Her case illustrates China's failure to live up to its Olympic promises, and how easy it is for even a well-qualified Tibetan to lose a job over a minor infraction.

CONGRESS AWARDS THE DALAI LAMA
ITS GOLD MEDAL

October is normally a splendid month in Washington, DC, and the fall of 2007 was no exception. The extreme summer humidity was gone, as were the summer crowds of tourists. In the off years, between elections, autumn is a season when Washingtonians ordinarily relax. But this October wasn't ordinary. Thousands of Tibetans and Buddhists had come in busloads from around the country, joining the estimated 10,000 Buddhists already living in the area, to be a part of history. At National Cathedral, Buddhist monks painstakingly made a sand *mandala*. Created for use in rituals of initiation and meditations, the tradition of sand mandalas has lasted throughout the generations.

To a Westerner, the *mandala* is simply a beautiful artwork, but to the Tibetans they are an integral part of Buddhism. Embodying the concepts of impermanence and nonattachment, the *mandala* is made over a period of days or weeks by applying one grain of sand at a time to a previously laid out sketch. At the conclusion of the initiation or meditation, the *mandala* is destroyed to symbolize the impermanence of life. To carry healing blessings throughout the world, the sand is poured into a nearby stream or body of water.

Inside the White House on October 16, President Bush and the Dalai Lama met for half an hour. It was not their first meeting. In fact, it was the fourth time President George W. Bush and Tenzin Gyatso had gotten together. The last visit had been in 2005, when the Dalai Lama was in Washington to speak at a conference of thousands of the world's top neuroscientists. But this occasion was different than their previous encounters. It was the day before the Dalai Lama was scheduled to receive a rare honor, the Congressional Gold Medal.

President Bush had stunned and outraged the Chinese government when he announced that he would personally bestow the medal in a ceremony on Capitol Hill in front of a phalanx of reporters and television cameras and Washington VIPs and celebrities. Never before had a U.S. president met publicly like this with the Dalai Lama, much less presented him with such a distinguished honor.

When reporters pressed for details about the private meeting, White House Press Secretary Dana Perino, was atypically reticent.

"There is no way we want to stir the pot and make China feel we are sticking a stick in their eye," Perino said when asked to release White House photos of the meeting. "This might be one thing we can do, but I don't believe it's going to soothe the feelings of the Chinese."

It was the understatement of the year. In September 2007, just before German Chancellor Angela Merkel met with the Dalai Lama, Chinese officials warned that she "was playing with fire." Chinese authorities routinely pressure world leaders not to meet officially with the Dalai Lama. Unswayed, Merkel went ahead with the meeting. During a subsequent official visit to China, Beijing retaliated by snubbing Germany's top economic officials and refusing to meet with them.

The Congressional Gold Medal is one of America's highest honors, the civilian equivalent of the Medal of Honor. It takes two-thirds of the members of the House and the Senate to cosponsor a proposed award. Then, the award goes to the floor of the House and the Senate for a full vote.

For months, Chinese diplomats had lobbied Congress, going door to door in House and Senate offices pressing Hill staffers to persuade their bosses to vote against giving the Dalai Lama the medal. They had competition from two elected officials, both Democrats from California. Senator Dianne Feinstein and Congressman Tom Lantos were jointly responsible for proposing the award.

Lantos, a Holocaust survivor who was born in Budapest and immigrated to the States in 1947, was chairman of the House Foreign Affairs Committee. He knew firsthand what it was like to suffer religious persecution, military occupation, and an oppressive regime. Among his achievements in a long congressional career was to be founder and cochair of the Congressional Human Rights Caucus in 1983. Moreover, he was an activist. In 2006, Lantos was arrested, along with other members of Congress, protesting human rights abuses in Darfur at the Embassy of Sudan.

Feinstein and Lantos put muscle into the effort to get members to sign on to the award. Republican Senator Larry Craig was another original cosponsor. Representative Ileana Ros-Lehtinen, a Cuban-American and conservative Republican from Florida, aided by instructing her staff to line up backers and identify wavering members of Congress with unresolved questions about the award's impact.

Members who needed extra persuasion got a visit from Lodi Gyaltsen Gyari, the Dalai Lama's special envoy to Washington. Gyari, a reincarnated lama whose mother, Dorjee, was prominent in the Tibetan resistance beginning in the 1950s, went from office to office patiently explaining the Dalai Lama's Middle-Way approach. He reassured lawmakers that the Dalai Lama didn't propose splitting Tibet from China. When the votes were counted, the Dalai Lama became the 133rd recipient of the coveted medal in the country's history.

China's reaction to the news that President Bush intended to give the Dalai Lama the congressional award was immediate and harsh. Foreign Minister Yang Jiechi, "solemnly demanded" that the White House cancel the ceremony. A Foreign Ministry spokesman warned it would "seriously damage" United States-China relations.

"China resolutely opposes the U.S. Congress awarding its so-called Congressional Gold Medal," the spokesman said, "and firmly opposes any country or any person using the Dalai issue to interfere in China's internal affairs."

Despite the Chinese threats, the ceremony went forward as planned on October 17 in the Capitol Rotunda, a small chamber that made the award presentation more intimate. House Speaker Nancy Pelosi hosted the event. The Rotunda was filled to capacity with Republicans as well as Democrats, Tibetans and Americans, and actors and musicians. Political dignitaries mingled with celebrities like Richard Gere, seated in rows of chairs before the dais.

After remarks by the political leaders and the president, the Dalai Lama took the podium. For a brief moment he had trouble with the folds of his robe but characteristically laughed it off. As he spoke about his homeland and hopes for peace and autonomy for the Tibetan people his warm smile, contagious laugh, and engaging personality kept the audience both entertained and captivated.

"Many of the world's problems are ultimately rooted in inequality and injustice, whether economic, political, or social," the Dalai Lama said. "Whether it is the suffering of poverty in one part of the world, or whether it is the denial of freedom and basic human rights in another part, we should never perceive these events in total isolation. Eventually their repercussions will be felt everywhere . . . the time has come to address all these global issues from the perspective of the oneness of

humanity, and from a profound understanding of the deeply intercon-
nected nature of today's world."

In the space of about an hour, the ceremony was over. The Dalai
Lama moved to the West Front of the Capitol. Spread out on the lawn
below were thousands of people waiting patiently to hear him speak. The
day's events were followed by a peace concert at the National Cathedral.
Several thousand people gathered to hear David Crosby, Graham Nash,
Jackson Browne, Emily Saliers of the Indigo Girls, and other artists per-
form. The inspiration for the concert stemmed from a 2003 speech the
Dalai Lama delivered at National Cathedral. Episcopal Bishop John
Bryson Chane noticed Crosby and Nash in the audience and after the
speech he struck up a conversation with them. When the Congressional
Gold Medal award was being planned, Chane, a fellow musician, asked
Crosby and Nash to host a peace concert, with the proceeds going to
benefit the ICT and the Cathedral Center for Global Justice and
Reconciliation. The 2008 concert was a success, and in a line that echoed
the 1960s, Crosby thanked the concert-goers "for coming to give peace a
chance."

The following night the Dalai Lama was feted at a gala hosted by
Senator Feinstein. Richard Gere, Martin Scorsese, Marvin Hamlisch,
and nearly 500 others attended the black-tie event. Scattered around
Washington were more plebeian gatherings, ranging from a film festival
to meditation sessions and Buddhist teachings. The events in Washington
were carried all around the world by television, cable, and Web cast, and
experienced by millions. Nothing happens in isolation, and the
Congressional Gold Medal award was no exception. Even inside Tibet, a
group of monks tried to celebrate the auspicious award.

THE START OF THE 2008
TIBETAN NATIONAL UPRISING

The stage was set in October 2007 for the riots that exploded across
Tibet the following March. And contrary to what the Chinese have purported, it wasn't the Dalai Lama or the "Dalai clique" that caused the
riots. It was the Chinese themselves.

When the Dalai Lama received the Congressional Gold Medal,
Tibetans throughout the world rejoiced. While Gold Medal celebrations
took place in Washington, DC, Dharamsala, India, and 36 Tibetan com-

munities scattered around the world, the Chinese Communist party banned any acknowledgment of the award inside Tibet.

The monks of Drepung monastery hoped to celebrate the award with a festival. When the authorities denied them permission, they decided instead to paint the monastery's walls to honor the Dalai Lama. On the appointed day, the monks set about cheerfully whitewashing the monastery's walls. But even this innocuous, apolitical expression of pride in honor of the Dalai Lama was too much for the authorities. Chinese police intervened in force, bloodying the monks with their batons, pulling some aside and pummeling them to the ground where they were kicked in the head and ribs and groin by groups of police officers.

The savagery stopped the whitewashing. Some monks lay bleeding on the ground, others sat beaten and stunned, as the police went through their ranks. As many as 30 monks were hustled out of the monastery for detention and questioning under a rain of punches and kicks from police thirsting to demonstrate their control. Drepung monastery was then sealed off and surrounded by China's People's Armed Police, paramilitary troops, often young, whose unlined faces made for deceptive masks of innocence. Pilgrims and tourists were turned away.

MARCH TO FREE THE DREPUNG FIVE

Eventually, most of the monks seized in October were released and returned to Drepung. But five remained in custody, a polite euphemism which masks the reality of conditions for a political prisoner of the Chinese. The winter of 2007 to 2008 was especially harsh in the Himalayas. Hundreds froze to death in nearby Afghanistan, while western China was brought to a halt by ice storms which stalled trains on their tracks and stranded millions of travelers trying to return home for the Chinese New Year celebrations.

In Tibet, the cold posed a deadly threat to political prisoners, who receive only threadbare blankets to huddle under in sparsely heated cells. Those lucky enough to have cellmates could at least share the warmth of another body. But in solitary confinement, after weeks of harsh interrogation, weakened from inadequate food, the cold can mean hypothermia. After uncontrollable shivering, lucid thought evaporates, and in a state of mental delusion bordering on hallucination, hypothermia causes one to drift into a fatal sleep. This is what the monks of the Drepung monastery knew faced five of their fellow men, the prisoners of the October white-washing, when they decided to march in unison and demand that the authorities release the inmates.

On March 10, 2008, some 300 monks assembled at Drepung monastery to march toward the historic Barkhor quarter of Lhasa, near the Jokhang temple, where they planned to issue their demands. They had chosen the date of the 49th anniversary of the Tibetan National Uprising to symbolize that the Tibetan spirit could not be crushed.

The marchers never arrived at their destination. Before reaching the city center they ran into a barricade manned by the People's Armed Police. Refusing to be stymied, the monks shouted in unison their demands to free the detainees. Unlike previous protests in Tibet, however, they did not demand independence.

The police responded savagely, wading into the ranks of yellow and burgundy-robed monks with truncheons, firearms at the ready, determined to break their formation. The scenes of brutality from the previous October were repeated. Fifty or more monks were apprehended. Hundreds more refused to be intimidated, and staged a sit-in on the street.

The police were posed with a stark choice: detain hundreds, risking a flare-up, or try to wait it out. Word of the sit-in spread and as many as 100 more monks joined those already gathered at the police checkpoint. For 12 hours, the two sides faced off uneasily.

ZHANG QINGLI DECLARES WAR

The battle of wills was a direct challenge to Zhang Qingli, China's top administrator in Tibet. The previous fall, Qingli had warned the United States of dire consequences if the Dalai Lama received the Congressional Gold Medal. Qingli, who describes his stance toward the Dalai Lama as a state of war, was responsible for the October 2007 crackdown at the Drepung monastery.

Now the protestors were openly disrespecting Qingli's authority. Left to his own discretion, Qingli no doubt would have ordered the use of deadly force. Without approval from higher authorities in Beijing, however, such a move would be hazardous to his career. Qingli was already in a delicate situation. There had been no protests on the streets of Lhasa for a decade. To Beijing, it might seem he had lost control. He needed time to consult his superiors.

News of the protests spread while police negotiators tried to persuade the monks to abandon their sit-in. At Barkhor Square in the city center, a group of about 15 monks unfurled the Tibetan national flag amid shouts for independence. This was dangerous. In 1988, before China's crackdown on democracy protestors in Tiananmen Square, two men who waved the Tibetan flag in Lhasa were immediately shot by police. Twenty years later, the monks weren't shot at, but they were arrested with the customary rough treatment from Chinese police.

At the checkpoint outside the city center the stand off continued until, their point having been made, the throng of monks dispersed. On March 11, the day after the initial protests, 500 monks from the Sera monastery marched in protest, demanding that the fifteen flag bearers be released. They too staged a sit-in. This one lasted seven hours before breaking up.

March 14, 2008, was to be a fateful day. The Drepung monks marched again, repeating their initial demands. Meanwhile, the Chinese had taken the decision to break up new protests swiftly. Qingli ordered the police to use heavy force. This time sufficient vehicles stood by to handle the mass arrests, beatings were severe, and Qingli was authorized to shoot Tibetans who bucked his authority.

A cluster of monks from the Ramoche monastery in the heart of Lhasa decided to join the protests. When police confronted them on a thriving commercial street in a predominantly Tibetan neighborhood, passersby incensed by the brutality thronged to their defense. In the melée, Chinese plainclothes officers who had blended into the crowds only seconds before suddenly made themselves known.

Now all Chinese were suspect. The Tibetans used stones to drive off the police, freeing the monks from their clutches. An empty police car was overturned and set on fire. Next the crowd took aim at the Chinese-owned businesses that had crept relentlessly into the Tibetan neighborhoods, expanding along with the growth of the Han Chinese population.

It was easy to distinguish which shops were Chinese and which were Tibetan. For years, Tibetan shop owners complained that Chinese authorities permitted Chinese entrepreneurs and business owners to erect large display signs, while Tibetans were limited to signage with small print. Now the prominent Chinese signs drew unwanted attention. Using gasoline and cylinders filled with fuel for stoves, the Tibetans set fire to Chinese-owned shops. Almost a thousand Chinese-owned businesses went up in flames. Foreign tourists saw ethnic Chinese being beaten by Tibetans, and while some were plainclothes police or informants, others were innocent victims of the violence.

TIBETAN RAGE BOILS OVER

The denial of human rights is so severe in Tibet that free people can hardly imagine the simple acts that constitute a crime. Tibetans can be imprisoned for speaking about a free Tibet or mentioning the Dalai Lama's name. Talking about the Chinese repression among friends is a criminal offense. Speaking with a foreign tourist about politics can land a Tibetan in jail for violating state secrets. Holding a peaceful gathering to commemorate an international award for the Dalai Lama is a crime. There is no freedom of the press, freedom of speech or religion, right to assemble, or freedom to petition government—rights that are taken for granted in democratic countries.

Even though Chinese officials claim that Tibetans are exempt from the "one-child rule," Tibetan women are reportedly forced to have abortions if they exceed the "one-child rule." Those who are unable to pay the fine levied by Chinese authorities for exceeding the rule with more than one birth face forced sterilization, usually carried out under barbaric conditions using no anesthesia or pain killers. After the sterilization, the women are left to care for themselves without nursing or postoperative care.

Tibetans who are imprisoned are beaten and tortured. Being hung from the ceiling by one's wrists and beaten with lead pipes is a typical form of Chinese torture reported by former prisoners. So, too, is being shocked with electric batons and whipped with braided steel wire on naked flesh.

Many Tibetans find they simply can no longer live with the human rights infractions that have been constant in their country since the 1950 Chinese invasion. The Tibetans have seen their rights winnowed away and their way of life and freedom of expression oppressed. Tibetan neighborhoods, livelihoods, and lands are continuing to be overtaken by the masses of Han Chinese migrants. It was only a matter of time before this frustration would, once again, take on the human face of protest.

Richard Gere summed it up in a March 14 interview with Wolf Blitzer on CNN.

"The sad reality is that the Tibetans have to be in a violent situation for people to notice," Gere said, "An incredibly peaceful, non-violent people—how do they find a way to get into the news, to capture the world's attention? It's sad it has had to come to this."

CHINA TRIES TO BLACK OUT THE NEWS

As the fires raged in Lhasa, dense smoke filled the air and stung the eyes and nose and throat. Exploding glass and collapsing timbers mingled with the sharp crack of high-velocity bullets as the Chinese paramilitary police started shooting Tibetans.

Photos of bloodied corpses, smuggled out to the world by cell phone and digital cameras over the Internet, showed neat little round holes squarely in the chests of many of the dead, evidence of precise, aimed fire. The vital zone of heart and lungs is where soldiers are taught to aim. It takes good marksmanship to make these kinds of wounds on people in a crowd, especially if they are moving, running, or using cover. It isn't easy, even for the steadiest of marksmen in the chaos of a riot or a firefight to score such neat hits, except at close range on a still target, or execution style.

"When they [the Tibetan monks] were shot at," Robert Thurman explained in a March 20, 2008 interview on the radio program, *Democracy Now*. "And when they were suppressed violently and beaten, then the Tibetan community exploded, because they are a tinder box, because China has been smothering them. . . ."

The protests began to radiate out from the Barkhor. Monks, nuns, and ordinary Tibetans spread through Lhasa's streets chanting, "Free Tibet, Free Tibet," "Tibet is Not Free," and, "Long Live the Dalai Lama." Chinese police ushered tourists away from the Barkhor, Lhasa's main shopping and gathering place, to keep foreigners from photographing or witnessing their crackdown. Anyone trying to take photographs or video of the protests was confronted by police or plainclothes officials and ordered to erase the photos and return to their hotels or homes. For tourists, hotels had become places of confinement. Police forces stood guard in front of hotels to keep the tourists inside until transportation was arranged to whisk them out of Tibet. This involuntary detention of tourists contributed to the blackout on news imposed by the Chinese.

Journalists, too, were barred from traveling to Tibet to get both sides of the story of the riots. With events spiraling out of control, the Chinese government began shutting down the news coming out of Tibet. Cell phone signals became harder and harder to get, restrictions on e-mail and the Internet inside China (including Tibet) were tighter than usual, and the popular Web site, YouTube, was shut down inside China.

The only images that the Chinese government released of the riots were of Tibetans seemingly wreaking mayhem in the city. Nowhere in the first days did the world see pictures of Tibetans being beaten, shot, or, arrested and hauled away to jail.

While the protests continued inside Lhasa, military police instituted a curfew throughout much of the city. By Saturday night on March 15 military police and tanks blocked streets in the city center. A handful of tourists managed to post information and comments on online travel Web sites. Some reported hearing gunfire, while others reported seeing violence erupt throughout the city, with police and military stationed everywhere.

Calling for an end to the violence, the Dalai Lama threatened to step down as Tibet's political leader if it continued. He appealed to the world for help and called for an international investigation of the situation inside Tibet.

The Chinese persisted in blaming the riots on the Dalai Lama and the Dalai clique. Chinese officials and news outlets accused the Dalai Lama of planning and inciting "splittist" actions to divide Tibet from China. In response, the Dalai Lama offered to open up the files of the Tibetan government-in-exile to any credible international body to prove that there had been no conspiracy to instigate the protests.

Reacting to the Dalai Lama's strong denials, Chinese Premiere Wen Jiabao labeled the Dalai clique hypocritical liars. Adding personal insult, Zhang Qingli called the Dalai Lama "a monster with a human face." Over the following weeks, the Chinese stepped up their campaign of vilification, charging the Dalai Lama with masterminding the riots to mar the 2008 Beijing Summer Olympics.

It was a severe distortion of the truth. The Dalai Lama, in fact, was well known for supporting the Beijing Olympics. He sincerely believed hosting the Olympic Games might boost the confidence of China's leadership sufficiently to change its behavior. The Olympics, the Dalai Lama hoped, would have a moderating effect and perhaps lead at last to a breakthrough in the hoped-for talks about his Middle-Way Approach. From the Dalai Lama's vantage, disrupting the Olympics would be counterproductive to the Tibetans' longstanding diplomatic objectives.

AS THE UPRISING SPREADS, CHINA TRIES TO SPIN THE STORY

Demonstrations in Lhasa were just the beginning. The unrest quickly spread to Eastern Tibet, where protests sprang up in Kardze, Tongkor, Macchu, and Ngaba. In the first week following the Lhasa protests, there were at least 63 demonstrations throughout Tibet and Western China.

The protests and demonstrations were a reality check. They jarred sharply with the image China was projecting to the world, the image of a rapidly developing country with an increasingly better standard of living for its people and a stable and reliable trading partner whose economic growth would soon make it one of the world's most powerful countries. Cognitive dissonance set in; if China was so attractive, why were Tibetans rioting and risking death to protest?

Taking a page from the past, Chinese authorities responded in late March by inviting a select group of international journalists on a government-sponsored trip to Lhasa. The Chinese government clearly hoped that the journalists would corroborate their version that the riots were an outburst of ethnic hatred instigated by the Dalai Lama.

Accompanied by watchful Chinese officials, the reporters were allowed to see the city and interview selected Tibetans and Han Chinese. They were not allowed independent access in Lhasa or elsewhere and were prohibited from speaking freely with Tibetan or Han Chinese citizens. Instead, they were led on a highly structured and scripted media tour orchestrated by Chinese officials.

One of the stops on the media tour was the Jokhang temple. On the morning of the journalists' scheduled visit, military trucks and personnel who had kept the Jokhang surrounded since the first protests on March 10 were withdrawn.

As journalists neared the temple approximately 30 monks surrounded them, calling out "Tibet is not free! Tibet is not free!" As some monks broke into tears, others told the foreign press that the Dalai Lama was not behind the protests or violence that had shaken their city. A few monks even told the reporters that they knew they were taking a great risk by speaking the truth but were willing to bear the consequences. Crying, one monk alerted the reporters to the fact that some of the so-called "monks" milling around the Jokhang talking to the journalists weren't monks at all. They had been planted there by the authorities for the purpose of spewing the official line to the reporters, who, the Chinese had hoped, would be gullible enough to report the contrived interviews as truth.

The monks' candor caught the Chinese by surprise. Officials quickly pushed and pulled the journalists away, but it was too late. The correspondents had the story and it was widely reported around the world. In retaliation, Chinese officials posted the journalists' names, physical descriptions, and cell phone numbers on a Web site, subjecting them to a campaign of abuse, intimidation, and death threats by Han Chinese nationalists.

The monks' protests and speaking out to the foreign journalists may have helped to redeem their reputation within Lhasa's Tibetan community. It is well known within the community that the approximately 120 monks who live in the Jokhang are among the best treated inside Tibet. The temple is carefully watched by the Chinese government but its monks are also well cared for and the temple's income is reportedly supplemented by the large amount of donations received from pilgrims who visit the temple from throughout Tibet. Monks living in Tibet's other temples and monasteries do not receive the same benefits or treatment. Because of this positive treatment given to the Jokhang monks by the Chinese, the monks' outbursts are all the more startling. Even though the Chinese assured the public that nothing would happen to the monks after their confrontation with the journalists, it is hard to believe that those who spoke out in favor of the Dalai Lama and a free Tibet were not arrested and imprisoned after the foreign journalists were cleared from the area.

As the March protests continued, Woeser's blog was one of the best sources for news about what was really happening in Tibet. Using her many contacts, she was able to report on developments across the region despite the Chinese news blackout. To silence her voice, computer hackers—presumably Chinese—tried unsuccessfully to shut down her U.S.-hosted Web site.

NANCY PELOSI SPEAKS OUT IN DHARAMSALA

On March 21, 2008, Representative Nancy Pelosi, Speaker of the House, arrived in Dharamsala, India, to meet with the Dalai Lama. Her visit had been scheduled before the outbreak of violence, but she used it now to urge an international investigation into the causes of the unrest. Echoing the Dalai Lama's conviction about speaking out against the Tiananmen Square massacre, Pelosi warned that if freedom-loving people failed to condemn Chinese oppression, they would forfeit the right to protest any human rights abuses.

Around the world, people who had not thought about Tibet or the reality of life under an oppressive communist regime suddenly took a second look at China. There were international protests in cities as far afield as Katmandu, New Delhi, Chicago, New York, San Francisco, Paris, and London. The Tibetan cause had not been embraced so tightly in years. The display of international solidarity was alarming to the Chinese, but heartening to those inside Tibet who got the news through sources like Radio Free Asia and the Voice of Tibet.

THE CHALLENGE TO CHINA GROWS

Over the ensuing weeks, protest built on protest. Tens of thousands of Tibetans demonstrated or held vigils. Another 40 Tibetans died at the hands of the police and military. In some areas, police outposts were attacked, and at least one policeman was killed. The number of incidents that could be counted inside Tibet and China rose to almost 100. There may have been more, but where Chinese efforts to suppress the news succeeded they went untallied. More than 5000 Tibetans were arrested.

It was the most serious challenge to Chinese authority in decades. The Chinese government reported 22 people killed in the Lhasa riots, all Han Chinese. Sources inside Tibet, however, were able to account for more than 80 Tibetans killed in Lhasa by Chinese police, paramilitary forces, and the PLA. The Tibetan government-in-exile documented a total of 203 Tibetans killed by Chinese authorities over the two months of unrest.

Aggressive actions in Tibet were a black eye for the Chinese. The last thing the Chinese government wanted was for Tibetan protestors, or any other critics of Chinese policy, to tarnish the upcoming Olympic Games. So China resorted to what it does best. They limited the news coming out of Tibet, as well as the people allowed to enter Tibet. Tourism was suspended. When Chinese news programs reported on the violence inside Tibet, they showed only one side of the story. Newscasts repeated the government line that the protests had been organized by the Dalai clique.

The Han Chinese were said to have been targeted by the Tibetans for no reason and were the only ones to suffer death or injury. Nowhere in the Chinese narrative could the Tibetan side of the story be found. Chinese citizens weren't told that under Chinese rule, Tibetans were second-class citizens in their homeland. Chinese audiences didn't know that Tibetans could no longer conduct business in their native language because Mandarin had been made Tibet's official language or that they were relegated to living in the urban slums and ghettos while the Han Chinese lived in newly built apartments and homes. Tibetans could not even get construction jobs building the new dwellings; they went instead to Chinese immigrants.

None of these frustrations or grievances that helped spark the violent protests were known to the Chinese audiences of state-controlled media. The lack of awareness made it easy for the Chinese government to stoke nationalistic fervor amongst the Han Chinese majority, a fervor which found its outlet in protests against the international news media and foreigners perceived to be meddling in China's internal affairs.

The tragedy is that one result of burying the truth about the riots is that little, or nothing, will be done to address the underlying grievances and prevent future deaths. In Tibet, where the Han and Tibetans live in close proximity to each other, they are often at odds on a daily basis. Relationships between the two ethnic populations are strained by mutual disdain and distrust. The Tibetans resent the droves of Chinese taking over their homeland and what they perceive as preferential treatment in getting jobs and opening businesses. They see the prosperity of the Chinese immigrants as proof that the Chinese government is one sided in its development initiatives in Tibet. Conversely, many Han feel the Tibetans are lazy, ungrateful for the Chinese government's help, and unclean. Left unresolved, this friction is a recipe for future conflagrations.

FOREIGN LEADERS WEIGH IN
WITH HU JINTAO

President Bush called Chinese president Hu Jintao after the riots erupted in Lhasa. He urged Hu to speak with the Dalai Lama in the hopes of finding a peaceful solution to the Tibet situation. Other foreign leaders added their voice to the appeal for China to open a dialog. When British Prime Minister Gordon Brown announced that he would not attend the opening ceremony for the Beijing Olympics, allegedly due to a scheduling conflict, public pressure escalated on other heads of state to boycott the ceremony.

Chinese Cardinal Joseph Zen also spoke out against the violence in Tibet. The Chinese supporter of religious freedom and human rights said that acts of violence could only serve to damage China's hosting of the Summer Olympic Games.

As the linkage between Tibet and the Olympics grew, China kept up its unremitting attacks on the Dalai Lama. But it was beginning to look like a diversionary tactic, an effort to deflect criticism of China's human rights record.

The fact that the protests were spontaneous and not coordinated by Tibetan exiles was also confirmed by Tsewang Rigzin, president of the Tibetan Youth Congress and a detractor of the Dalai Lama's Middle-Way Approach. Rigzin was part of the Tibetan People's Uprising Movement, formed in January 2008 to plan a march that was to start on March 10 and take its followers on a route from Dharamsala, India across the border into Tibet. The group never called for marches or protests inside Tibet. The marchers were stopped inside India, where at least 100 of them were detained by Indian authorities. The Dalai Lama said he feared the exile march would do little more than anger the Chinese.

CONTROVERSY FOLLOWS
THE OLYMPIC TORCH RELAY

The embers had barely cooled in Lhasa when the Olympic Torch relay began on March 24, 2008, in Olympia, Greece, site of the first modern Olympics in 1896. The lighting of the torch was the start of an 85,000 mile worldwide torch relay. The torch-bearer hadn't traveled ten yards before a pro-Tibet protestor burst into the frame of the television cameras covering the event. It was the beginning of a campaign that would dog the relay across continents.

Meanwhile, in Dharamsala, India, Tibetans lit their own "Independence Torch" on March 25. Launched by the Tibetan Youth Congress, the largest Tibetan nongovernmental organization in Dharamsala, the Independence Torch embarked on its own tour of the world. The goal was for the Independence Torch to ultimately end up inside Tibet sometime around the start of the Olympics in Beijing on August 8, 2008.

China's reputation wasn't helped when the 2008 Olympic Torch relay reached London and Paris. In London people protesting China's actions in Darfur and Tibet crowded around the torchbearers, resulting in 37 arrests. Many of the protestors were manhandled by a phalanx of young Chinese men known as the "Beijing Olympic Games Sacred Flame Relay," who were running alongside the torchbearers.

They were members of the People's Armed Police, the Chinese paramilitary organization normally used for riot control and border enforcement. "Thugs" is the word used by Lord Coe—chairman of London 2012, the British committee currently organizing the London Summer Olympics—to describe the Chinese paramilitaries. The Sacred Flame Relay repeated their strong arm tactics in Paris, France, where a protestor tossed a water bottle at a Chinese paraplegic athlete who was relaying the torch and the flame was extinguished several times. Chinese officials defended the use of the paramilitary police as necessary to "maintain the safety, purity, and dignity of the Olympic Games."

By the time the torch reached San Francisco, the battle lines were drawn. The Washington, DC-based International Campaign for Tibet held vigils and rallies in the Bay Area. Richard Gere, chairman of ICT, made an appearance and spoke at one of the rallies. Pro-Tibet activists scaled the Bay Bridge to unfurl banners reading "One World One Dream. Free Tibet" and "Free Tibet".

Chinese counterprotestors, including groups like the Northern California Chinese Culture-Athletic Federation, staged rallies to support the Beijing regime. According to STRATFOR, a widely respected private intelligence publication, Chinese intelligence agents helped develop plans to bus thousands of pro-China demonstrators to San Francisco. Provocateurs waving large Chinese flags were instructed to walk into groups of pro-Tibet or pro-Darfur demonstrators to provoke a clash, which other Chinese supporters would capture instantly on video or cell cameras. Reinforcing the propaganda line that disruptive protestors were attacking innocent Chinese, television programs inside China broadcast the resulting images. It was a classic example of the use of *agent provocateur* tactics.

To prevent events from spiraling out of control, San Francisco Mayor Gavin Newsom, under advice from chief of police Heather Fong, made surprise last-minute changes in the torch relay route. The nearly 80 San

Francisco torchbearers led the Olympic torch on a virtually deserted six-mile route along the San Francisco Bay, ending up at the airport rather than Justin Herman Plaza as previously planned. The change in course, called a "fake-out" by many, left thousands of frustrated protestors and supporters on one end of San Francisco while the torch took off for its next stop in Buenos Aires, Argentina.

Aaron Peskin, Board of Supervisors President and a vocal critic of Mayor Newsom, was quoted in the *San Francisco Chronicle* as saying, "Gavin Newsom runs San Francisco the way the premier of China runs his country—secrecy, lies, misinformation, lack of transparency, and manipulating the populace. He did it so China can report they had a great torch run."

CHINESE INVITE DALAI LAMA
TO SEND AN ENVOY

Under growing international pressure, on April 26, 2008, Hu Jintao invited the Dalai Lama to send an envoy to discuss conditions in Tibet. Lodi Gyari was sent to Beijing, where the Chinese made it clear that they were only interested in the Dalai Lama's help in quelling the unrest in Tibet. They continued to reject the creation of an autonomous Tibetan political entity as an unacceptable demand for one-quarter of China's territory. They criticized the Dalai Lama's international activities, which consist mainly of Buddhist teachings and appearances as a spiritual leader, as anti-Chinese agitation. And they dismissed the Dalai Lama's proposal that Tibet be a demilitarized zone as a "de facto" form of Tibetan independence.

Just before the Olympic Opening Ceremony, *New York Times* columnist Nicholas Kristof reported that the Dalai Lama offered China a new concession. Modifying his Middle-Way approach, Tenzin Gyatso suggested that an autonomous Tibet would remain within China's socialist political system. It was a significant concession, and Kristof urged Hu Jintao to respond by inviting the Dalai Lama to Beijing in November for serious talks. There was no immediate response from China.

The lack of clear progress gave rise to widespread suspicion within the Tibetan exile community that the two sides are merely talking past one another. Many believe that the Chinese are simply running out the clock, stringing the Tibetans along in endless, and fruitless, dialogue, waiting for the 73-year-old Dalai Lama to die, hoping that the cause of a free Tibet will expire with him.

POSTSCRIPT TO THE BEIJING OLYMPICS

Part of the construction boom for the 2008 Beijing Olympics included a new museum about Tibet. In a prime location close to the National Stadium, China's newly constructed Olympic arena, the museum's opening was timed to coincide with the influx of tourists coming to the Olympic Games. Run by the China Tibetology Research Center, its purpose was to display reproductions of documents, antiquities, and records from Chinese dynasties, all driving home the message that Tibet was an integral part of China. The museum's exhibits depicted pre-1950 Tibet as a land in which serfs were abused by their masters and the people suffered under an exploitive theocratic government.

The Dalai Lama barely figured in the new museum. The museum contains no image, display, or even mention of him after 1959. He was literally edited out of the museum narrative. According to a Chinese scholar involved in the museum's creation, China no longer recognizes the Dalai Lama as part of Tibet's history. It is as if the Dalai Lama walked out to India, and disappeared. Foreign visitors to the museum got an entirely one-sided version of Tibet's history.

In April 2008, IOC president, Jacques Rogge said that freedom of expression was an absolute human right and that Olympic athletes would be allowed to speak freely in on-site media interviews taking place after their competitions. He also insisted that Chinese officials enforce a media law designed before the Olympics began to allow journalists full access for reporting while inside China, including Tibet. Recalling Chinese promises in 2001 to use the Olympic Games as a means to "advance the social agenda of China, including human rights," Rogge maintained that the Games would bring positive change to China.

The previous month, Icelandic singer Björk tested the limits of China's tolerance for free speech during a concert in Shanghai. In her song, *Declare Independence*, the young singer ended by softly saying, "Tibet, Tibet. Tibet, Tibet. Tibet, Tibet," swirling her body across the stage in large circles. The Ministry of Chinese Culture responded to Bjork's actions by tightening their control over foreign singers and performers. In April, Canadian singer Celine Dion was forced to cancel a Beijing concert when her promoters (who also had been Björk's promoters) were unable to acquire proper permits from the authorities, an apparent act of reprisal.

Repression at the Olympic Games was more extreme. Two elderly women who applied for a public demonstration permit to protest the seizing of their homes to make way for Olympic construction were sentenced to a hard labor "reeducation" camp. Eight Americans affiliated with Students for a Free Tibet were seized and detained for ten days for trying to display pro-Tibet banners. John Ray, a correspondent for Britain's ITV News, was jumped by Chinese plainclothes police in a restaurant near the Olympic Park, knocked down, and dragged forcibly to a police vehicle for attempting to shoot video footage of the protestors. Chinese officials apologized for the rough treatment after learning he was a reporter, explaining that they had mistaken him for one of the demonstrators.

The Foreign Correspondents Club of China reported multiple cases of interference with reporters. A Finnish journalist simply asking people if they liked the Games was blocked by police. In Xinjiang, photographers and a reporter were detained by security officials. Police damaged the camera of a journalist trying to photograph a pro-Tibet activist.

"BRAND CHINA" TAKES THE HIT

Instead of showcasing China's strengths, the 2008 Olympics spotlighted China's weaknesses. At a time when "Brand China" is still emerging on the world scene, the March protests and Beijing Games awakened world awareness of China's deficiencies.

A Harris Interactive poll, taken in May 2008, showed that public opinion in most European countries had turned dramatically against China. From 53 percent of the English to almost 75 percent of Italians and Germans, the poll reported that a majority of Europeans believe Tibet should be free of Chinese rule. These results constitute a severe setback for China in world opinion.

But the March protests also posed challenges for the Dalai Lama. The presence of Tibetan flags and shouts for independence indicate that support for the Dalai Lama's Middle-Way Approach is wavering. If opinion inside Tibet has soured on autonomy and a new independence movement is emerging, it could be difficult for the Dalai Lama to control. If

Tibetans are losing patience with nonviolent tactics, the deaths in Lhasa may be a forewarning of what could come when the Fourteenth Dalai Lama is no longer on the scene and able to contain the frustration. Both inside Tibet and outside, a new generation of younger, more militant Tibetans may be emerging, with tactics that more closely resemble those of the Palestinians than those of Gandhi. If the polarization continues, both China and Tibet will lose. In an interdependent world, China cannot afford to insist that what happens in Tibet is a purely internal matter.

Chapter 16

The Last Dalai Lama?

Just after the end of the Beijing Olympics, Lodi Gyari left Washington, DC, bound for France. Special envoy to the Dalai Lama, Gyari planned to meet him in southern France, where His Holiness would inaugurate the Lerab Ling Buddhist temple. The Dalai Lama also planned to meet with Carla Bruni, the glamorous wife of French President Sarkozy, at Lerab Ling. Following his visit to France, Tenzin Gyatso's schedule called for him to go to Mexico, the Dominican Republic, and then for a meeting with former Costa Rican president and Nobel Prize winner Oscar Arias.

Instead, he flew from France back to India, where he was hospitalized in Mumbai after experiencing severe stomach pains. Pending the outcome of medical tests, all the events on the Dalai Lama's schedule for the coming months were canceled.

It was not the first time medical problems caused a sudden shift in plans for the 73-year-old Tibetan leader. In January 2002, while visiting some of India's most important Buddhist sites, he fell ill in Bodh Gaya. Two hundred thousand pilgrims had gathered for a teaching of the Kalachakra ritual by His Holiness, but his malady was acute. A helicopter flew to Shechen Monastery, where he was staying, to take the Dalai Lama to a hospital. He spent most of January and February bedridden. It was March 2002, before he recovered sufficiently to resume his rigorous daily schedule.

These episodes bring to the forefront the questions that usually stay in the recesses of many people's minds: What will happen on the death of the Fourteenth Dalai Lama? Will he reincarnate? If so, where? In Chinese occupied Tibet, or outside? What hand will the Chinese government play in trying to identify the Dalai Lama's successor? And, will the inner politics of Tibet's four Buddhist sects—Nyingma, Sakya, Kagyu, and Gelug—play a role in identifying the Fifteenth Dalai Lama?

THE DALAI LAMA AND
TIBETAN IDENTITY

With Tibet occupied and fragmented by artificial boundaries meant to prevent any social or political cohesion, and the Tibetan exiles in diaspora spread across 37 different communities, the Dalai Lama is more important now than perhaps ever before in Tibet's history. More than any other figure, the Dalai Lama provides a sense of shared purpose for Tibetans, whose sense of national identity would otherwise be hampered by regionalism. Historically, Tibetans have had a stronger sense of belonging to the regions from which they come—Kham, Amdo, or U-Tsang— than a sense of nation. This is partly because Tibet's central government was always relatively weak, but also due to the immense distances on the Tibetan Plateau and the difficulty of movement over high mountain divides and barren valleys and gorges filled with whitewater.

Nomads traveled their ranges with their herds and families, merchant caravans sojourned the trade routes to India and back, monks and pilgrims made their way to and from Lhasa for religious observances, but most Tibetans stayed put. Their sense of being was rooted in family, village, tribe, and region. Nation came a distant last.

Embodying spiritual and secular authority, the Dalai Lama is the main unifying force of Tibetan identity. This makes the question of the Dalai Lama's succession crucial to Tibet's future. Yet it is a topic that is rarely discussed publicly. When the Tibetan Charter's provisions for a transfer of political power after his death were made public, there were angry protests. Tibetans considered it disrespectful to the point of insulting to even raise the matter of the Dalai Lama's passing. To mollify the public, Tibetan politicians explained that the reasons for the Dalai

Lama's absence that might trigger the Charter's mechanism for a transfer of government power could be as simple as him going on a prolonged retreat. The uproar over the mere mention of a political transition illustrates the passions Tibetans attach to His Holiness.

GOVERNMENT PERMISSION
NEEDED TO REINCARNATE

The fact of the matter is that the battle to identify the Dalai Lama's rightful successor will be the most critical test facing the Tibetans in the 21st century. There is no question about China's intent. Chinese authorities have long signaled that they plan to hijack Tibetan Buddhism by controlling the successor to the Dalai Lama and other reincarnate lamas.

In September 2007, China's State Administration on Religious Affairs announced that Tibetan Buddhist teachers, including the Dalai Lama, cannot be reincarnated without the permission of the central Chinese government. To clarify precisely how this bureaucratic recognition is to occur, the Chinese issued Order No. 5, containing 14 articles under the umbrella title of *Management Measures for the Reincarnation of 'Living Buddhas' in Tibetan Buddhism.*

"It is an important move to institutionalize the management of reincarnation of Living Buddhas," the new law states, "No outside organization or individual will influence or control the reincarnation of Living Buddhas."

In a swift response, Tibet's government-in-exile rejected the legitimacy of Order No. 5. In a statement issued from Dharamsala, the Tibetans attacked the order as a new weapon employed by the Chinese government to undermine Tibetan Buddhism and to insult and oppress the Tibetan people.

These new regulations are completely contrary to Tibetan traditions and longstanding religious practices. Nonetheless, Order No. 5 sets the stage for Chinese authorities to take charge of selecting the Dalai Lama's next incarnation. The timing of the order—issued one month before awarding the Congressional Gold Medal to the Dalai Lama and on the eve of the Communist Party Congress that appointed Hu Jintao to a second five-year term—heralded a continuation of China's hardline policy toward Tibet.

Fifty years ago, when she went to Tibet on a government-sponsored trip for journalists in the aftermath of the 1959 Tibetan National Uprising,

Anna Louise Strong reported that Chinese officials were already planning to control the succession of Tibet's lamas.

"All incarnations have to have the approval of the central government of China," Strong wrote, quoting a Chinese official named Chao Puchu, who was then head of the Buddhist Theological Research Institute in Beijing. From the era of Mao Zedong to the rule of Hu Jintao, China's efforts to control the Tibetans by controlling their religious leaders has been consistent.

THE CASE OF THE ELEVENTH
PANCHEN LAMA

The mystery of the Eleventh Panchen Lama reveals how China is likely to use Order No. 5 when the time comes to find the Dalai Lama's successor. As with any reincarnation of a Tibetan lama, the story must begin with the Tenth Panchen Lama.

When the Dalai Lama fled Tibet in 1959, the Tenth Panchen Lama remained behind at his monastery, Tashilhunpo. Some believe he collaborated with the Chinese occupation. Initially, he seemed to back the Chinese as they embarked on a program of building modern schools, hospitals, roads, and agrarian reform.

But by the 1960s it became clear to him that Chinese reforms caused terrible suffering. Collective farming was imposed, and Tibetans were ordered to plant wheat, which was preferred in China, instead of their native barley. But wheat was hard to grow on the Tibetan Plateau, and the harvests were poor. Still, Tibetans were forced to export what little wheat they had to China. The result was famine and widespread death.

The Panchen Lama thought that if he could convey the dire effects of the misguided agricultural policies to China's leaders they would be halted. He began writing what became known as his "70,000 Character Petition." Concerned that the Chinese would interpret the criticisms as subversive, his tutor, Ngulchu, tried to dissuade him from putting them on paper. Instead, he counseled keeping the critique verbal.

But the Panchen Lama was determined to put it in writing. He entitled it, *A report on the sufferings of the masses in Tibet and other Tibetan regions and suggestions for future work to the Central Committee through the respected Premier Zhou* and had it translated into Chinese.

On May 18, 1962, the Panchen Lama delivered an abbreviated, summarized version to a group of Chinese senior military and Party officials. A chill descended on the room by the end of his report. By putting the critique in writing, the Panchen Lama had created a damning indictment of Communist Party policies and their impact on Tibet. In the uncertain context of Chinese party politics, the document could be used against the very officials he had addressed, many of whom took the criticism personally. It was a document that could end careers, or worse, if it ended up in the hands of bureaucratic rivals. Alternately, if the critique found its way to the outer world, it would serve as a scathing refutation of China's international propaganda. Either way, what the Panchen Lama had written posed a potent threat.

Ironically, he had not intended the document to threaten the party cadres. He sincerely believed that if higher echelons knew about the adverse impact of their well-intentioned, but flawed, policies they would change course. The reward he received for putting his faith in the good will of Mao Zedong and the Chinese Communist Party was jail. From 1968 until 1977, he was imprisoned.

After his release, the Tenth Panchen Lama refrained from further involvement in political criticism—for a while. In 1989, Chinese authorities allowed him to make a number of public appearances around Tibet. In the city of Shigatse, Tibet's second-largest town and home to a notorious Chinese detention center for political prisoners, the Panchen Lama called for Tibet's independence. The outburst was deeply embarrassing to Chinese administrators, especially Hu Jintao, just climbing his way up the rungs of party leadership.

On January 28, 1989, at the relatively young age of 50, Tibet's Tenth Panchen Lama died. Chinese doctors certified that the cause of death was a heart attack. However, suspicions that the true cause of death was poisoning remain unalloyed to this day. The real political theater, or perhaps one should say spiritual theater, began after his death.

CHINA MANEUVERS TO PICK THE PANCHEN LAMA'S SUCCESOR

The symbiotic relationship between the Dalai Lama and the Panchen Lama meant that if China could control the selection of the Eleventh

Panchen Lama, it would be in a better position to determine who would succeed the Fourteenth Dalai Lama when he dies. The Tibetans also understood the stakes. At issue was not only the legitimacy of the Eleventh Panchen Lama, but in all probability the legitimacy of the Fifteenth Dalai Lama as well. Both sides, Tibetan and Chinese, were determined to find the Eleventh Panchen Lama first.

A few days after the death of the Tenth Panchen Lama, China's Xinhua news agency published an article on reincarnation. The article purported that the selection of the Panchen and Dalai Lamas—central features of Tibetan Buddhism—had historically been the prerogative of the Chinese government, as far back as the Qing dynasty. (The Qing dynasty, it should be mentioned, was not Chinese at all but a Manchu dynasty). In any event, Beijing was setting the propaganda stage to announce its recognition of the Panchen Lama's reincarnation.

A five-year hiatus followed, during which a child was born in Tibet and grew to an age when he could, with the proper divine guidance and tests, be recognized as the reincarnation of the Panchen Lama. In 1994, the search to find that child began in earnest.

It looked as though China held all the cards to name the reincarnation. Tibet was firmly under Chinese control. Political commissars closely monitored the monasteries and regulated the activities of the monks and nuns. In theory, the Chinese could have easily used their influence to select a child, and, with assistance from cooperative monastic officials, recognize him as the Panchen Lama.

But the Dalai Lama had his own weapon. Even though he had been in exile for 35 years, the people of Tibet still held him in the highest regard and esteem. Despite decades of repressive measures, China had not been able to destroy the people's reverence for their religious traditions. Unless the Dalai Lama affirmed the reincarnation of the Panchen Lama, the Tibetan people would simply ignore China's choice.

This posed a dilemma for China. The utmost effort had to be made to create a veneer of legitimacy around the selection of the Panchen Lama. The Chinese might not be able to persuade all Tibetans that their designated choice was right, but they might deflect some criticism by going through the motions of a traditional process for finding the reincarnation.

To identify reincarnations of Tibet's higher lamas, such as the Dalai or Panchen Lamas, high ranking monks visit the shores of Lhamo Latso to meditate. The lake yields clues, sometimes in the form of visions, of where the reincarnation has been born. The information gleaned may be a geographical direction, one of the points of the compass, in which to begin the search. It might be the color of the house where the child lives or a hint as to the type of work the mother and father do. Combined with other information from previous instructions that may have been left prior to the death of the previous high lama, or revelations through meditation, search groups are able to start the hunt and identify likely matches.

Once a child who might be the true reincarnation is identified, teams of monks are sent to examine the child and parents. They ask specific questions about unique, odd, or special circumstances under which the child was born. Neighbors are also interviewed. Finally, the child is observed and then asked to identify possessions of the previous incarnation. For example, the Fourteenth Dalai Lama was only three years old when monks first visited his family's home and presented him with certain objects, some of which were owned by the Thirteenth Dalai Lama. As the young boy identified those that had belonged to the previous Dalai Lama he immediately said, "It's mine! It's mine!" This certitude helped convince the monks that he was the true reincarnation.

For the Dalai Lama, exile complicated identifying the correct reincarnation of the Panchen Lama. Normally, he would rely heavily on a team of senior lamas from Tashilhunpo monastery, the Panchen Lama's traditional home inside Tibet, in the search. Along with these monks, the Dalai Lama conducts meditations, divinations, and consultations with Tibetan oracles to arrive at the correct choice of the rightful heir. Isolated from the Tashilhunpo monastery, the task of researching with the monks was slow and complicated. The Dalai Lama could not easily communicate with the Tibetan teams of monks carrying out the searches. Tenzin Gyatso offered to assist the Chinese in finding the Eleventh Panchen Lama, but they rejected his help. Neither he nor his India-based search team were allowed inside Tibet.

Despite the severe limitations, there were ways around the obstacles. Tibetan monks held clandestine meetings, taking care to exclude all but the most trustworthy so as to minimize the potential for Chinese spies and agents, infiltrated into their own ranks, to compromise their work. Couriers carried secret messages by hand over the mountain passes and across the borders from Tibet to India and back. It was a highly risky business. If a messenger was intercepted, the Chinese would discover that the

Tashilhunpo monastery was in communication with the Dalai Lama, and the monks would be in grave danger. Not every message or reply got through, leading to prolonged lapses in communication and heightening the tension.

The Tashilhunpo monks had to play a double game inside Tibet. In their effort to create a consensus around the selection of the Eleventh Panchen Lama, the Chinese went through pro-forma sessions with the monks about the correct way to identify the reincarnation.

The discussions were not in good faith. In fact, the Chinese had already settled on making the final choice by using a lottery system called the Golden Urn. Names of several children who appeared to match the information gleaned from divination rituals, meditation, and other signs were to be inscribed on ivory tablets. The tablets, wrapped in yellow silk so that the names were no longer visible, would then be dropped into the Urn. They would be jumbled and then drawn and the name thus chosen was that of the reincarnated Panchen Lama.

The Chinese hoped to get the monks to buy into this method for recognizing the reincarnation. By assuring that only politically-acceptable names went into the Urn, China would control the outcome. This approach—one of co-opting in order to control—had been used by Chinese emperors on conquered peoples throughout the centuries.

The Golden Urn system had rarely been resorted to throughout Tibet's history. It was used to identify successors to the Dalai Lama and Panchen Lama as well as to identify junior incarnations in a handful of instances. But it had never been the sole method of identifying a reincarnated lama. The few occasions in which the Golden Urn was used were in combination with other time-honored techniques, including divination rituals and the observance of six days of prayer before drawing the chosen candidates from the Urn.

Despite the Chinese interference, the Tashilhunpo monks had carefully conducted their investigations and searches. They had a strong instinct about a particular child and sent his name and picture along with those of other leading contenders secretly over the Himalayas to the Dalai Lama. When he got the list, the Dalai Lama consulted the Tsangba and Nechung oracles. He also conducted further meditations and divinations. Finally he simply sat, looking at pictures of the chosen candidates.

As he looked at the photograph of one boy, Tenzin Gyatso felt a sense of certainty. After further meditation, the Dalai Lama recognized Gedhun

Choekyi Nyima, a six-year-old who was born April 25, 1989, in Nagchu, a district in central Tibet, as the Eleventh Panchen Lama. He did not know that his choice was the same as that of the Tashilhunpo monks.

Even though the Dalai Lama had identified him, he made no public announcement. The Tibetans, too, were trying to achieve a consensus around the choice of Choekyi Nyima. The Dalai Lama wanted to give the monks who were negotiating with the Chinese ample time to try to ensure the legitimate candidate was recognized by both sides. He sent a message to Tashilhunpo telling of his recognition of Choekyi Nyima and waited for a response.

At Tashilhunpo, the monks had grown so certain about their identification that they proposed Choekyi Nyima as a candidate to the Chinese delegation. They presented strong evidence of the boy's authenticity, but the Chinese would not add his name to the short list of candidates. They did agree, however, to put him on a back-up list.

When the monks received confirmation from the Dalai Lama that they had chosen the right boy, they became more determined than ever to dissuade the Chinese from using the Golden Urn. They continued to push the boy's name forward, saying that numerous divinations and meditations invariably revealed Choekyi Nyima as the reincarnation of the Tenth Panchen Lama. The Chinese refused to budge. They had their own candidate and were adamant about the Golden Urn.

Months passed and the Dalai Lama heard nothing from Tashilhunpo. He began to worry that China would try to preempt matters by naming their choice first. He considered his options with his advisers in Dharamsala before deciding to announce the boy's name on the next "auspicious date." The announcement would state that the boy would be left inside Tibet to be educated at the Tashilhunpo monastery. The Dalai Lama believed that by declaring this as his intention, the Chinese might accept his choice, since the monastery was under their control.

On May 14, 1995, the Dalai Lama still had not heard from Tashilhunpo. But the day was deemed auspicious. After praying and consulting the Nechung oracle a final time, he told a small gathering of dignitaries from the government-in-exile, high lamas from the Gelug and Nyingma sects, the medium of the state oracle, and representatives from the Tashilhunpo monastery in India (sister monastery to the one in Tibet) that the search was over. The Eleventh Panchen Lama was six-year-old Gedhun Choekyi Nyima.

The Dalai Lama's recognition of the boy was met with joy and immediate acceptance by Tibetans, but Beijing was ominously silent. The
announcement caught the Chinese flat footed. The boy's family in Tibet
was also taken by surprise. They had not been forewarned that their son
was the reincarnation of the Panchen Lama.

Then, two days after the Dalai Lama's announcement, the Chinese
declared that they would not accept Choekyi Nyima as the Panchen
Lama's reincarnation. The lottery using the Golden Urn would go ahead
as planned. Moreover, the Chinese government would be the ones to
announce the correct Panchen Lama. Gedhun Choekyi Nyima did not
meet the proper criteria and his name would not be included in the lottery. The Dalai Lama's recognition was, as far as Beijing was concerned,
null and void.

This was a fateful turn of events for Choekyi Nyima and his family.
Excluding him from the lottery meant the Chinese were left with three
options of how to deal with him—kill him, banish him, or imprison him.

On November 29, 1995, the Golden Urn lottery was held. Although
it was attended by Buddhist monks, the Chinese called the shots. They
declared that the true Eleventh Panchen Lama was Gyaltsen Norbu. Like
Choekyi Nyima, he too had been born in the Nagchu region of Tibet, sat-
isfying some of the divinations that pointed to this as the place where the
Panchen Lama would reincarnate. Norbu's family, however, were loyal
members of the Communist party.

Meanwhile, Choekyi Nyima and his family had simply fallen off the
face of the earth. No one had seen them or knew of their whereabouts
since the Dalai Lama's announcement six months earlier in May. A full
year passed before the Chinese government finally acknowledged on
May 28, 1996, that the boy and his family were in "protective custody."
This has not been independently corroborated by foreign diplomats,
international human rights organizations, independent journalists, or
relief organizations such as the Red Cross. For all anyone knows, Choekyi
Nyima and his family, like the Romanovs after the Russian revolution,
were executed.

The case of the Eleventh Panchen Lama shows the extraordinary
extent to which China will go in trying to control Tibet. Nothing is out
of bounds, not even distorting the sacred traditions of Tibetan Buddhism,
in accomplishing their goal. The Chinese have already removed one of
Tibet's highest spiritual lamas from Tibetan society and installed their

own puppet as the Eleventh Panchen Lama. One can only imagine the lengths to which China will go when the Fourteenth Dalai Lama dies and the search for his reincarnation begins.

That is, if he decides to reincarnate at all.

THE CHOICE TO REINCARNATE

For some, the reincarnation of the Dalai Lama is beyond question, more certain even than the rising of the sun in the morning. But this certitude is misplaced. The belief that the Dalai Lama will reincarnate is more of an assumption, and a hopeful one at that, than a foregone conclusion.

The Dalai Lama himself has said on numerous occasions that reincarnation is a choice, unlike rebirth which is a reality. Reincarnation, His Holiness says, is the power granted to certain worthy individuals, like the Buddha himself, to control their future birth.

In an effort to thwart a repeat by the Chinese of the episode with the Eleventh Panchen Lama, in November 2007 the Dalai Lama declared that he is considering a referendum on how to pick his successor before he dies. This announcement came two months after China issued Order No. 5. In a shameless twist, this time it was the Chinese who denounced the Dalai Lama's statement about a referendum as a violation of religious practice.

The concept of the referendum is similar to the approach used with the Tibetan Charter. First, Tibetan Buddhists would be polled on whether they preferred to maintain the Dalai Lama as their spiritual and secular head. If a majority supported the Dalai Lama system, Tenzin Gyatso said he would reincarnate—but his reincarnation would either take place outside China or he might choose a new Dalai Lama before his death.

"There is this idea in Buddhism," explains Dr. Robbie Barnett, a professor of Modern Tibetan Studies at Columbia University's Weatherhead East Asian Institute, "that a high lama doesn't impose his ideas on other people. It is the other people who ask for their teachings. Thus, the people pray for the reincarnation of the lama and the lama's reincarnation then fulfills the wishes, the prayers of his people."

The transition from the Fourteenth Dalai Lama to his successor has many possible variations. If the search for the successor has a similar outcome to the search that found Tenzin Gyatso, there will be a period as long as two decades in which the next Dalai Lama will not exercise full powers. It may take several years to locate the child who is the reincarnation of the Dalai Lama. He or she will then undergo spiritual training and secular education. Only after passage of key monastic exams does the new Dalai Lama exercise full spiritual authority, and the assumption of secular authority as head of state comes on maturity. What this means is that there may be a vacuum of leadership in Tibetan Buddhism during the succession period.

In terms of political leadership, any void will be filled by the democratic mechanisms this Dalai Lama established for the Tibetan government-in-exile. The Tibetan Charter specifically provides for an orderly transfer of power. The Dalai Lama has even laid out a transition plan for the eventuality, however remote, that China gives autonomy to Tibet.

THE ROLE OF THE
SEVENTEENTH KARMAPA

To glimpse who may fill the spiritual void during the transition between the Fourteenth and Fifteenth Dalai Lama, one has to travel to the Indian town of Sidhpur. There, in a monastery set against the backdrop of steeply rising mountains off in the middle distance, resides the twenty-two-year-old Ogyen Trinley Dorje, better known as the Seventeenth Gyalwang Karmapa, head of the Karma Kagyu School of Tibetan Buddhism.

Uniformed Indian soldiers guard his monastery, rifles slung on their shoulders, ready to fire from behind sandbag barricades on the monastery rooftop. Visitors must confirm their identity and register their passport with Indian and Tibetan security authorities to gain admittance to the monastery. More guards stand vigilantly by a metal detector. Plainclothes officers are omnipresent, and the security details are composed of Tibetans and Indians, especially at times when the Karmapa holds audiences and long lines of people form. Inside the monastery temple, where the audiences take place and blessings are bestowed on Buddhists who come from around the world, no cell phones or photography are permitted.

The highly visible security prompts speculation. Some believe the Indian military presence is to keep the Karmapa and his followers under control, a form of house arrest. Rumors swirl that in Indian government circles in New Delhi some believe the Karmapa is under the control of Chinese intelligence, a sleeper agent biding his time.

To a trained eye, there is a simpler, yet also sinister, explanation for the high security enveloping the Karmapa. A credible threat of assassination exists. The positioning of armed guards at checkpoints and on rooftops, the security precautions, the plainclothes officers, and the use of magnetometers and hand searches of visitors are familiar to anyone who has entered the White House or attended a presidential event.

And who would want to harm this Karmapa?

The still unsolved, grisly murder of Lama Lobsang Gyatso—a favorite of the Dalai Lama—along with two of his students in the heart of Dharamsala on February 4, 1997, hints at the hidden dangers lurking around Tibetan Buddhism. Some believe he was killed by members of a rival sect, while others maintain Chinese agents were behind the murders.

Indian security is taking no chances with the Karmapa. As with the Panchen Lama, there is more than one Karmapa. There are, in fact, two Karmapas, although only one of them can be legitimate. Ogyen Trinley Dorje has been recognized by both the Dalai Lama and Chinese authorities as the true reincarnation of the Sixteenth Karmapa, a distinction his rival, Trinlay Thaye Dorje, lacks.

Ogyen Trinley Dorje was found in 1992 by a delegation of monks searching for the reincarnation, armed with a letter from the previous Karmapa predicting where the boy lived and how to recognize him as the legitimate successor. Among a family of nomads from the Kham region of Eastern Tibet, the monks found Dorje. He was seven years old.

The Seventeenth Karmapa was taken to a monastery and, soon thereafter, visited by an official delegation from Beijing. The Chinese, probably believing that they could influence his monastic education, gave their bureaucratic seal of approval by confirming that Dorje was in fact the Seventeenth Karmapa. They cultivated him, giving him ample freedom of movement in Tibet and China, and in general treated him well.

It was therefore all the more shocking when, in December 1999, the Seventeenth Karmapa set off on a daring escape. His route took him more than 1000 miles to India. He covered the distance on horseback and on foot, by auto and truck, on trains and in taxis, and even by helicopter. It took a month before he emerged in India, a voluntary exile, and the highest profile refugee from Tibet since the 1959 National Uprising. He was just 14 years old.

In Dharamsala, the Dalai Lama took the young Karmapa under his wing, no doubt seeing in Dorje a kindred, plucky spirit. Their closeness has fueled speculation that the Dalai Lama could do something unprecedented by transferring power to the Seventeenth Karmapa as his successor. Over the centuries, the Gelug School and the Kagyu School have more often been rivals for power, and their struggles for ascendancy have sometimes degenerated into violence. By mutually acknowledging one another's legitimacy, the Dalai Lama and the Karmapa have at a minimum forged a clear alliance.

That alliance leaves out a rival Karmapa, the 25-year-old Trinlay Thaye Dorje. In broad strokes, the essence of the rival claim is based on a dispute over the authenticity of the "prediction letter" left by the Sixteenth Karmapa.

When Ogyen Trinley Dorje was found in 1992, he was recognized by Tai Situ Rinpoche, the third ranking lama in the Kagyu lineage of Tibetan Buddhism, and Gyaltsab Rinpoche. But conflict arose in 1992 when Situ Rinpoche presented a letter to fellow Kagyu lamas which he claimed to be the prediction letter from the Sixteenth Karmapa (typically, the Karmapas are the only lamas in Tibetan Buddhism to leave written instructions about how or where to find their reincarnation). Shamar Rinpoche, the second ranking lama in the Kagyu lineage, rejected the letter's authenticity.

To resolve the dilemma over the letter, Shamar Rinpoche suggested forensic examination of the handwriting and paper so as to prove or disprove its authenticity. His suggestion was rejected, however, and Ogyen Trinley Dorje was recognized and enthroned as the Seventeenth Karmapa without Shamar Rinpoche's approval.

In 1994, Shamar Rinpoche was among those who found and recognized Trinlay Thaye Dorje and proclaimed him as the rightful Seventeenth Karmapa. Even though many high ranking Kagyu lamas support him, the lineage is split into two camps—those who support the Dalai Lama's recognition of Ogyen Trinley and those who support Shamar Rinpoche's choice of Trinlay Thaye Dorje.

It may be out of an abundance of precaution that the Indians take measures to safeguard the Seventeenth Karmapa's monastery at Sidhpur. The dispute over the legitimate Seventeenth Karmapa may never become violent. Nonetheless, the guards and guns are there. It is unlikely that their purpose is house arrest. In the spring of 2008 the Indian government gave the Seventeenth Karmapa permission to travel outside the country for the first time. On May 15, he arrived in the United States on a two-week journey that took him to New York City, Boulder, Colorado, and, Seattle, Washington. In addition to his own security, the U.S. Department of State provided a diplomatic security detail for the Karmapa.

Naropa University and Shambhala International, the institutions founded by Chögyam Trungpa in the 1970s, hosted the Karmapa's trip. Diana Mukpo, Trungpa's widow, was on hand at a private reception held for the Karmapa at Boulder's St. Julien Hotel. Nawang Khechog gave a solo performance in front of a small gathering that included Lama Sarah Harding. Peter Volz, now employed by Shambhala International, was one of the principal organizers of his introductory U.S. tour, "Karmapa in America 2008."

At a teaching the following day, Diana Mukpo introduced the Karmapa to a sell-out audience of approximately 5000 people. In a glancing reference to her late husband, she reminisced briefly about the "informal and chaotic" days of Shambhala's founding. Throughout her introduction and the Karmapa's teaching, the agents from the State Department's Diplomatic Protection Group stood vigil.

Coming as it did in the immediate aftermath of the March protests in Tibet and international demonstrations during the Olympic Torch relay, Indian approval of the Karmapa's travel risked provoking China. Before his departure, Indian officials made clear that they expected the Seventeenth Karmapa to keep from making political statements during his U.S. debut and instead stick to spiritual affairs. Even in the private receptions, he stayed away from political controversy.

Curiously, the Chinese refrained from trying to block or criticize the visit. In fact, Chinese officials have displayed unusual restraint in their comments about Ogyen Trinley Dorje since his 1999 flight from Tibet. Official statements have downplayed his decade-long absence as a "study mission" abroad, possibly indicating that the Chinese are leaving the door open for his eventual return.

FISSURES WORK IN CHINA'S FAVOR

Two Panchen Lamas, two Karmapas—will there be two Dalai Lamas one day? In mandates like Order No.5, the Chinese government has specified that the reincarnation of the Dalai Lama must be born inside

China, which in China's view also includes Tibet. There is no other allowable form of reincarnation. However, much to China's dislike, the Dalai Lama says that if he reincarnates his successor will be born outside of China, and outside of Tibet.

With these two conflicting statements in plain view, the stage is set for there to be two Dalai Lamas in the future—one appointed by the Chinese government, and one recognized by the Tibetans. This bifurcation of spiritual leadership would play into China's hands. It is a recipe for conflict that could affect the leadership of Tibetan Buddhism at many levels.

Tibetans take at face value that Choekyi Nyima is the Eleventh Panchen Lama because the Dalai Lama has recognized him. Their trust in his authority makes Tibetans believe Choekyi Nyima is the true Panchen Lama. But if there are two claimants as Dalai Lama, it could get tricky as to which Dalai Lama reincarnation the Tibetans will recognize as legitimate. In this game of spiritual chess, the Chinese have already taken out one of the authorities Tibetans rely on to resolve such matters by replacing the rightful Panchen Lama with a puppet.

In late 2007, while in Milan, Italy, to hold teachings, the Dalai Lama mischievously added a new wrinkle to the riddle of his reincarnation. He said he would not rule out returning as a female, if it should be revealed to him that reincarnating as a woman would be more useful. He added, perhaps in jest and perhaps not, that he might come back as a "beautiful" woman, because of the attention she could command.

It is extremely rare for a reincarnation to be a different sex than their predecessor. But it is the mind, not the soul or body, which reincarnates. So, while there are far fewer female lamas in Tibetan Buddhism than male lamas, it is not impossible that the Fifteenth Dalai Lama will be found as a female child. Unlike many religions, Tibetan Buddhism is flexible, sometimes surprisingly so. This pliability is likely to be tested.

Unless Tibet's future is resolved before the death of the Fourteenth Dalai Lama, it is inevitable that China will try to create a schism in Tibetan Buddhism. This reality has created a growing sense of urgency among Tibetans that the clock is running out.

Chapter 17

What Is to Be Done to Free Tibet?

The Fourteenth Dalai Lama's concept of interdependence is the key to freeing Tibet. China has never been more dependent on the rest of the world than now. This dependence, especially on sales of products made in China in export markets, has strengthened its economy. Simultaneously, it has made China vulnerable. Ordinary people have the ability to use China's vulnerabilities as a force to bring about change to benefit not only Tibetans, but also the Chinese. The conditions under which China will finally give Tibetans freedom are the same conditions which will create democracy across China, making it a safer, fairer trading partner. The power to compel this change is in the hands of millions of European and North American consumers and voters.

One of the greatest impediments to taking action is the false hope that the problem will resolve itself. The faith that economic development in China will result in democracy is, to paraphrase Karl Marx, the opiate of the masses. By shedding our thinking of false premises, it becomes easier to see how China can be compelled to change. Before spelling out how average people can free Tibet, let's examine some of the fallacies about change coming automatically to China.

CONSTRUCTIVE ENGAGEMENT
WITH CHINA DOESN'T WORK

One of the Nixon Administration's principal justifications for establishing relations with the People's Republic of China was linkage. The concept of linkage is that when nations build ties, they are less likely to risk disrupting those ties during times of friction. Linkage has a moderating effect on behavior. By constructively engaging an estranged country like China in 1972, the growth of linkages starting from diplomatic ties and eventually extending to economic cooperation and trade will convert a hostile regime. Over time, mutual cooperation increases and can even create interdependence.

Democratic and Republican presidents have clung to the rationale that constructive engagement with China will inevitably lead to democratic change. The premise is that a market economy drives political reform. But there is no basis in political science to support this contention. It is an ideological premise, blind faith that capitalism has some magical quality to transform China from a one-party communist state to a multi-party democracy. Yet it is a bipartisan article of faith among America's foreign policy elite. The decision of the IOC to hold the 2008 summer Olympics in Beijing was premised on the equally unfounded rationale that merely by hosting the Games, China would improve human rights.

In the four decades since Nixon's constructive engagement with Beijing, there has been an explosion of trade with China. Its economy is now one of the fastest growing in the world. In sheer numbers, China's middle class is as large as the American middle class. The development of modern infrastructure, funded through trade surpluses with the United States and the European Union, has been phenomenal. China has moved from a severely undeveloped country in 1972 to a rapidly modernizing society.

Despite the upward improvement in its economic indicators, the direction of political change in China has been negative. The Chinese Communist Party's control over the state is as tight as ever. No other political parties are tolerated. There is no constitutional freedom of speech, assembly, or the right to petition government. The casual visitor to China may hear his or her hosts express controversial opinions in a café or club, but if those views are posted on the Internet or put on a placard for a public protest the result will be arrest.

China's leaders are intent on managing an economic transformation without any parallel political liberalization. The free trade policies of Western governments, eager to find fresh markets and sources of inexpensive labor for their corporate interests, have made China's economic growth possible. China's rise is not an inevitable development, akin to a force of nature. It is a consequence of political and economic agreements, based on a fragile consensus that China's entry into the family of nations would produce positive results for China and for the world.

INTERNET ENTREPRENEURS BECOME CHINA'S COLLABORATORS

Another naive premise for automatic, effortless change in China came about in the 1990s during the initial euphoria over the Internet. The premise, advanced largely by self-proclaimed visionaries, was that computer technology and Internet access would empower hundreds of millions of Chinese citizens, resulting in a transformation of China's government from a repressive state into a democracy. To date, this is the most disappointing of the premises for automatic change.

The most outrageous aspect of the Internet's failure to transform China lies not with the failure of technology, but the moral failure of leading "Netizens." To do business in China and gain access to its consumers, executives at technology firms have become willing enforcers for China. Microsoft and Google have both helped China block information through their search functions or block access to blogs the Chinese government wants to restrict. Yahoo! has exceeded this by helping China convict political dissidents for exercising basic human rights.

Take the case of Chinese journalist Shi Tao and engineer Wang Xiaoning, who were each sentenced to ten years in jail for the crime of writing articles promoting democracy and posting them on a Yahoo! Groups Web site. The evidence used to convict the men was handed over to Chinese authorities by Yahoo, Inc., after the Chinese asked for details of their Internet and e-mail usage. Yahoo! routinely tracks the Internet usage of all its customers in order to market the data, mainly to advertising firms. Microsoft's gmail is worse in that it scans the contents of every e-mail and reads key words.

When Congress looked into the matter in 2006 after prompting from human rights organizations, Yahoo! CEO Jerry Yang, whose net worth is an estimated $1.9 billion, had his company deny any knowledge that the Chinese request was for the purpose of prosecuting the democracy activists. Yang changed his tune after congressional investigators determined that the Chinese request stated explicitly that the purpose was a probe of the "illegal provision of state secrets," a catch-all category frequently used to prosecute political dissidents.

Under grilling by the House Foreign Affairs Committee, Yang's corporate attorney claimed that Yahoo! was merely complying with the "lawful demands" of Chinese authorities. Yang's arrogance prompted the late Congressman Tom Lantos, a human rights champion, to berate him and the attorney as "moral pygmies."

Instead of the Internet transforming China's government, China has transformed the Internet. The Internet in China is an extension of state power. The Chinese government has harnessed the Internet to harass and intimidate foreign journalists. Chinese government hackers use it to access sensitive computer systems, including the Pentagon, to launch paralyzing cyberattacks in a rehearsal for asymmetrical warfare. Internet sites containing information the Chinese government doesn't want its citizens to see are blocked, chat rooms are monitored by authorities, and e-mail accounts are used to track and find dissidents who are then charged and jailed.

It is not only Chinese citizens who are subject to their government's cybersnooping. At this writing, the FBI is investigating Chinese hackers who intruded on the e-mail accounts and Web server of the Save Darfur Coalition, showing that foreign citizens are not immune from Chinese repression.

SOUTH AFRICA AS A CASE MODEL
FOR HOW TO CHANGE CHINA

Back in 1984, Tony Blankley, a then-obscure White House aide, sat at his desk in the bullpen of Room 350 of the Eisenhower Executive Office Building pondering poll data. Blankley was a staffer in the Office of Planning and Evaluation. OPE, as insiders knew it, was nestled among National Security Council offices just down the hallway from CIA Director William Casey's White House hideaway office and PFIAB, the President's Foreign Intelligence Advisory Board.

Ross Perot, whom Reagan named to PFIAB, popped into Room 350 when he was at the White House to say hello to Marion Droll, the woman who had been his date at the 1953 Army-Navy game. It was normal to run into CIA Director Bill Casey ambling by on his way to the West Wing to brief the president or attend Cabinet meetings, accompanied even in the secure confines of the White House by a CIA security detail. Down the hall and around the corner an eye-popping assistant named Fawn Hall greeted visitors to the office of a gap-toothed Marine with the perpetually haggard look of heavy responsibility, Lt. Col. Oliver North.

Because of its location on the third floor and the nature of neighboring offices, many White House staffers assumed that OPE was part of the national security apparatus. In fact, it was an in-house think tank, with a broad mandate to review and assess high-priority presidential policies. OPE also conducted briefings for the president, convening panels of outside experts to meet with Cabinet officials and discuss policy issues. In the early 1980s, it was one of the first White House offices involved in formulating the government's response to a newly discovered and enigmatic disease—AIDs.

Fresh polls taken for the White House were delivered to OPE, where the analysts poured over them eagerly to see whether public support for high presidential priorities was waxing or waning. These polls were unlike the headline-variety polls that appeared in daily newspapers. Many were as thick as telephone books. Care was taken to phrase key questions identically from poll to poll, so that analysts could accurately compare the answers over time to spot developing trends in public opinion.

Of greatest interest were the detailed tables in the back of the books that followed the poll questionnaire and methodology. They tabulated people's responses to the poll questions against a rich variety of social, demographic, geographic, and economic variables. Experts refer to these tables as "cross-tabs" and go straight to them when analyzing poll data.

Blankley noticed something interesting in the cross-tabs regarding Reagan's South African policy. At the time, South Africa was governed by apartheid, a policy of rigid racial segregation through which the country's white minority dominated the black majority. The Reagan Administration officially opposed apartheid as a violation of human rights, but it maintained diplomatic and commercial relations with South Africa on the grounds that continued ties gave the United States leverage to press for changes.

This policy was called "constructive engagement." Its chief proponent was an official in the State Department, Assistant Secretary for African Affairs Chester A. Crocker. Liberals and African-Americans had long been opposed to the policy of constructive engagement. But, compared to other burning issues of the day, constructive engagement generated little interest one way or the other from the majority of the public. Polls showed they were more concerned with the economy, relations with the Soviet Union, and the increasingly controversial wars in Central America, where the Reagan Administration was supporting arms sales and the CIA-backed "contras." Dewey Clarridge, who had cut his teeth as a junior spy in Nepal and India, was now in charge of the covert war in Nicaragua.

What Blankley saw in the cross-tabs concerned him. Disapproval of constructive engagement was growing. If confined to liberals, the growth in negative opinion wouldn't have been so worrisome, but the cross-tabs showed suburbanites, especially women, were souring fast on the apartheid regime. This was a core constituency, and its erosion meant constructive engagement was endangered.

In a pointed memorandum for Counsellor to the President Edwin Meese, one of Reagan's closest advisers, Blankley carefully outlined the negative trend. With public support for constructive engagement crumbling, Blankley cautioned, Congress could seize control of South Africa policy, directly challenging the President's command of foreign affairs.

Meese took the memo seriously and forwarded it to Secretary of State George Shultz, who sent it down the line to Crocker. Predictably, Crocker defended his own policy. Vigorously rebutting Blankley's critique, Crocker asserted that there was ample support for constructive engagement and nothing to be worried about. Shultz sent a note to Meese saying he concurred, thus repelling the White House intrusion on the State Department's turf.

At the time Blankley wrote his 1984 memo on constructive engagement, divestment legislation had passed in 16 states and the District of Columbia. The idea behind the divestment campaign was to put economic pressure on South Africa by passing laws requiring public pension funds, universities, and state agencies to sell the stock of any corporations doing business in the country.

Randall Robinson, an African-American with a Harvard law degree, was one of the driving forces behind the divestment campaign. His not-for-profit organization, TransAfrica, brought pressure on state and local governments to pass divestment laws. Similar campaigns played out on college campuses, where students formed the backbone of the effort to bar universities from investing endowment funds in corporations with operations in South Africa. They had unusual allies. In California, the International Longshoremen Workers Union joined by refusing to unload South Africa cargo at the port of San Francisco.

In the fall of 1984, the South African government of President Pik W. Botha carried out mass arrests of South Africa's black labor union leaders. The arrests catalyzed opposition and made transparent the failure of constructive engagement to moderate the behavior of the apartheid regime. The United Nations voted a resolution censuring South Africa.

In response to the arrests, Randall Robinson and two supporters—Congressman Walter Fauntroy and former U.S. Civil Rights Commissioner Mary Frances Berry—met with South Africa's ambassador. The meeting was held at the South African Embassy in Washington, DC, in late November.

As the ambassador lectured his guests on the benefits of apartheid, he was interrupted by an aide. Reporters were gathering on the sidewalk outside the Embassy. When his staff called the State Department to report the development, they were told that Robinson and the others intended to be arrested at the Embassy. The ambassador returned to the meeting and asked his guests if it was true, and they confirmed that they would not leave the Embassy of their own free will.

It was a carefully staged media ambush. When the ambassador had the police arrest the trespassers, it was just the beginning. Day after day, protestors descended on the Embassy to hold vigils and block access. Being arrested at the South African Embassy became a badge of honor for many, including politicians and celebrities. Over the next 12 months, 5000 people were arrested at the South African Embassy.

At Harvard University, students erected a makeshift squatter's village patterned after those in the townships of Johannesburg and took up residence to protest until the university sold its investments in companies doing business with South Africa. On campuses around the country the protests were repeated. The tactics unleashed a cascade of publicity that further eroded support for constructive engagement.

In 1985, Republican Senator Richard Lugar introduced legislation to impose trade sanctions on South Africa. Lugar's sanctions bill passed, but was vetoed by Reagan. In a rare rebuke, Reagan's veto was overridden by the Senate. In 1986 the sanctions became law.

The era of constructive engagement was over. As Blankley had foreseen two years earlier, the fabric of public opinion required to sustain constructive engagement had frayed beyond repair.

Although it tried, South Africa's apartheid government couldn't withstand the economically punishing combination of trade sanctions and an international divestment campaign. On February 11, 1990, Nelson Mandela was freed from prison after 20 years of confinement. In the spring of 1994, South Africa held the first elections in which the black majority was permitted to cast votes. The South African precedent shows that activism can change the policies of a popular president, as well as a repressive regime.

TIME IS RIPE FOR A DIVESTMENT
CAMPAIGN AIMED AT CHINA

Just as polls gave the first indication in 1984 that support for constructive engagement with the South African regimes had eroded, polls taken in 2008 show that China has lost crucial support. According to a Harris public opinion poll completed one day before the Olympic torch relay in San Francisco, China is now perceived as the biggest threat to global stability by pluralities of Americans and Europeans. The poll reversed a five-year long trend dating to the start of the Iraq War, in which most Europeans identified the United States as the greatest threat to world peace. In just a year, the number of Europeans who see China as the major threat to stability increased 50 percent. In Germany, the number doubled, rising from 18 percent in 2007 to 35 percent in 2008.

This dramatic reversal of China's image in the eyes of the world is not simply due to its handling of human rights in Tibet, the Darfur crisis, or the controversy over the Beijing Olympic Torch relay. China's negative image is also growing because of the country's abysmal record on product safety issues. It is that factor that has the potential to unite consumer organizations with human rights groups in a campaign targeting corporations which manufacture goods in China.

China's failure to enforce even minimal regulations has resulted in hazardous exports ranging from pet food to cold medicine to sophisticated pharmaceutical products. In 2007, the number of dangerous goods removed from store shelves in Europe rose by 53% in one year. China was the country of origin in the majority of these recalls, more than one-third of which involved children's toys and products.

In March 2008, the U.S. Consumer Product Safety Commission initiated the recall of 2,500,000 Chinese-made toys sold by Wal-Mart and Toys'Я'Us because of the danger of children dying by swallowing magnets used in their manufacture. The year before, the Mattel Corporation had to recall millions of toys decorated with lead-based paint. Based on recall statistics, Chinese toys pose a disproportionate safety threat to American and European children.

Chinese exporters, however, have done far more serious damage in Panama. Almost 120 Panamanians died, many of them infants and children, and many more were disabled when a Chinese chemical company substituted diethylene glycol for the more expensive glycerin used in cold syrup. The result was a toxic dosage that proved lethal. Toothpaste sold mainly in foreign markets, but also in dollar-stores in the United States, was similarly tainted by Chinese manufacturers deliberately substituting cheaper, toxic products to increase their profit margins.

In the United States, 81 Americans died after receiving tainted heparin, a drug commonly administered during heart surgery or kidney dialysis. Investigators from the U.S. Food and Drug Administration believe the heparin was deliberately adulterated with chondroitin sulfate by Chinese suppliers. Heparin costs $900 a pound, but chondroitin sulfate costs only $9 a pound. In the same week that Chinese paramilitary police were safeguarding the "purity" of the Olympic torch relay by manhandling human rights protestors, FDA officials told the House Subcommittee on Oversight and Investigations that their working hypothesis is that the heparin contamination was "intentional."

According to FDA investigators, Changzou SPL, suppliers of heparin to Scientific Protein Laboratories, was the source of the chondroitin sulfate that ended up being administered to Bonnie and Randy Hubley, two of the Americans who died. They were the wife and son of LeRoy Hubley. Both had a genetic condition requiring dialysis. After receiving the tainted heparin, they died within weeks of one another, leaving a grieving

LeRoy to grapple with what he calls his "anger that an unsafe drug was permitted to be sold in this country."

In addition to the United States, heparin was also recalled in Japan, Italy, Denmark, France, and Germany. China is the world's largest supplier of heparin ingredients, which originate in the mucous membranes of pig intestines.

When confronted with the FDA findings, Chinese regulators refused to take responsibility for the contaminated heparin. Jin Shaohong, a top official of China's National Institute for the Control of Pharmaceutical and Biological Products, rejected the FDA's findings and denied that oversulfated chondroitin caused patients' lethal reactions. In a news briefing at the Chinese Embassy in Washington, DC, the Chinese official demanded the right to inspect American pharmaceutical firms connected with the heparin.

Safety concerns are a key reason why the U.S. Olympic Committee sent a caterer to China in 2007 to test food products for the more than 600 American athletes participating in the Beijing games. After the caterer found enough steroids in poultry to result in athletes testing positive for banned drug use and thereby being disqualified from competition, the USOC decided to ship 12 tons of protein to China instead of relying on local sources for meat, fish, and poultry.

UNITING CONSUMERS, UNIONS, AND ENVIRONMENTALISTS

It is a bitter irony for European and American workers and consumers that one of China's competitive advantages as a manufacturing center is the lack of regulation. Many regulations which exist on the books are not enforced. The result is that compliance costs for health, safety, and environmental regulations are dramatically lower in China than in the United States or the European Union. This means that American and European corporations which build plants and factories in China or that procure products and parts from Chinese suppliers have the advantage of avoiding higher costs that come from measures to improve health and safety for workers and consumers.

These concerns have the potential to unite environmentalists, consumers, and organized labor in a divestment campaign targeted on China. Until the regulatory and environmental playing field is level, China will have an unfair advantage in the global economy. By uniting with human rights groups to bring economic pressure to bear on China, a broad coalition could force democratic change. Once the Chinese people have their own fundamental human rights restored, Chinese citizens will be able to organize to improve environmental and workplace conditions. This leveling of the economic playing field will benefit citizens everywhere, while introducing real competition to the global economy.

By allowing China to enter the World Trade Organization without requiring fundamental changes in the government, the stage was set for multinational corporations to roll back a century's worth of progress in workplace safety, consumer safety, and environmental legislation. By shifting production, manufacturing, and outsourcing to low-cost countries like China—and then selling finished, branded products into the markets of advanced industrial nations, such as the United States, Canada, and members of the European Union—corporations have reaped windfall profits.

Defenders of globalism see this as a conundrum. Classic economic theory holds that free trade should result in price competition and thereby benefit consumers. Not even former Federal Reserve Chairman Alan Greenspan can explain why prices for goods made in China but sold in the United States or European Union member nations have remained so high when costs of production in China are so low.

The answer, however, is simple. There really is no free trade with China. Major corporations can afford the initial high cost of relocating manufacturing to China and the necessary pay offs to Chinese officials. Potential competitors are shut out by these barriers to entry, creating an artificial monopoly which works to the benefit of established firms.

Meanwhile, the United States and European Union are steadily losing manufacturing jobs. In 2008, General Electric, the world's biggest industrial company, announced plans to invest $2 billion by 2011 to increase its production capacity in China. Also in 2008, Timken announced that it would shift manufacturing of its ball bearings from Ohio to China.

This is more than a job issue; safety is also at stake. Nowhere is this more dramatically illustrated than in the case of nuclear power plants. Currently, utility companies have filed applications with the Nuclear Regulatory Commission to build a total of 15 new nuclear plants in eight U.S. states. But the trend toward shifting industrial fabrication to China, combined with the Chinese propensity to pawn off counterfeit products as legitimate, has U.S. utility managers worried.

In 2006 and 2007, Chinese suppliers produced more than 140,000 counterfeit circuit breakers, designed to prevent damage from electrical surges, which were then sold in the United States as the legitimate products of Schneider Electric, a French company. The counterfeit Chinese circuit breakers, however, were faulty and posed a fire hazard. According to the Nuclear Regulatory Commission, some of these flawed circuit breakers found their way into U.S. nuclear power plants. In another case, crucial valves installed in a nuclear reactor in Georgia were found to be fakes. If there is ever an American Chernobyl, the cause is likely to be the inadvertent use of counterfeit parts made in China in a U.S. nuclear power plant.

CHINA'S UNFAIR ADVANTAGES
HURT THE MIDDLE CLASS

Former Treasury Secretary Lawrence Summers, currently an economics professor at Harvard University, is among those who understand that untrammeled trade with countries like China is in trouble. Summers detects what he calls a "gnawing suspicion of many that the very object of internationalist economic policy—the growing prosperity of the global economy—may not be in their interests." He also notes that globalism has created "stateless elites whose allegiance is to global economic success and their own prosperity rather than the interests of the nation where they are headquartered." It is no accident that the majority of the richest 1% of households in America are headed by corporate CEOs whose pay has soared in recent years, due largely to the global economy.

While the "stateless elites" grow immensely wealthy, family income of the American middle class is shrinking. Between 2000 and 2006, incomes of the richest 1% of families in the United States rose by 22 percent. At the same time, for 90% of American families, incomes decreased by 4 percent. A study by the Economic Policy Institute and Center on Budget and Policy Priorities over the time span between 1988 and 2006 found that the richest 5 percent of Americans saw their incomes grow an average of $82,607, compared to an increase of only $5,784 for the middle class. Income inequality is growing dramatically in advanced industrial societies around the globe.

Advocates of globalization and free trade across a "flat" world characterize this state of affairs as if it were the result of natural evolution, instead of the result of political agreements reached incrementally over three decades of free trade negotiations under the General Agreement on Trade & Tariffs (GATT), the WTO, and bilateral trade talks. Today's global trading system isn't inevitable, or irreversible. It wasn't created by the Internet or technology suddenly leveling the playing field, or more accurately, tilting the playing field toward less-developed countries with low wages and negligible environmental and safety regulatory enforcement. This situation was created by political action, and it can be reversed by political action. Barriers to trade can come up, just as barriers to trade have come down.

CHINA ONLY RESPONDS TO PRESSURE

Just as "constructive engagement" with South Africa failed to yield political equality and enfranchisement for that country's black majority, neither linkage, trade, nor the Internet will cause China to grant autonomy to Tibet or freedom to its own citizens. There is evidence, however, that concerted political action can force China to change its policies.

Take the case of the An Yue Jiang, a Chinese vessel loaded to the gills with weapons destined for the repressive regime of Zimbabwe's Robert Mugabe. After an election in which Mugabe's ruling ZANU-PF party clearly lost but refused to concede, China shipped millions of rounds of ammunition, assault rifles, mortars, and mortar shells to the regime. The weapons were intended for use against Mugabe's political opposition and would have created a bloodbath in Zimbabwe.

But Zimbabwe is landlocked. For the weapons to reach Mugabe, they would first have to be offloaded at another country's port and then shipped by land. Zambian president Levy Mwanawasa called on neighboring African countries to refuse to unload the deadly cargo. When South African union dockworkers heeded the call, the An Yue Jiang searched for friendlier ports. Finding none, it returned to China fully laden.

The episode shows that China will back down when confronted. It proves that those who say it is counterproductive to criticize publicly or put international pressure on China are dead wrong. It is particularly apt that the dockworkers of South Africa showed the world that China bows to pressure. South Africa's black majority has finally won freedom with the help of an international campaign of sanctions, boycotts, and divestment. The same tactics, if used against China today, would be just as effective as they were in South Africa two decades ago.

Ironically, China's growing economy is both its strength and its weakness. China is still dependent on foreign trade to sustain its economic growth. The government's massive infrastructure plans and economy cannot function without equally massive imports of commodities ranging from concrete and oil to copper and steel. Whether the target of pressure is a company selling to China, or one investing in China in order to sell exports abroad, China depends on foreign commerce to sustain its economic growth.

China's leaders understand this, which is why they tried to quash demands for a boycott of French firms in the aftermath of the disruption of the Olympic torch relay in Paris. Chinese nationalists, mistakenly believing that the French supermarket company Carrefour gave financial support to the Dalai Lama and Tibetan government-in-exile, called for protests and boycotts. Chinese officials urged instead that citizens display their patriotism through hard work and forego the boycotts. China's leadership doesn't want to sanction a tactic that can be used against it with devastating effect.

In military terms, China is a "target rich" environment for an international divestment and sanctions campaign. The climate of public opinion is ripe. Corporate leaders, already under fire for exorbitant CEO compensation packages and outsourcing jobs, are in a poor position to defend their business interests in China against increasingly hostile public opinion.

A divestment and sanctions campaign doesn't have to be waged only by human rights organizations. A coalition with a broad agenda for change in China could conceivably include labor unions, environmentalists, and consumer safety advocates. Middle class Americans, uneasy over job losses and angry at dangerous Chinese products, could easily be motivated to support the goals of a divestment and sanctions campaign, especially if it was geared toward enforcement not only of fundamental human rights in China but also basic safety regulations.

The struggle is not between the Chinese people and the rest of the world. Nor is it between the Chinese people and the Tibetan people, although Chinese government propagandists are more than willing to whip up nationalistic and ethnic tensions to distract from the real issues. The fight is between freedom and dictatorship. For the Tibetan people to win their struggle, the Chinese people will also have to find liberation.

In Chinese-dominated Tibet, the exercise of freedom of speech is punishable by a decade in prison, but in Dharamsala, there is ample freedom to question the Dalai Lama's policy of autonomy instead of independence for Tibet.

DEMOCRACY IN CHINA IS THE CIVIL RIGHTS BATTLE OF THE 21ST CENTURY

On October 25, 2008, in remarks for the forty-eighth anniversary of the founding of the Tibetan Children's Village, the Dalai Lama announced that he wanted the Tibetan people to determine the best course for dealing with China. Coming just days before a Tibetan delegation went to China for the eighth round of talks since 2002, the Dalai Lama's comment hinted at a possible shift in policy if the negotiations failed to produce concrete progress.

Four days later, British Foreign Minister David Miliband announced that Britain was withdrawing its recognition of Tibet's suzerainty status with China, a status that recognized Tibet's traditional autonomy. Britain had conferred this recognition in 1914, an outcome of Col. Younghusband's 1904 treaty with Tibet. Its withdrawal is a severe diplomatic setback, and it cast a pall over the talks in China.

Emboldened by Britain's policy reversal, the Chinese continued their foot-dragging tactics. The final round of talks ended November 5 with the Chinese adamantly refusing to discuss autonomy for Tibet. Frustrated, the Dalai Lama called on leaders of the Tibetan exiles from communities across the globe to convene in Dharamsala for a week-long "special meeting" to debate how to respond to China. Characterizing his efforts to negotiate autonomy as a failure, the Dalai Lama urged the Tibetans to review all options.

"Taking into account the inspiring courage being shown by people all over Tibet this year, the current world situation, and the present intransigent stance of the government of the PRC," the Dalai Lama said, "all the participants, as Tibetan citizens, should discuss in a spirit of equality, cooperation, and collective responsibility the best possible future course of action to advance the Tibetan cause."

In the aftermath of disappointment over the failure of the Olympic Games to moderate China's behavior, the brutality of the crackdown in Tibet after the March protests, and the failure of the talks begun in 2002 to yield any concrete result, the "special meeting" was a political necessity. Tibetans needed a forum to vent their frustration and reach a new consensus. To avoid influencing their deliberations, the Dalai Lama declined to attend the special meeting. His presence, he said, might stifle open discussion.

581 Tibetans attended the Nov. 17-22 special meeting. Dividing into working groups of about 40 members each, they addressed the full range of issues affecting Tibet. The discussions were frank and candid, and no issue was sacrosanct, not even the Dalai Lama's Middle-Way Approach and reliance on non-violence. Advocates of independence were given equal say, as were those who favored stronger tactics for pushing China out of Tibet.

Each working group prepared position papers for presentation to the entire assembly. Over two days at the meeting's end, the papers were debated before the whole assembly and a resolution summarizing the results prepared for the Dalai Lama. Rather than producing an immediate change in policy, the special meeting heralded the start of a search for fresh ideas. That process is now underway. Its outcome will determine whether Tibet will regain freedom within the Dalai Lama's current lifetime.

The contrast between the practice of democracy and tolerance for dissent and questioning in the Tibetan government-in-exile and China could not be clearer. And this is one of the principal impediments to China's ability to accommodate the Dalai Lama's demands; China will have to give freedom of speech to all its citizens if it grants genuine autonomy to Tibet, and that is something China's Marxist, one-party state is not prepared to permit.

The great civil rights struggles of the 20th century focused on an end to imperialism, colonialism, and racial and gender inequality. With the collapse of the Soviet Union's empire in the 1990s, hundreds of millions of people in Russia and Eastern Europe were liberated as democracies replaced totalitarian governments across an immense portion of the earth spanning twelve time zones. The epic civil rights struggle of the 21st century is to create democracy for the more than one billion people who live in China and the annexed territories on its fringes. China must join the world community of free societies if it is ever to fulfill its potential. Freedom in China will mean freedom for Tibet.

By leveraging its growing interdependence with the world community, an international movement to put economic pressure on China will succeed where constructive engagement has failed.

"Tibet's struggle is not for land but for a way of life," says Lhasang Tsering, a Tibetan activist and poet. He sums up his feelings, and those of many fellow Tibetans, about their struggle in the following poem from his book, *Tomorrow and Other Poems*.

Something to Live For

I know I am Homeless—still I have a house.
Though I was an Orphan—now I have my wife and children.
I have something to live for.
I have Freedom to fight for.
I know I've lost my Country—still I have my people.
Though they call me Stateless—still I have the world.
I have something to live for.
I have Freedom to fight for.
I know China is mighty Today—this will not last Forever.
Though long and dark the Night—the Day will surely come.
I have something to live for.
I have Freedom to fight for.
I know I must not give up—my cause is true and just.
Though governments side with China—people are on the
side of Tibet.
I have something to live for.
I have Freedom to fight for.
I know Tibet will be Free—I will not give up my Birthright.
Though Power may side with China—Truth is on the
side of Tibet.
I have something to live for.
I have Freedom to fight for.

For information on how you can make a difference, go to www.FreeingTibet.com.

Appendix

NSC Directive 5412/2

NOTE BY THE EXECUTIVE SECRETARY
to the
NATIONAL SECURITY COUNCIL
on
COVERT OPERATIONS

References: A. NSC 5412/1
            B. Memo for NSC from Executive
                Secretary, subject: "Report
                of the Planning Coordination
                Group", dated December 20,
                1955
            C. NSC Action No. 1497

The President has this date approved the amendment of paragraph 7-a of NSC 5412/1 as submitted to and approved by the other statutory members of the National Security Council by Memorandum Approval in response to the reference memorandum of December 20, 1955. The President and the other statutory members of the Council have also approved the recommendation that paragraphs 4-a and 7-b of NSC 5412/1 be amended as necessary to take account of the termination of the Planning Coordination Group and to conform to the substance of the language in paragraph 7-a thereof.

Accordingly the enclosed National Security Council directive, incorporating the above-mentioned amendments to NSC 5412/1, is transmitted herewith for implementation by all executive departments and agencies of the U. S. Government concerned, as indicated therein.

The enclosed directive, as adopted and approved, supersedes NSC 5412/1.

It is requested that special security precautions be observed in the handling of the enclosed directive, and that access to it be very strictly limited on an absolute need-to-know basis.

It is further requested that all copies of NSC 5412/1 be returned to this office for destruction upon receipt of this directive.

JAMES S. LAY, JR.
Executive Secretary

Distribution:
    The President (via Mr. Anderson)
    The Secretary of State
    The Secretary of Defense
    The Chairman, Joint Chiefs of Staff
    The Director of Central Intelligence
    The Executive Officer, Operations Coordinating Board

NSC 5412/2

~~T O P   S E C R E T~~

COPY NO._____1 of 15

NSC___5412/2_____

December 28, 1955
_____

NATIONAL SECURITY COUNCIL

NSC 5412/2
_____

```
ATTENTION

THE ENCLOSED TOP SECRET CONTROL
FORM MUST BE COMPLETED BY EACH
INDIVIDUAL (1) WHO READS THIS
DOCUMENT WHOLLY OR IN PART OR
(2) WHO PERSONALLY HANDLES IT
AND HAS ACCESS TO ITS CONTENTS
```

DECLASSIFIED

Authority _NSC LIST - MAY 1977_

By __DJH_ NLE DATE _6/2/77_

~~T O P   S E C R E T~~

NATIONAL SECURITY COUNCIL DIRECTIVE

on

COVERT OPERATIONS

1. The National Security Council, taking cognizance of the vicious covert activities of the USSR and Communist China and the governments, parties and groups dominated by them (hereinafter collectively referred to as "International Communism") to discredit and defeat the aims and activities of the United States and other powers of the free world, determined, as set forth in NSC directives 10/2 and 10/5, that, in the interests of world peace and U. S. national security, the overt foreign activities of the U. S. Government should be supplemented by covert operations.

2. The Central Intelligence Agency had already been charged by the National Security Council with conducting espionage and counter-espionage operations abroad. It therefore seemed desirable, for operational reasons, not to create a new agency for covert operations, but, subject to directives from the NSC, to place the responsibility for them on the Central Intelligence Agency and correlate them with espionage and counter-espionage operations under the over-all control of the Director of Central Intelligence.

3. The NSC has determined that such covert operations shall to the greatest extent practicable, in the light of U. S. and Soviet capabilities and taking into account the risk of war, be designed to:

   a. Create and exploit troublesome problems for International Communism, impair relations between the USSR and Communist China and between them and their satellites, complicate control within the USSR, Communist China and their satellites, and retard the growth of the military and economic potential of the Soviet bloc.

   b. Discredit the prestige and ideology of International Communism, and reduce the strength of its parties and other elements.

   c. Counter any threat of a party or individuals directly or indirectly responsive to Communist control to achieve dominant power in a free world country.

   d. Reduce International Communist control over any areas of the world.

   e. Strengthen the orientation toward the United States of the peoples and nations of the free world, accentuate, wherever possible, the identity of interest between such peoples and nations and the United States as well as favoring, where appropriate, those groups genuinely advocating or believing in the advancement of such mutual interests, and increase the capacity and will of such peoples and nations to resist International Communism.

    f. In accordance with established policies and to the extent practicable in areas dominated or threatened by International Communism, develop underground resistance and facilitate covert and guerrilla operations and ensure availability of those forces in the event of war, including wherever practicable provision of a base upon which the military may expand these forces in time of war within active theaters of operations as well as provision for stay-behind assets and escape and evasion facilities.

4. Under the authority of Section 102(d)(5) of the National Security Act of 1947, the National Security Council hereby directs that the Director of Central Intelligence shall be responsible for:

    a. Ensuring, through designated representatives of the Secretary of State and of the Secretary of Defense, that covert operations are planned and conducted in a manner consistent with United States foreign and military policies and with overt activities, and consulting with and obtaining advice from the Operations Coordinating Board and other departments or agencies as appropriate.

    b. Informing, through appropriate channels and on a need-to-know basis, agencies of the U. S. Government, both at home and abroad (including diplomatic and military representatives), of such operations as will affect them.

5. In addition to the provisions of paragraph 4, the following provisions shall apply to wartime covert operations:

    a. Plans for covert operations to be conducted in active theaters of war and any other areas in which U. S. forces are engaged in combat operations will be drawn up with the assistance of the Department of Defense and will be in consonance with and complementary to approved war plans of the Joint Chiefs of Staff.

    b. Covert operations in active theaters of war and any other areas in which U. S. forces are engaged in combat operations will be conducted under such command and control relationships as have been or may in the future be approved by the Department of Defense.

6. As used in this directive, "covert operations" shall be understood to be all activities conducted pursuant to this directive which are so planned and executed that any U. S. Government responsibility for them is not evident to unauthorized persons and that if uncovered the U. S. Government can plausibly disclaim any responsibility for them. Specifically, such operations shall include any covert activities related to: propaganda, political action; economic warfare; preventive direct action,

including sabotage, anti-sabotage, demolition; escape and evasion and evacuation measures; subversion against hostile states or groups including assistance to underground resistance movements, guerrillas and refugee liberation groups; support of indigenous and anti-communist elements in threatened countries of the free world; deception plans and operations; and all activities compatible with this directive necessary to accomplish the foregoing. Such operations shall not include: armed conflict by recognized military forces, espionage and counter-espionage, nor cover and deception for military operations.

7. Except as the President otherwise directs, designated representatives of the Secretary of State and of the Secretary of Defense of the rank of Assistant Secretary or above, and a representative of the President designated for this purpose, shall hereafter be advised in advance of major covert programs initiated by CIA under this policy or as otherwise directed, and shall be the normal channel for giving policy approval for such programs as well as for securing coordination of support therefor among the Departments of State and Defense and the CIA.

8. This directive supersedes and rescinds NSC 10/2, NSC 10/5, NSC 5412, NSC 5412/1, and subparagraphs "a" and "b" under the heading "Additional Functions of the Operations Coordinating Board" on page 1 of the President's memorandum for the Executive Secretary, National Security Council, supplementing Executive Order 10483.

About Sources

Many of the primary sources we relied on for the book are mentioned in our acknowledgments, and secondary sources are listed in the bibliography. *Freeing Tibet* contains new details about the CIA's covert operations in Tibet, including the existence of a black propaganda campaign, which may be controversial. Where classification details are reported, our sources were one or more individuals we interviewed. These individuals had direct access to information about or personal involvement in the events themselves. Where possible, when a conversation is recounted, we have verified its accuracy with more than one source. In some instances, notably the exchange between Howard Bane and Ambassador Galbraith over aid to an encircled group of Tibetan freedom fighters, an account of the conversation from both parties was not possible because one of the individuals involved had died. In such instances, the conversation is reconstructed as faithfully as possible, given that the recollection of it is necessarily one sided. In his own writings, Ambassador Galbraith was clear about his dim view of the CIA's Tibet operation.

Howard Bane was a primary source for this book. Over our friendship of approximately thirty years, we had dozens upon dozens of conversations about intelligence matters and shared many confidences. Howard was, however, not the only intelligence officer to assist us. In addition to getting help from a number of former CIA officials, we also interviewed military officers, such as General Aderholt, who were involved in special operations in Tibet. These interviews took place over the course of many years, beginning in the 1990s. Other insider details, including anecdotes about the planning of President Nixon's trip to China, are based on discussions with Nixon White House staff members. Some of these stories, such as the true origin of the "Bring Us Together" campaign placard, have never been published.

Whenever possible, especially for sensitive information, we have identified the individual sources in the text. However, some sources requested anonymity, particularly when discussing or characterizing still-classified information, and those requests have been honored. Gaining the trust of those entrusted with secret information is a matter of patiently building contacts and demonstrating personal integrity in the use of classified information. We have refrained from publishing anything which might needlessly jeopardize any individual's safety or reputation, compromise intelligence means or methods, or harm national security or the struggle to free Tibet.

Other interviews for the book were conducted face to face in Dharamsala, India, home to the Dalai Lama and the Tibetan Central Administration. In the United States, interviews were conducted in person whenever possible and at other times over the telephone. In certain instances, follow-up questions or clarification was sought by email, but in no case were interviews ever done entirely by e-mail.

Bibliography

Agee, Philip, *Inside the Company: CIA Diary.* New York: Stonehill, 1975.

Alme, Oystein, and Vagen, Morten, *Silenced: China's Great Wall of Censorship.* Stockholm: Amaryllis, 2006.

Ambrose, Stephen E., *Eisenhower the President, Volume Two, 1952–1969.* London: Allen & Unwin, 1984.

Avedon, John F., *In Exile From the Land of Snows: The Dalai Lama and Tibet Since the Chinese Conquest.* New York: HarperPerennial, 1997.

Baker, Deborah, *A Blue Hand, The Beats in India.* New York: Penguin, 2008.

Barnett, Robert, and Akiner, Shirin, ed., *Resistance and Reform in Tibet.* Bloomington and Indianapolis: Indiana Univ. Press, 1994.

Bell, Charles, *The People of Tibet.* New Delhi: Munshiram Manoharlal Publishers, 2000.

Brown, Mick, *The Dance of 17 Lives, The Incredible True Story of Tibet's 17th Karmapa.* New York: Bloomsbury, 2004.

Carnahan, Sumner, with Lama Kungpa Rinpoche, *In the Presence of My Enemies: Memoirs of Tibetan Nobleman Tsipon Shuguba/* Santa Fe, NM: Clear Light Publishers, 1995.

Clarridge, Duane R., *A Spy for All Seasons: My Life in the CIA.* New York: Scribner, 1997.

Clifford, Terry, *Tibetan Buddhist Medicine and Psychiatry, The Diamond Healing.* New York: Samuel Weiser, 1990.

Conboy, Kenneth, and Morrison, James, *The CIA's Secret War in Tibet.* Lawrence: Univ. Press of Kansas, 2002.

Dalai Lama, His Holiness, with Carrière, Jean-Claude, *Violence and Compassion; Dialogues on Life Today.* New York: Image Book/Doubleday, 2001.

Dalai Lama, His Holiness, with Chan, Victor, *The Wisdom of Forgiveness*. London: Hodder and Stoughton, 2005.

Dalai Lama, His Holiness, with Rowell, Galen, *My Tibet*. Berkeley and Los Angeles: Univ. of California Press, 1990.

Department of Information and International Relations, *International Resolutions and Recognitions on Tibet (1959 to 2004)*. Dharamsala, India: Central Tibetan Administration, 2005.

Department of Information and International Relations, *The Middle-Way Approach, A Framework for Resolving the Issue of Tibet*. Dharamsala, India: Central Tibetan Administration, 2006.

Department of Information and International Relations, *Souvenir: His Holiness the 14th Dalai Lama of Tibet*. Dharamsala, India: Central Tibetan Administration, 2005

Department of Information and International Relations, *Tibet Under Communist China, 50 Years*. Dharamsala, India: Central Tibetan Administration, 2006.

Department of Information and International Relations, *Travellers to Tibet, A Selection of Eyewitness Accounts by Tibetans and Others, 1959–2004*. Dharamsala, India: Central Tibetan Administration, 2004.

Dhonden, Dr. Yeshi, *Healing from the Source, The Science and Lore of Tibetan Medicine*. Ithaca, NY: Snow Lion Publications, 2000.

Dunham, Mikel, *Buddha's Warriors, The Story of the CIA-backed Tibetan Freedom Fighters: The Chinese Invasion, and the Ultimate Fall of Tibet*. New York: Jeremy P. Tarcher/Penguin, 2004.

Galbraith, John Kenneth, *A Life in Our Times*. Boston: Houghton Mifflin, 1981.

Ginsberg, Allen, *Howl and Other Poems*. San Francisco: City Lights Books, 1956.

Ginsberg, Allen, *Indian Journals*. New York: Grove Press, 1999.

Govinda, Anagarika, *Foundations of Tibetan Mysticism*. London: Rider & Company, 1959.

Gyatso, Lobsang, *Memoirs of a Tibetan Lama*. New York: Snow Lion Publications, 1998.

Harris, Clare, *In the Image of Tibet: Tibetan Painting after 1959*. London: Reaktion Books, 1999.

Hilton, Isabel, *The Search for the Panchen Lama*. New York: W.W. Norton 7, 2000.

Institute of National Affairs, *Dalai Lama and India*. Hind Book House, 1959.

International Commission of Jurists, *The Question of Tibet and the Rule of Law*. Geneva, 1959.

Kelly, Orr, *From a Dark Sky: The Story of U.S. Air Force Special Operations*. Presidio Press, 1996.

Kerouac, Jack, *Some of the Dharma*. New York: Viking Penguin, 1997.

Kerr, Blake, *Sky Buria: An Eyewitness Account of China's Brutal Crackdown in Tibet*. New York: Snow Lion Publications, 1997.

Kissinger, Henry, *Does America Need a Foreign Policy? Toward a Diplomacy for the 21st Century*. New York: Simon & Schuster, 2001.

Kissinger, Henry, *The White House Years*. New York: Weidenfeld & Nicholson, 1979.

Knaus, John Kenneth, *Orphans of the Cold War: America and the Tibetan Struggle for Survival.* New York: PublicAffairs, 1999.

Kongtrul, Jamgon, and Taye Lodro, *Enthronement, The Recognition of the Reincarnate Masters of Tibet and the Himalayas.* Ithaca, NY: Snow Lion Publications, 1997.

Laird, Thomas, *Into Tibet, The CIA's First Atomic Spy and His Secret Expedition to Lhasa.* New York: Grove Press, 2002.

Leary, Timothy, Metzner, Richard, and Alpert, Richard, *The Psychedelic Experience: A Manual Based on the Tibetan Book of the Dead.* New York: Citadel Press, Kensington Publishing, 1995.

Logan, Pamela, *Tibetan Rescue, The Extraordinary Quest to Save the Sacred Art Treasures of Tibet.* Boston: Tuttle Publishing, 2002.

Malraux, Andre, *Anti-Memoirs.* New York: Holt, Rinehart and Winston, 1968.

Mangold, Tom, *Cold Warrior, James Jesus Angleton: The CIA's Master Spy Hunter.* New York: Simon & Schuster, 1991.

Margolis, Eric S., *War at the Top of the World, The Struggle for Afghanistan, Kashmir, and Tibet.* New York: Routledge, 2001.

Marshall, S.L.A., *Infantry Operations & Weapons Usage in Korea.* London: Greenhill Books and The Institute for Research on Small Arms in International Security, 1988.

McCarthy, Roger E., *Tears of the Lotus, Accounts of Tibetan Resistance to the Chinese Invasion, 1950–1962.* North Carolina and London: McFarland, 1997.

Medhurst, Kenneth, *The Basques and Catalans.* London: Minority Rights Group, 1977.

Morreale, Don, *The Complete Guide to Buddhist America.* Boston: Shambhala Publications, Inc., 1998.

Morris, James, *Heaven's Command: An Imperial Progress.* London: Faber and Faber, Folio Society Edition, 1992.

Morris, James, *Farewell the Trumpets: An Imperial Retreat.* London; Faber and Faber, Folio Society Edition, 1993.

Nixon, Richard M., *The Real War.* New York: Warner Books, 1980.

Osanka, Franklin Mark, *Modern Guerrilla Warfare: Fighting Communist Guerrilla Movements 1941–1961.* New York: Free Press, 1962.

Pachen, Ani, and Donnelley, Adelaide, *Sorrow Mountain: The Journey of a Tibetan Warrior Nun.* New York: Kodansha International, 2000.

Paine, Jeffery, *Re-Enchantment, Tibetan Buddhism Comes to the West.* New York: W.W. Norton, 2004.

Pema, Jetsun, *Tibet: My Story.* Rockport, MA: Element Books, 1997.

Phillips, David Atlee, *The Night Watch.* New York: Atheneum, 1977.

Powers, John, *Introduction to Tibetan Buddhis.* New York: Snow Lion Publications, 1995.

Rajesh, M. N., and Kelly. Thomas I., *The Buddhist Monastery.* New Delhi: Roli Books and Lustre Press, 1998.

Rapgay, Dr. Lopsang, *The Tibetan Book of Healing.* Varanasi, India: Pilgrims Publishing, Durga Kund, 1996.

Ranelagh, John, *The Agency: The Rise and Decline of the CIA*. New York: Simon and Schuster, 1986.

Reed, John, *Ten Days That Shook the World*. New York: Boni & Liveright, 1919.

Rhie, Marylin M., and Thurman, Robert F., *Wisdom and Compassion: The Sacred Art of Tibet*. New York: Asian Art Museum of San Francisco and Tibet House, New York with Harry N. Abrams, 1991.

Ricard, Matthieu, *Monk Dancers of Tibet*. Boston and London: Shambhala, 2003.

Roosevelt, Eleanor, and Smith, Huston, *The Search for America*. New York: Prentice-Hall, 1959.

Seager, Richard Hughes, *Buddhism in America*. New York: Columbia Univ. Press, 1999.

Schwartz, Ronald D., *Circle of Protest: Political Ritual in the Tibetan Uprising*. New York: Columbia Univ. Press, 1994.

Snellgrove, David, and Richardson, Hugh, *A Cultural History of Tibet*. Boston and London: Shambhala, 1995.

Strong, Anna Louise, *When Serfs Stood Up in Tibet*. Beijing: New World Press, 1960 and 1965.

Suyin, Han, *Eldest Son: Zhou Enlai and the Making of Modern China, 1898–1976*. New York: Kodansha Globe, 1994.

Tibetan Centre for Human Rights and Democracy, *Human Rights Situation in Tibet: Annual Report 2007*. Dharamsala, India, 2008.

Thomas, Evan, *The Very Best Men, Four Who Dared: The Early Years of the CIA*. New York: Simon & Schuster, 1995.

Thomas, Lowell Jr., *The Silent War in Tibet*. New York: Doubleday & Company, 1959.

Thurman, Robert, and Wise, Tad, *Circling the Sacred Mountain: A Spiritual Adventure Through the Himalayas*. New York: Bantam Books, 1999.

Thurman, Robert A.F., *Essential Tibetan Buddhism*. New York: HarperSanFrancisco, 1995.

Thurman, Robert A.F., *Inner Revolution: Life, Liberty, and the Pursuit of Real Happiness*. New York: Riverhead Books, 1998.

Trungpa, Chögyam, *Born in Tibet*. Boston: Shambhala Publications, Inc., 1995.

Tsering, Diki, *Dalai Lama, My Son: A Mother's Story*. New York: Viking/Arkana, 2000.

Tsering, Lhasang, *Tomorrow & Other Poems*. New Delhi: Rupa & Co., 2003.

Wheatcroft, Andrew, *The World Atlas of Revolutions*. New York: Simon and Schuster, 1983.

Willis, Michael, *Tibet: Life Myth and Art*. New York: Stewart, Tabori & Chang, 1999.

Index